THE CRAFT OF THE Weaver

Ann Sutton
Peter Collingwood
Geraldine St Aubyn Hubbard

Ann Sutton

Peter Collingwood

Geraldine St Aubyn Hubbard

Edited by
Anna Jackson

BRITISH BROADCASTING CORPORATION

Black and white photography

The following black and white photographs were taken by Ed Buziak:
Portraits on title page, plates 4, 7, 8, 10, 11, 13, 15, 18–28, 32–65, 68–77, 80, 81, 92–94, 99, 100, 102, 108, 110–118, 122, 123, 128, 129, 136, 137, 139–142, 149, 150, 152, 163–193, 197–208, 210, 213–218, 228–233, 235, 250, 258, 259, 261, 263–265, 272–275, 278–281, 283, 288–291, 293–296, 298–300, 302, 307–311, 315, 319–322, 324–327, 332–336, 348–350, 353–355, 371–385, 392, 394.

Acknowledgement is due to the following for permission to reproduce photographs:

© A.D.A.G.P. Paris 1981, 396; Barnaby's Picture Library 9; Berne Historical Museum, Ethnography Department (photo S. Rebsamen) 370; Tadek Beutlich 16; Bolton Museum and Art Gallery (photo F. Davies) 401; Peter Collingwood 284, 301, 305, 317, 325, 348, 363; Council of Industrial Design 234; County Museum, Liverpool 398; Crafts Council 5, 274, 291; Rosemary Ellis 104–106; Harris Looms 143, 144; Horniman Museum 392; Diana Hughes 274; Anna Jackson 335; Kunstindustrimuseet, Oslo 266; Venice Lamb 14, 394; Lauros-Giraudon/Cluny Museum, Paris 395; Metropolitan Museum of Art, New York 389, 390, 397; Museum of English Rural Life, Reading 283; National Gallery, London 276; Norsk Folkemuseum, Oslo 391; Petrie Museum, University College, London (UC 9547) 388; Philadelphia Museum of Art 404; Morfudd Roberts 273; Chloe Sayer 337; Scottish National Gallery of Modern Art (photo Crafts Council) 124; Shipley Art Gallery 385; Howard Sochurek/The John Hillelson Agency (from '*The book of looms*') 338; Southwest Museum, Los Angeles 103; Ann Sutton (photo Sam Sawdon) 361; The Textile Museum, Washington, DC 403; TFH. Crafts 287; The Trustees of the British Museum 6 (Courtesy Joan Wescott), 386, 393, 402; Victoria and Albert Museum, London 12, 78, 79, 138, 399, 400, 405, 406; West Surrey College of Art 216, 275, 277.

Colour photography

The following colour photographs were taken by Ed Buziak:
Front cover, 1–10, 12–19, 21 and 22, back cover 1, 2 and 4.

Acknowledgement is due to the following for permission to reproduce the colour photographs:

David Black and Clive Loveless Collection 24; City of Leeds Museums (Lotherton Hall) and Ann Sutton (photo Jessica Strang) 20; Crafts Council 1, 6, 7, 19 & 35 (photo Michael Freeman); Erzbischöfliches Diözesan Museum, Cologne 33; Sonia Halliday 36; Diana Hughes 15; Kunstindustrimuseet, Oslo 37; Museum of Fine Arts, Boston (Gift of Mrs. Walter Scott Fitz) 29; National Museum of Finland 27; Novosti Press Agency 26; Marjory Parr Gallery 10; Photographie Giraudon 11; Scottish Arts Council 12; Southern Arts Regional Art Association 4; The Textile Museum, Washington DC 28, 31 & back cover 3; The Trustees of the British Museum (Museum of Mankind) 30; Victoria and Albert Museum, London 23, 25, 32 & 34; West Surrey College of Art 14; Lindsay Wilcox 22.

Illustrations by Hayward and Martin Limited.

Acknowledgement is also due to the following:

British Wool Marketing Board for the diagram *The correct way to fold a fleece* on page 16.
Mike Halsey for permission to reproduce six illustrations from his book *Tapestry weaving* on pages 50 and 51.

The Yarn Count on pages 12 and 13 is taken from *Handweaving and cloth design* by Marianne Straub and reprinted by permission of the publishers as follows: Pelham Books Limited for British Commonwealth, Viking Press Inc. for USA and Rainbird Publishing Group for the rest of the world.

Unless otherwise stated, all fabric samples are by the authors of their own chapters.

Foreword

For thousands of years man has interlaced threads to weave cloth with which to clothe himself, and to provide warmth, shelter and decoration. The fibres, equipment and techniques used have varied greatly, and the results include textiles such as delicate gauzes woven on backstrap looms in Peru, glowing rugs from the Middle East, fine Coptic tapestries from Egypt and double cloths from Scandinavia.

Today in the West machinery has taken over many of the repetitive tasks of weaving, and the hand weaver is free to explore the effects of particular yarns, designs and weaves not economic for the industrial process. Weaving an article for use or for pleasure can be a very satisfying experience, and we hope that this book helps you to enjoy the craft of the weaver.

This is not a book of rules; every technique has many variations, and the guidelines we give are those found useful by the writers. We are grateful to Bobbie Cox, Fiona Mathison, Roger Oates and Fay Morgan who appeared in the programmes, and some of whose ideas are incorporated in the book.

Anna Jackson

Ann Sutton trained as an embroiderer and woven textile designer for industry, at Cardiff College of Art. She then taught weaving for seven years at West Sussex College of Art, and has since taught and assessed at colleges and polytechnics throughout Britain. She has her workshop in Arundel, West Sussex, where she specialises in architectural hangings based on permutations and systems, often relating to new textile structures. She started the 'International Exhibitions of Miniature Textiles', chaired the Fibre Section of the World Crafts Council in Mexico, wrote *Tablet-weaving*, with Pat Holtom, and was the presenter of the BBC Television Series 'The craft of the weaver'.

Peter Collingwood OBE qualified as a doctor, then turned to weaving after having been inspired by local weavers in Jordan. He began training in the weaving workshops of Ethel Mairet, Barbara Sawyer and Alastair Morton. He has his own workshop in Nayland, Suffolk, where he specialises in the weaving of floor rugs, and his distinctive macrogauze wall-hangings. He makes yearly teaching trips to America or the Continent, and has written detailed books on rugs, *The techniques of rug weaving*, and on sprang, *The techniques of sprang*; another on tablet weaving is in preparation.

Geraldine St Aubyn Hubbard trained pre-diploma at Goldsmith's College School of Art, London. Diploma AD in Woven Textiles at West Surrey College of Art and Design, Farnham. Taught part-time at Farnham. Has been a full-time weaver since 1977, with occasional guest teaching at West Dean College and Farnham. Makes fabric for clothes and scarves from wool, silk and cashmere, using simple weave structures, and relying on the colours and textures of the yarns for interest and variety. Much of her yarn is dyed in her own workshop with either natural or synthetic dyes.

This book accompanies the BBC Television series 'The craft of the weaver', first broadcast on BBC2 from 24 March 1980 and repeated on BBC1 in January 1982 and produced by Anna Jackson.

Published to accompany a series of programmes prepared in consultation with the BBC Continuing Advisory Council.

This book is set in 10/12 point Times Monophoto.
Printed in England by Jolly & Barber Limited, Rugby.
© The authors 1982.
First published 1982.
Published by the British Broadcasting Corporation
35 Marylebone High Street, London W1M 4AA.
ISBN 0 563 16363 1 (paperback)
ISBN 0 563 16507 3 (hardback)

Contents

All the measurements given are metric,
with imperial measurements in brackets.
These are only exact equivalents
where necessary, otherwise they are convenient
approximations. If possible it is preferable
to keep to either metric or imperial
measurements throughout a particular process.

Introduction

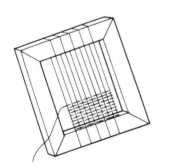

1 The simple over-one, under-one interlacing of plain weave.

Weaving is quite simply the interlacement of two sets of threads to form a cloth. The *warp* threads run the length of the fabric. The *weft* threads are woven in across the width of the warp, from side to side, usually at right angles (1). The simplest weaving consists in weaving the weft over and under every other warp thread; the next weft thread passes over and under the alternate warp threads and is beaten down to hold the first one in place.

It is nearly impossible to weave unless the warp is held taut, and any apparatus, simple or complicated, large or small, which holds the warp under tension during weaving is called a *loom* (2).

It is useful to get to know certain weaving terms: the warp threads are called *ends*. Each weft thread is called a *pick*. The opening formed by lifting the warp threads, or ends, through which the weaver passes the next weft, or pick, is called a *shed*. The line of the newest pick, at the growing edge of the cloth, is called the *fell* (3).

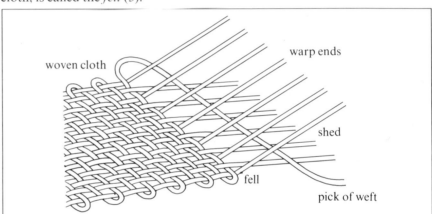

3 A piece of weaving, showing the warp ends, the weft pick, the shed and the fell.

The number of warp threads, that is, ends per centimetre in a piece of weaving is often written as ends/cm or e/cm (ends per inch is ends/inch or epi); the number of weft threads, that is, picks per centimetre is picks/cm or p/cm (picks/inch or ppi). The relationship between the number of threads per cm or per inch in warp and weft is the *sett* of a cloth. Other terms will be explained as they arise in the book.

All types of weaving are variations on this simple beginning, and the range of variation is enormous: the weaver can vary the interlacement, so that it is not just over-one, under-one, to achieve an elaborate weave; the weaver can organise the interlacement so that the cloth is *balanced* (colour 8), that is, where both warp and weft show equally; or *weft-faced* (colour 6), that is, where the warp threads are completely hidden by the weft threads, as is common in tapestry and rugs; or occasionally so that the weft is hidden by the warp, to make a *warp-faced* fabric (colour 7). In addition, there are endless possible permutations of yarn, colour, and density.

Given time and patience, all types of technique can be used on the very simplest loom. However, aids to faster and more efficient weaving have evolved over the years, first for hand looms, then for industrial looms, right up to the present day, when the fastest looms have a weft inserted by jets of air or water. Nevertheless, no matter how expensive and elaborate the equipment used for this process, or how simple and basic, the most important element in a good piece of weaving will always be the careful attention given by the weaver to every detail of the process.

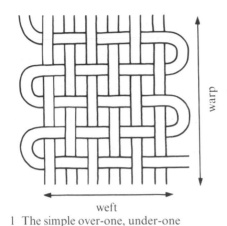

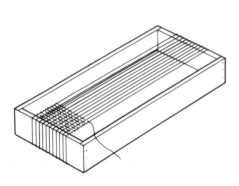

2 A wooden box, a strong frame, even a car roof-rack, can all be used as looms.

4 Carefully placed striped areas enliven this plain weave jacket by Shirley Lawn.

It is well worth keeping a record in a notebook of the methods you use, and their result, whether spinning, dyeing or weaving. Include as many details as possible, information on yarns, sett, amounts of dye used and so on, and stick a sample of the result onto the page. In this way you will build on your experience and learn from your mistakes. To save wasted effort and disappointment, make a small sample of a weave before trying it on a large piece: this way you will make sure the result is what is required. This sample will also give you vital information about the qualities of yarn needed.

5 'Mr Adam's apple', a tapestry by Archie Brennan.

Chapter One

Fibres and yarns

6 Woollen blanket from Mali, Africa, woven from six strips sewn together; plain weave and brocading.

Almost all pieces of weaving are made out of yarn, and almost all yarns are made out of fibres of some kind. Weavers can buy yarns ready-made, or spin fibres themselves; or hand-spun yarns can be mixed with machine-spun yarns – this is something which is often done by professional weavers who can't afford the time to spin all their own yarns.

Although most weavers work with spun yarns, it is quite possible to use the longer fibres, such as some wools, sisal and jute, in an unspun state, but only as weft.

Fibres can be obtained from natural sources or be man-made, and each one has properties and characteristics that are very different; when planning a piece of weaving, it is vital to choose the best fibre for the job, according to the type of weaving and end-product that you want.

Natural fibres

Most natural fibres come from either animal or vegetable sources.

All the natural fibres except silk occur in *staple* form – that is in short lengths which may be from about 2 cm to 36 cm ($\frac{3}{4}$ in to 14 in) and they have to be spun together to form a yarn before they can be used for weaving.

Wool from the sheep is the most popular fibre with both hand-spinners and hand-weavers, mainly because it is good-tempered in use, it 'covers' well,

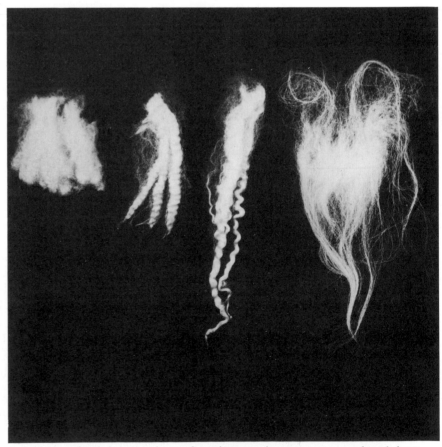

7 *Left:* downland sheep produce soft, springy wool; *two centre:* some breeds have fleece with lustrous waves; *right:* coarse harder fibres come from mountain sheep.

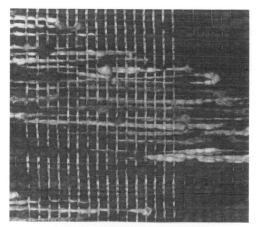

8 Detail of rug by Barbara Mullins, using unspun fleece weft and linen warp.

9 The popular Jacob's sheep, with black and white fleece.

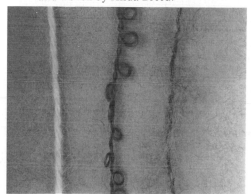

10 A knee-rug of Jacob's wool, spun and woven by Hilda Breed.

it takes dye easily, and it is elastic (6, colour 37). There are many kinds of wool: variety of climate, diet and breed produce different fleeces which contain fibres suitable for specific purposes. Some fleeces have a long, straight staple, some are naturally crimped, or short. A downland breed will have soft fibres suitable for luxury clothing, while a sheep from the mountains will have a harsher fleece, suitable for rugs or hard-wearing upholsteries (7). However, most fleeces contain a mixture of both harsh and soft fibres, which must be sorted carefully before spinning by hand. People usually think of wool as naturally creamy-white, and are surprised at the variety of natural greys and browns in a fleece; 'black' fleece (really a very dark brown), formerly scorned because it does not show coloured dye, is now sought after by hand-spinners for its pleasant natural colour. Small flocks of Jacob's sheep are kept by enthusiasts because their soft fleece grows in patches of black, grey and white (9, 10).

Most wool is spun *in the grease* or *in oil* and it is easier to weave in this lubricated state: you can tell if it is in the grease by smelling it – it smells like plasticine. After weaving, the cloth is *finished* in water and the grease is removed. The cloth then *fulls* – that is, thickens – and is much softer.

The hand-weaver may also use the hairs of other animals:

Mohair, from the Angora goat, is a long, lustrous fibre, and is often spun into a loop form of yarn. These loops are ideal for brushing out after weaving to make the familiar, soft, raised surface. Some mohair yarns have these loops brushed out in the yarn stage; when these yarns are used for weaving, they must be spaced well apart, or the result will not be soft, but hard and spiky. Mohair is used for hard-wearing fabrics such as upholstery fabrics or rugs in its straight spun form, and soft luxurious clothing fabrics, scarves, and so on, in its loop form (11).

Angora, from the Angora rabbit, is an expensive fibre which is often mixed in with wool to give a soft but cheaper yarn. A high percentage of angora

11 *Left:* soft angora yarn; *centre:* mohair loop and *right:* mohair yarn where the loops have been brushed out.

12 Corner of a Kashmir shawl, woven with pashmin wool, early nineteenth century.

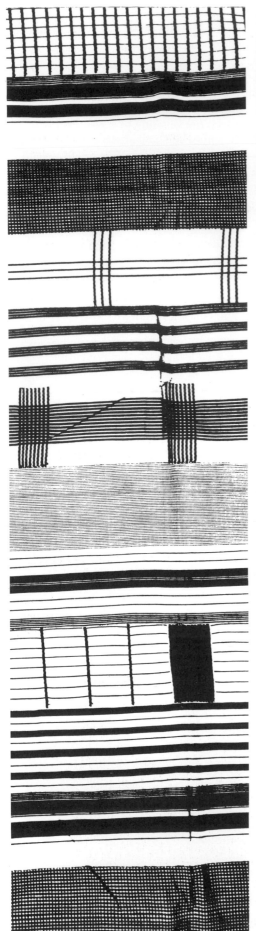

13 A cotton boll – the pod has exploded to show cotton fibres surrounding the seeds; and a silk cocoon – the moth has emerged, and so this silk cannot be reeled off as a filament, but must be torn up and spun as a staple fibre.

fibres gives the softest yarn available, and the fibres project so that the cloth keeps warmth in the body. Sometimes an angora yarn will shed its fibres annoyingly; this can be controlled by putting the cloth or garment in a deep-freeze for a few hours. This has the effect of slightly felting the fibres together, and making them hold into the cloth. Angora is often used for luxury dress fabrics or scarves where a very soft handle is required (11).

Cashmere, alpaca, camel hair are all animal fibres which are liked by the hand-weaver because they are very soft and come in a lovely range of natural colours through white and cream to rust, grey and cinnamon brown (12). They can be used when a very special dress fabric is being woven. Sometimes the long fibres of camel hair are spun into a hard yarn which can be used for rug warps.

Cow hair is very hard-wearing, and can be used for rugs. Some hand-spinners use **dog hair**, of various breeds, and occasionally **human hair** can be suitable for spinning. Any animal fibre will produce some type of yarn, but it may not be strong enough to weave, especially as warp thread.

Some terms are useful to know when buying wool yarn: *all new wool* or *pure new wool* means that the yarn is made of fibres which have come straight from the sheep. If a wool yarn is not called by one of these terms it may well be reprocessed wool – sometimes from off-cuts of new fabrics, but often from used fabrics such as torn-up sweaters. This wool yarn will be much cheaper, but will not be as elastic or as long-lasting as the one made of new wool, and will probably be dingier in colour; it may well be labelled *all wool*, or *100 per cent wool*.

Silk comes in filament form – that is, a continuous length. It comes from the cocoon of the silk worm – 1 to 2 km (a mile or a mile and a half) in length from one cocoon (13). Silk is the only fibre which occurs naturally in fila-ment form, though it can also be chopped into small lengths, combed and spun like cotton; this is often done with the short lengths left over from the cocoon or broken cocoon: it is then called *spun silk*, and is slightly less lustrous. Silk has always been used for fine fabrics (colour 1, colour 3), and today it is used for luxury dress or furnishing fabrics or accessories (back cover 4). The staple form, spun silk, is much rougher and cheaper than the thrown filament yarn.

Cotton fibres surround the seeds in the boll, or pod of the cotton plant (13). They are normally white in colour and take dye very well (14). Cotton is a strong fibre, and very suitable for beginners to use. It can also be bleached to a bright white, and is sometimes *mercerised* to give it a permanent gleam:

14 Cotton textile from Ashanti, Ghana, woven in narrow strips, using indigo and undyed yarn in many different patterns.

this is done by treating it in a caustic soda solution while the fibres are under tension. Cotton is useful for all forms of weaving to be used as furnishing – table cloths and mats, cushions, curtains and so on – as it washes well.

15 Stems of flax, bent to show the linen fibres inside.

Linen fibres lie inside the stem of the flax plant, and have to be extracted by rotting away the unwanted outer part of the stem (15). Linen yarns are very strong indeed, and are good yarns for the experienced weaver, but they lack elasticity. They are difficult for beginners to use as a warp because the fibres expand or contract according to changes in humidity, which can produce areas of varied warp tension. Linen has uses varying from the finest table linen to heavy rug warps. It is cool, heavy and flexible (283).

Jute is another *bast* fibre – that is, from the stem of the plant – and although the yarns have attractive qualities of texture and colour, and are popular for wall hangings (16) or even rugs, it should be used with caution as it deteriorates rapidly, especially in damp conditions.

Sisal is also popular with some hand-weavers, for hangings and mats, but it is difficult to use because it is very stiff and bouncy. Its attractive creamy-white colour will turn yellow quite quickly, and although it takes dye well initially, the colour will usually fade rapidly.

In addition, there are a few **mineral fibres:** *metal*, usually used in wire form; *asbestos*, which is now recognised as too dangerous to use in any form; and *glass*, which as glassfibre yarn has interesting and useful properties as yet little explored by the hand-weaver. Great care must be taken in handling this fibre: plastic gloves are essential – leather ones have permeable pores.

Man-made fibres

Man-made fibres are made in continuous filament form, and are sometimes used like that, often to imitate silk; or they are crimped with heat and cut up into shorter lengths to imitate wool or other natural fibres and are spun in that form. Most man-made fibres lack the qualities of the real thing.

On the other hand, some man-made fibres possess qualities which can't be found in natural fibres, and these will probably be the most interesting ones for the hand-weaver: for example *alginate fibres*, made from sea-weed, dissolve in water, and can be used to support other yarns temporarily during the weaving of a very open cloth; they can then be washed away during the finishing process. *Nylon monofilament yarns* are nearly invisible, and are very strong indeed (colour 20).

Always be alive to the possibilities of unconventional materials: newspaper, rags, metals, chain, grasses – any substance which comes in or can be formed into long lengths can be used for some weaving purpose.

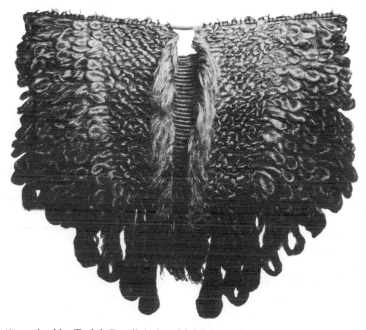

16 'Eruption' by Tadek Beutlich, in which he uses lustrous unspun jute fibres.

Types of yarn

The characteristics of a yarn are affected not only by the type of fibre, but by the way it is turned into a yarn: see Chapter Two for more detail about spinning and plying. Fibres are twisted or spun together to form a yarn, and this twisting can be *hard* with many turns to the centimetre (inch), or *soft* with only a few. A hard-spun yarn will be strong – unless too much twist has made it brittle – but can be difficult to weave and will make a harsh and wiry cloth. A yarn with only a few twists per centimetre (inch) can fall apart easily, and it certainly won't be suitable for a warp yarn, but it will be soft to the touch, and will help a fabric to drape well.

Wool fibres can be spun in two very different ways (17): the fibres can be prepared so that they form a spiral along the length of the yarn (18); when they are twisted together the yarn has projecting fibres; this is called a *woollen* yarn, and makes for a soft, springy, warm cloth. The fibres can also be prepared by combing them parallel before spinning so that a smooth yarn results: this is called a *worsted* yarn (19); the resulting weaving will not be as warm a cloth but it will be smoother, and smarter-looking.

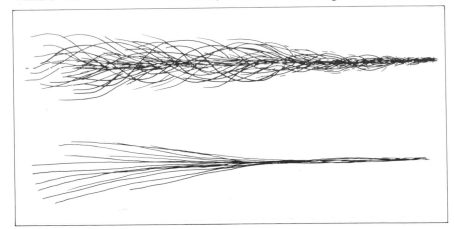

17 Structure of yarn; *top:* woollen-spun; *below:* worsted-spun.

18 Spiralling wool fibres make a warm woollen-spun yarn.

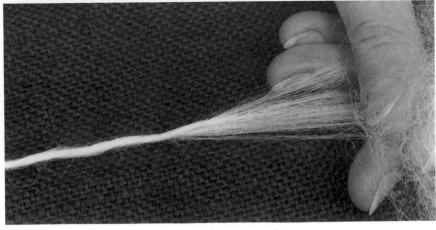

19 Parallel wool fibres are worsted-spun into a smooth yarn.

When fibres are spun into a yarn, that yarn is called *singles*. Two singles can be twisted together to form a two-ply, or two-fold yarn, three make a three-ply yarn, and so on (20). This does not indicate the thickness of the yarn (a confusion which has arisen through the common way of describing knitting wools). A singles yarn is always trying to twist with something, and a singles yarn in the warp will bed in well with a singles weft; tweeds are usually woven with singles yarns for this reason. However, singles yarn is more difficult to handle and beginners should avoid using it for the first few warps. Singles linen in the warp is one of the most difficult yarns to weave, and only suitable for experienced weavers.

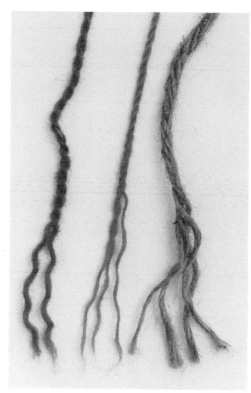

20 Two, three, or four singles are plied into two, three or, four-ply yarns.

Thickness

A special system is used to describe the exact thickness of a yarn (see Page 12) and this will also indicate the length per kilo (pound), that it is necessary to know when the weaver is ordering for a project. Basically, singles yarn can be spun in any thickness, from hair-fine to the thickness of a finger, and the resulting thickness of several of these plied together will obviously vary according to the thickness of the original singles.

Fancy yarns

One type of fancy yarn occurs when two singles of very different thicknesses are plied together. This forms a yarn known as *spiral*. If one of the singles was a *slub* yarn – that is, uneven in thickness, *spiral slub* would result. If, during plying, one more highly twisted yarn was released at intervals at a much faster rate than the other, then a *snarl* would result. Other variations include *knop, flake, gimp* and *crêpe* (21). *Chenille yarn*, looking like its name (French for caterpillar), is an oddity, being the only yarn which is actually a woven fabric first, cut between the warp threads to form the furry yarn. None of these fancy yarns should be used as a warp yarn by beginners, as they tend to catch in the heddles and reed, and can break.

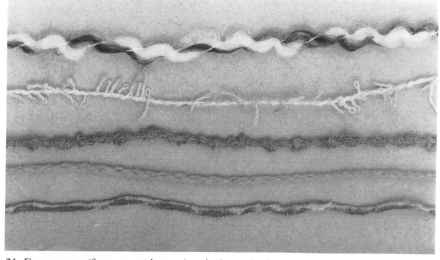

21 Fancy yarns (from *top* to *bottom*): spiral, snarl, gimp, crêpe, chenille.

Which fibre and yarn to use?

This is one of the most important, and difficult, questions for the handweaver. With such a wide variety of fibres and yarns available, you can narrow down the choice by asking yourself a few questions about the fabric which is to be woven:

1 What will its function be? Is it to be worn, hung, sat upon, walked on, or just looked at?

2 Will it be washed regularly? Cotton washes well, but wool may felt.
3 Should it be hard or soft?
4 Does warmth matter? Woollen spun yarn is warmer than worsted.

Some of the answers to these questions will indicate a yarn type as well as a fibre. Thickness will probably be obvious; a plied yarn, especially for the warp, is desirable. Any fancy yarns should be reserved for the weft.

In your notebook, keep a page for each project, and record all the details of the yarns you choose, the weave, sett, and later finishing. It is always a good idea to weave a few extra centimetres (inches) on a piece, so that you can keep a sample, preferably in the book. This way you will start to build up your experience of yarn behaviour (277).

Buying yarn

Although there are a few specialist shops scattered around the country, most yarns suitable for weaving can only be bought by post, by choosing from a sample card. A few yarns in knitting shops, especially the cotton and fancy yarns, are suitable for weaving, but in general yarns designed for knitting should *not* be used for weaving. They are spun with less twist, and are suitable for looped structures such as knitting and crochet, but when woven together they tend to make an unsatisfactory cloth.

Most suppliers of weaving yarns will supply small quantities, but it is a good idea to buy a little more than you think you need for a project. Not only is this a safeguard, in case calculations were not quite accurate, but also you can add any left-overs to a growing store of oddments, very useful when planning future weaving.

How much yarn to buy?

How much yarn to buy depends on a number of variables such as the kind of cloth to be woven. Instructions for calculating the amount are given on Pages 60 and 98. Once you have determined the length of yarn you need, the length has to be converted into weight, as yarn is sold by weight.

The Count systems

The numbers, such as 10/2s, 8 cut, 10 skein, by the side of yarn samples in spinners' lists baffle some weavers, but they are there to describe the yarn, and to enable you to calculate how much to buy. The system is complex, and it is made more complicated by the fact that not only does the system vary according to the fibre being used, but it also has regional variations, especially in the woollen yarn category. Wool can be 'counted' by the Galashiels system of *cuts*, or by the Yorkshire *skein* and there are many other methods.

Marianne Straub describes the 'Yarn count system' in her book 'Hand weaving and cloth design':

'The yarn count expresses the thickness of the yarn, and must be known before calculating the quantity of yarns for a known length of fabric. The yarn-count number indicates the length of the yarn in relation to the weight.

Three systems of yarn count are currently in use: the fixed-weight, the fixed-length, and the Tex systems. The fixed-weight system can be used with British and American weights and measures. The fixed-length system and the Tex system are based on metric weights and measures. Tex is an internationally agreed system of yarn numbering that applies to all types of yarns, regardless of the method of production.

The fixed-weight system

The fixed-weight yarn-count system is used for numbering spun yarns. It is based on the length of yarn per lb weight. The greater the length of yarn weighing 1 lb, the finer it is and the higher the count number. The count number gives the number of unit lengths, ie skeins, hanks, etc in 1 lb: for example, 10 hanks cotton (abbreviated to '10's cotton'); 12 skeins Yorkshire woollen spun (12's Y.sk).

The unit length of 1's count (ie one unit length to 1 lb weight) varies with different fibres and spinning systems:

Woollen spun	Galashiels	cut	200 yd
	Yorkshire	skein	256 yd
	West of England	hank	320 yd
Worsted		hank	560 yd
Linen		lea	300 yd
Cotton		hank	840 yd
Spun silk		hank	840 yd

Man-made spun yarns are numbered according to their spinning method.

To find the length of a yarn of a known count, the unit length is multiplied by the count number, eg, 10's cotton has $10 \times 840 = 8400$ yd per lb.

When a yarn is plied – that is, when two yarns of identical count are twisted together – the yarn is twice as thick and therefore the length of a lb weight is halved. The numbering of the yarn states both the count of the single component and the number of components that make up the ply, eg, 2/10's cotton; the length of this yarn would be:

$$\frac{10 \times 840}{2} = 4200 \text{ yd per lb.}$$

All plied yarns within the fixed-weight system state the number of components before the count of the yarn with the exception of spun silk. In this case the yarn count precedes the number of components, 30/2 spun silk. In this example the count is 30 made up of two components each having a count of 60, giving a total yarn length of $30 \times 840 = 25,200$ yd per lb.

The fixed-length system

This system is used to number continuous filament yarns, that is, reeled silk and man-made extruded yarns. It is based on a fixed yarn length to a variable weight, and is measured in deniers. The denier count of a yarn states the weight in grammes per 9000 metres. Thus a 10-denier yarn will weigh 10 grammes and measure 9000 metres. The coarser the yarn, the higher the denier count number becomes. Thus 9000 metres of a 30-denier yarn weigh 30 grammes.

The Tex system

The Tex system is also based on the fixed-length system, ie weight per unit length. The Tex count represents the weight in grammes per 1 kilometre (1000 metres) of yarn, ie a yarn numbered 10 Tex measures 1 kilometre and weighs 10 grammes. The Tex number increases with the size of the yarn.

The yarns are labelled according to an international code. The yarn count number is followed by the word Tex. The term 'folded' is used in preference to 'plied' yarn when two or more yarns are twisted together, and the direction of the twist is included in the information. Example: R 20 Tex/2 S; two threads of 10 Tex are folded in an 'S' direction, therefore the resultant count (R) will be 20 Tex because the weight is exactly doubled.'

(Y.sk. is also written ysw.)

Packaging the yarn

Yarn can come packaged in several forms, very often a hank or skein convenient for dyeing. Before using it to make a warp it must be wound into a ball. First of all be prepared to spend a little time making sure that the skein is straight and free from tangles. You will see that it is tied around at least once, usually twice or more; one of these ties will also have the beginning and end of the skein knotted to it. *It is very important not to remove these ties yet.*

Ideally, place the skein on a skein winder (22). Once the skein is firmly on the holder try to work out which of the two ends is the beginning, on the outside of the hank. If the skein is really tangled hang it over a smooth projection, like a door-knob, and bring the side of your hand sharply down inside the skein banging it into alignment. Revolve it around a little, bang it again, and repeat the process till it is straightened out. Then replace it on the holder, remove the ties and wind the skein off into a ball.

You can wind from the skein into a ball by hand, and then place the ball in a jar on the floor so that it can run freely during warping. Better still, and faster, is a cylindrical 'ball' made on the sort of ball-winder used by machine-knitters (23): when using this sort of ball, always take the thread from the *inside* of the ball.

Some weaving yarn arrives on a *cheese*, also called a *cop*; ideally this should be placed horizontally during warping, on a spool rack (24), or you can use a knitting needle pushed through a cardboard box (25), or placed vertically on a large nail driven through a piece of wood. This is ideal for *pirns* which are tapered, but the top of a cheese can sometimes catch the yarn as it comes off, especially when it's nearly empty.

22 A 'rice', to hold skeins.

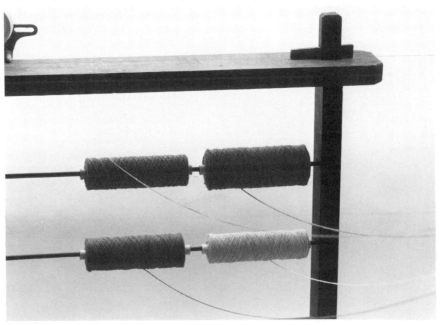

24 Cylindrical cheeses of yarn will run easily on a spool rack.

Sometimes yarn arrives *on cone*, which can sit on the floor during warping.

The main consideration is that, however the yarn arrives, it runs freely and easily to the hand holding it during the warping process.

Colour

Probably the remaining question is the choice of colour. Some weavers never buy dyed yarn, preferring the flexibility of keeping plenty of natural yarns in stock, dyeing them when needed. I like to have the inspiration of seeing coloured yarns around the studio, and often unexpected neighbours on my shelves spark off a colour scheme. Dyeing is dealt with in Chapter Three.

23 A device for winding balls which will stack for storage.

25 An improvised spool-rack: a knitting needle pushed through a cardboard box.

Chapter Two

Spinning

by Geraldine St. Aubyn Hubbard

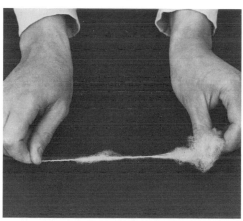

26 Fibres becoming yarn.

The nature of a cloth depends very much on the initial design of the yarn from which it is woven. Yarn is made by spinning – that is, by pulling out fibres and twisting them together (26). Of course, the weaver can buy yarns already spun, but many like to spin their own. If, therefore, you decide to spin your own yarn, keep the end-product firmly in mind from the beginning.

The differences in yarn depend on two factors: the character of the fibre used, and the method of preparation and spinning.

There are two main types of preparation and spinning. One is called the *woollen* system, which uses shorter fibres spiralling to give a warm, elastic, springy, bouncy yarn (17, 18). The other is called the *worsted* system, and this uses longer fibres lying parallel to give a smooth, sleek, lustrous, cool yarn (17, 19). You may want a yarn which is hard or soft, hairy or smooth, bouncy or limp. An understanding of the woollen and worsted systems and their results will give the spinner a basic vocabulary for designing an infinite variety of yarns, and so fabrics.

Wool

In this chapter we will deal with the preparation and spinning of wool, because wool is the most common fibre used by weavers, and one which displays a wide range of exploitable characteristics. Other fibres with similar characteristics can be treated in the same way, although preparation may need to be different – see Booklist for books dealing with other fibres.

The spinner can buy wool at various stages: the whole fleece, which needs preparation; or wool that has been ready-sorted, or wool in even later stages of preparation, though this will limit your scope for design, and will be more expensive.

Breeds of sheep

Within Great Britain there are about thirty-six pure breeds of sheep, and many cross-breeds developed for increased meat production. It is sometimes difficult to identify the exact breed of a fleece, but this may not matter providing one looks very hard at the character of the wool. Has it a long or short staple? Is it bouncy or limp, frizzy or sleek, soft or hard, elastic or not? Whichever characteristics it exhibits, these should be used in the designing of the yarn and may dictate which technique of preparation and spinning to choose. Always bear in mind the purpose for which the fabric will be used: is it to be soft for knitting or for a dress? Must it be resistant to abrasion for upholstery, or hard-wearing for floor rugs? Is it to be a warm or cool fabric, light or heavy?

British wool breeds fall roughly into three categories, but these should be used only as a guide, as there are exceptions, particularly as breeds are often reared on pastures far from their original habitat, and this can affect the characteristics of the wool.

Mountain and hill breeds, such as the Welsh Mountain, Rough Fell, Herdwick and Blackface. The length of staple is medium to long, 8 to 18 cm (3 to 7 in). May be coarse or hard, or open and softer, but usually contains *kemps* – short, wiry fibres, which may be white, red or black, will not take dye, and cannot easily be removed from the fleece. Some breeds may even

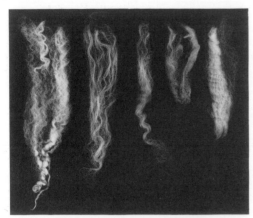

27 Longwools and lustres: Masham, Devon Longwool, Lincoln, Border Leicester and Kent.

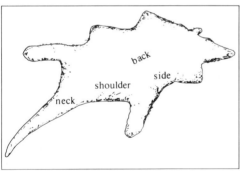

28 Short wools and downs: Hampshire Down, Southdown, Suffolk, Dorset Down.

contain two types of fibre growing at once: the Blackface has a long, hairy outer coat, and a shorter, softer undercoat or *bottom wool*. These two may be treated separately, in quite different ways.

Longwools and lustres These are generally long wools, 12 to 46 cm (5 to 18 in). Some are soft and semi-lustrous, like the Kent breeds and Border Leicester, others are harder but particularly lustrous and sleek – for example, Lincoln or Devon Longwool (27).

Shortwools and downs, such as Hampshire Down, Dorset Down, and Suffolk. Short staple wools – 10 cm (4 in) or shorter. These have bouncy wools – usually fine and close – much elasticity and are usually soft. Particularly fine and springy is the Southdown. Their wools show a marked degree of crimp (28).

Choosing a fleece

When buying wool it is important that it is sound – that is, that there are no weak places along the staple caused by illness or lack of food. There tends to be a period of weak growth at the end of the winter (less food) and then a spurt of strong growth in the spring. This particular weak patch very often disappears as the shears cut across this area, when the sheep are shorn – but if this is left too late it may show up.

Test a lock by taking it from the fleece, holding it at each end and giving it a sharp tug: it will pull apart at any weak point. You can also see weaknesses by holding the lock up to the light.

Unrolling and sorting the fleece

Usually the fleece is rolled up after shearing in such a way that the finest wool is on the outside, the coarser wool inside. The fleece is thrown on the ground cut side downwards, and folded into three lengthways. It is then rolled from the tail to the head, and generally wool pulled from the neck or back is twisted into a band, bound round the fleece and tucked in (29).

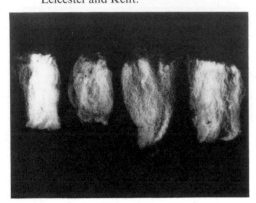

30 Parts of a fleece.

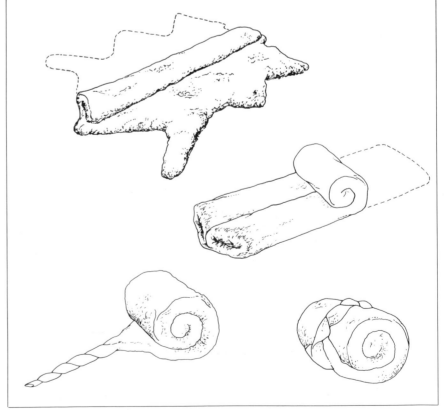

29 How a fleece is rolled.

16

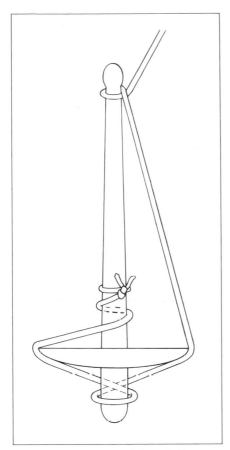

31 Path of yarn around the spindle.

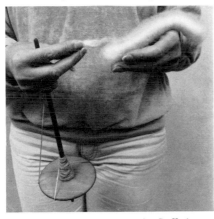

32 Woollen spinning: put the fluffed-out end of the yarn into the rolag.

33 Twist the spindle.

Unroll the fleece; if it has not been rolled as described, then undo it very carefully, and try to spread it out with the cut side on the floor (on polythene, not carpet) or on a large table. Having chosen a fleece, it is not enough simply to start spinning from wool on the outside and gradually work through, as there are many different qualities of fibre in the one fleece, and these need sorting out. Gentle shaking can help with some disentanglements. Sometimes it is almost impossible to spread it out so that front and back legs are obvious, and indeed it is more important to get like qualities together than to spread it out in a particular way. The finest fibres are found on the shoulders, the coarsest on the back legs – indeed these may be almost 'hairy'. The sides may have quite long fibres, graduating in fineness between front and back. The back often has slightly shorter fibres than the corresponding side area, and it may be drier – the oil is washed towards the sides by the rain (30).

Most fleeces can be sorted into at least three different qualities, many into five and some into eight or ten; it depends on the variety of fibres within one fleece, the sensitivity of the wool sorter and the uses to which the wool will be put. There are no hard and fast divisions – the diagram should act only as a guide; it is a matter of skill in judgement which will only improve with practice and time spent looking at and feeling the fibres. Often names like *britch* (back legs) and *diamond* (shoulders) may be given to the different divisions of the fleece, but these vary in different parts of the country. You may like to develop your own classification system for particular fleeces.

These qualities will produce very different types of yarn, both in the way they spin and in the way they react to washing in the final cloth. It is possible to blend fibres; this takes skill to do accurately, but is a normal practice in industry. However, it seems a pity for the hand-spinner not to take the opportunity of doing something that industry is not equipped to do – that is, to use the small quantities of sorted wool, exploiting their particular characteristics, rather than to use a general blend, as industry does.

If you need more of one quality of wool for a particular job than one fleece gives you, then instead of blending coarse and fine   the fine fibres occur all too seldom, and it seems a waste to lose them in a blend – spin two similar qualities from the fleece separately, and then ply them together; this will produce a more even and interesting blend than a mixture of coarse and fine.

Spinning tools

All the spinning tools provide a means of obtaining twist and somewhere to store the yarn when it is made. All sorts of tools are in use all over the world: there are three main groups.

The spindle A spindle consists of a central shaft of wood, and a weight or *whorl*, made of wood, ceramic or stone. Spindle whorls have been found in sites from 3 000 BC onwards (386). The whorl adds momentum to the spindle, and acts as a base on which to build up the yarn.

To use a spindle, tie a piece of yarn to the spindle immediately above the whorl. Then pass the yarn down over the whorl, round the shaft, back up over the whorl, and tie a half hitch at the top of the shaft (31).

Hold the prepared fibre in the left hand, the yarn from the spindle in the right hand. Fluff out the end of the yarn and put it into the prepared fibre (32). Twist the spindle. The most common way is clockwise, but you can spin it either way, as long as you continue to twist it in the same direction; if you don't, the twist will undo and the whole thing will land on the floor. Release the spindle and let it hang from the yarn, twisting it occasionally with your fingers to keep it spinning, leaving your hands free most of the time to manipulate the fibres. Allow the twist to travel up into the fibres (33–36). As the fibres begin to twist, begin to draw them out in the woollen or the worsted method (see Pages 20 and 22).

17

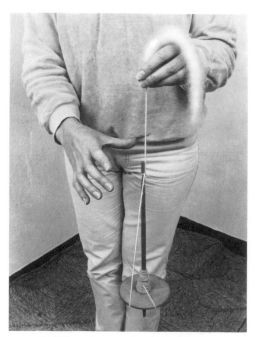

34 The twist travels up the fibres.

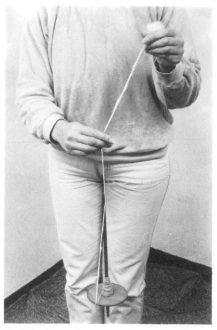

35 Woollen spinning: pull out the fibres to form the yarn.

36 Add twist to strengthen the yarn, before winding it onto the fingers in a figure of eight.

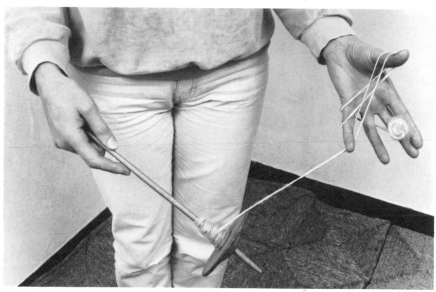

37 Unwind the yarn from the fingers onto the spindle.

When you can't stretch your hands any further apart, you may need to add a little twist to make the yarn stronger. Hold the spindle with the right hand to prevent it untwisting. Wind the yarn onto the fingers of your left hand in a figure-of-eight. Undo the half hitch on the spindle shaft, undo the yarn from the base of the whorl, and wind the yarn from your fingers on to the spindle, starting nearest the whorl and working backwards and forwards to make a cone shape, widest nearer the whorl (37): this helps to increase the momentum of the spin. Arrange the last few centimetres (in) of spun yarn around the whorl and shaft as described above and begin to spin again. The yarn must be strong enough to support the weight of the spindle. This method is widely used in peasant cultures of the world, as it provides mobility, so yarn can be spun while walking. Both woollen and worsted spinning is possible this way.

Another method of using this same spindle is to sit on the floor, or a wide seat, and rotate the spindle top against the shin or thigh, the other end resting on the floor, the whole spindle lying at an angle (38). In this case only one hand is available for drawing the fibres out, so this is most suited to the woollen method. As the yarn is at an angle of about 45° to the spindle shaft, twist is flipped off on to the yarn as the spinner rotates the spindle.

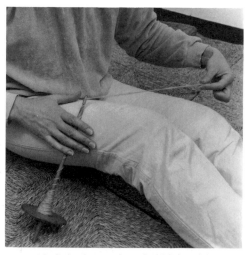

38 Spinning against the thigh, with the yarn at an angle of 45° to the shaft.

(If the yarn were parallel with the shaft it would unwind; if it were at right angles to it, it would wind onto the shaft.) After a length of yarn is made, unwind it from the shaft and then hold the yarn at right angles to the spindle to wind it on, starting nearest to the whorl as before. This supported spindle method demands a stationary spinner, but it does make it possible to produce a fine yarn that may not be capable of supporting the weight of a spindle; for example spinners making cotton for Dacca muslin support the spindle in a shell.

The spindle wheel This is really a spindle supported in a horizontal position, whose whorl is driven by a much larger wheel, which is turned by hand. It can also be used for winding bobbins for weaving. As with the spindle, the making of the yarn and the winding on are two separate processes. These wheels were in use until the last century in remote areas for the making of woollen yarn. This method was adapted for the *spinning jenny* and later the *mule* in industry.

The flyer wheel This is the wheel you are most likely to use. It has a device called a *flyer* which enables the wheel to twist the yarn and wind it onto a bobbin simultaneously. The flyer wheel was not invented until about 1520 – quite late compared to spindles. In order that the twisted yarn should wind onto the bobbin, it is essential that the bobbin and flyer rotate at different speeds, the bobbin either faster or slower than the flyer. Also, at times you will need to be able to twist the yarn without winding it on, so the speed at which it is wound on to the bobbin must be capable of variation.

There are two principal methods of achieving these aims:

i) The double drive band wheel (39) The bobbin and flyer each have a whorl of different diameters; usually the whorl on the bobbin is smaller than that of the flyer. They are driven by a band passing round the large wheel twice and once round each whorl. Of necessity this band itself crosses once and thus the bobbin is driven faster than the flyer, causing the spun yarn to be wound onto it. This effect is increased if the band is tightened, preventing slippage; this has to be done progressively as the bobbin fills and the circumference grows. Remember to slacken the band when starting an empty bobbin. The band tension needs constant adjustment according to the fibre being spun, and also according to the level of humidity in the air.

ii) Single band and friction brake (40) This wheel has only a single driving band going round the main wheel once and turning only the flyer, but the yarn running from the flyer drags the bobbin around at the same speed. The spinner slows down the bobbin, by applying a friction brake round its whorl, so that the yarn will wind onto the bobbin. This friction band has an adjustable tension, to control how fast the yarn will wind onto the bobbin.

The spinner can work quite fast on both these wheels, as the large driving wheel is turned by means of a foot treadle, which leaves both hands free for making the yarn.

39 The double drive band flyer wheel.   40 Single band and friction brake wheel.

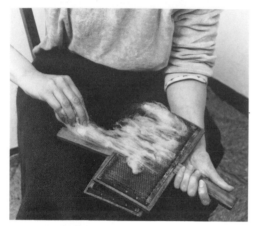

41 Teasing the fibres.

42 Pull the wool onto one of the carders.

Woollen spinning

This technique is for producing a light, warm, air-filled yarn, elastic and springy (17, 18), so fibres with some or all of these characteristics are best suited for this type of spinning. Use lengths of fibre from 2 to 12 cm (1 to 5 in); longer than this they become very difficult to handle successfully.

Teasing This means opening the fibres and actually drawing them apart so that they separate – particularly disentangling the tips, which are often glued together with grease and dirt. Do this carefully, without breaking the fibres (41). At this stage remove any very short lumps of fibre (for example, from second cuts of the shears), as they will cause lumps in the yarn; much of the vegetable matter, seeds, leaves, dirt and dust, will also fall out. Once you have separated the fibres, mix them together again as large handfuls, they won't stick to one another.

At this stage it is advisable to lubricate the wool; this lessens fibre breakage at the next stage and makes spinning easier, as the fibres are able to slide over one another more easily. You can use oil; olive oil is best though expensive. Cooking oil is a possibility, though it's difficult to wash out and get rid of that fish-and-chip smell. An olive oil and water emulsion is particularly good. Add a few drops – four to six drops to a handful of wool – and mix them well into the fibres.

Carding The next stage is carding – that is, spreading the fibres evenly and aligning them. Pull a handful of the teased and lubricated wool on to one of the carders (42). Don't put too much wool on at once – it makes thick bats of wool which are difficult to roll up later. Carders have angled metal wires set into leather or rubberised cloth; they should not be sharp nor set rigidly but be flexible, otherwise they tend to tear the fibres. Brush the fibres by working the teeth of the carders *against* each other. Do not engage the carders too much at the beginning of each stroke, but gradually increase the pressure: usually people are too fierce with the fibres, so imagine that you are brushing your hair with the carders (43–45). Then to ensure that all the wool is brushed, turn the underside to the surface – this also changes the wool from one side of the carder to the other (46–47), thus evenly spreading the fibres. Then strip the fibres off and re-card them by working the teeth *with* each other, starting at the edge of the carder and working gradually towards the handle.

Make about 6 to 8 strokes between each stripping action, and strip at least 4 times; the wool will end up alternately on one carder, and then the other. In fact, the grip of the hands need never change; the right wrist simply turns over for the stripping. I find that by resting the left carder on the left knee the knee acts as a lever, taking some of the strain, and the right hand and arm work diagonally across the body from left knee to right hip – you need plenty of elbow room. Try an experiment: start with black wool on half the carder, white on the other, and see how well they are blended by the end.

The rolag When the wool is evenly blended across the carders, strip it off, release it and turn it on to the back of the left carder (48). Roll it up, using

43 Begin the first stroke near the bottom of the carder.

44 Gradually begin subsequent strokes nearer the handle.

45 Near the end of the final stroke: the fibres are ready for stripping off.

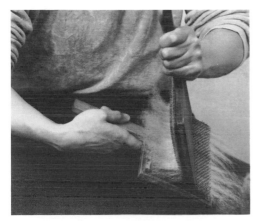

46 Begin to strip the fibres off one carder onto the other.

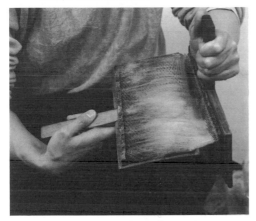

47 Stripping off: keep the carders open and the fibres flat.

the left hand and the back of the right carder (49). Once the initial curl is started, push down and roll (50). This roll is called a *rolag*; don't allow it to elongate at this stage by too much handling.

The twist To understand the principles of woollen spinning, take one end of the rolag between the thumb and forefinger of the right hand, twist (without letting go the twist), moving the left hand about 5 cm (2 in) away from the right hand, and pull between the two hands while twisting. You will see that as the fibres pull out the twist will go to the thinnest parts, the parts of least resistance, and bind them, preventing the fibres sliding any further apart. The lumps have little or no twist, so if you continue to pull, the fibres will slide past one another in these areas, which will become thinner, and the twist will bind them together. Eventually, if pulling and twisting are done at the right moment, you will get an even yarn. You will notice that the fibres spiral *into* the twist, enveloping pockets of air which will make the yarn warm and light. As the fibres are pulled out like a coiled spring, they make the yarn elastic and springy. In this pulling or *drafting* action, the yarn feels a little like chewing gum; if you go on too long the yarn will break, as it will not have enough twists per centimetre (inch) to hold it together. To prevent this, add more twist, just enough to make it firm.

Wheel-spinning woollen Start by attaching a long, 2-metre (2-yard) piece of spun yarn to the bobbin, and thread it round one of the hooks, or *hecks*, and through the hole in the flyer – making sure that it follows a straight path (if twisted it won't draw in properly when required (51)). Check the band tension and drawing-in speed of the yarn. Start the wheel clockwise (you can spin anti-clockwise if you wish, as long as you remain consistent) and with the yarn in the left hand hold the fluffy end of the rolag in the right hand next to the yarn. As the twist rotates the yarn, fibres from the rolag will be caught in (52). To prevent a lump at this stage, pull the rolag back slightly, drawing out the fibres. Let go the left hand – the twist will run up the fibres to the right hand (53). (Beginners may stop the wheel at this stage.) Re-grip with the left hand on or above the join – but ensure that there is space for plenty of twist between the two hands. Let go with the right hand and re-grip the rolag a little further up – taking care not to slide the fingers

48 Place the bat of wool on the back of the carder.

49 Start to roll the bat of wool.

50 Push down and roll the wool to form a rolag.

51 The path of the yarn through the flyer onto the bobbin.

52 The fibres from the rolag catch onto the twisting yarn.

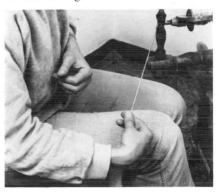

53 Twist running up the fibres to the right hand.

54 With the left hand on the join re-grip the rolag. Then pull out the right hand until the yarn is of the thickness you require.

55 Remove the left hand to add twist.

56 Collect twist for the next draft with the right hand over the right knee.

57 Re-grip with the left hand, half way between the right hand and the mouth of the wheel.

up or disturb the spiral structure (54). Then gently pull the right hand away from the left hand. Depending on the amount of twist on the fibres it will be easy or difficult to pull, so try this little test: allow a little more twist through the left fingers; if it is too easy to pull there is not enough twist – and you will get a thin, mean yarn with no body. If it is too difficult to pull, there is too much twist, so move the right fingers further up the rolag.

Pull out until the yarn is of the required thickness, then allow a little more twist onto it by removing the left hand (55); (beginners, re-start the wheel). All the twist will run up the yarn if it is taut. This is the stage at which you fix the amount of twist you want in your yarn. Let the yarn run swiftly but taut into the wheel, but stop short when the right hand is directly over the right knee; this allows for space for the twist to build up, ready for the next pull, or *draft* (56). Use the left fingers as a clamp – halfway between the right hand (point of twist) and the wheel mouth (57), and then repeat the drafting process. This drafting against the twist, together with the spiral structure of the rolag, is what gives woollen-spun yarn its warm, light, bulky and elastic characteristics.

Worsted spinning

This technique will produce a smooth, sleek, lustrous, cool yarn, so is best suited for fibres with those characteristics (17, 19). It is also used for spinning strong, resilient yarns from hard, non-lustrous fibres. Use lengths of fibre from about 10 cm (4 in) up to 50 cm (20 in). Some shorter fibres, if very fine, can be spun by this method – for example merino wool.

Washing Wash the wool first, by soaking in hand-hot water about 44 to 54°C (about 110 to 130°F) for 10 minutes, then in hot water with well-dissolved soap flakes, enough to form a lather. If the wool is very greasy, you may have to repeat this soap wash. Handle the fleece as little as possible and don't give it any sharp temperature changes. Rinse two or more times to remove all the soap, and then spread it out to dry naturally; if it dries too fast the wool will feel brittle.

Combing This process is designed to remove all the short fibres, leaving long fibres which are lying straight and parallel. Take a lock or staple from the washed fleece and pull it through a comb (clamped firmly to keep it stationary), starting at one end of the fibres and gradually working towards the middle (58, 59). If too many fibres are pulled through at once, some may break. Then turn the lock round and comb it from the other end. You may like to put a tiny drop of oil at the bottom of the comb. All the short fibres remain on the comb; the long fibres are kept straight and parallel. The long fibres are called *top* (60).

These fibres are then drafted to form a *roving*, as follows: pull them out a few fibres at a time, only half the length of the fibre at a time (61); continue

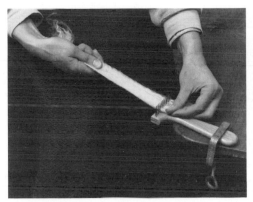

58 Place one end of the lock over the teeth of the comb.

59 Hold the fibres firmly and pull away from the comb.

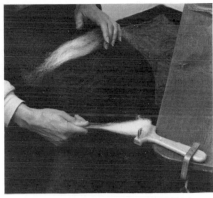

60 After combing, put any long fibres still on the comb parallel with the other combed fibres. These are called *top*; the short fibres left on the comb are *noil*.

61 Draft fibres to form a roving.

62 Turn the hand over to add a small amount of twist.

drafting the fibres until the whole roving has been dealt with. Put a small amount of twist into the roving by turning the hand over while drafting (62). To distribute the fibres evenly along the length of the roving, pull it apart in the middle, lay one half on top of the other and draft again in the same way. This will blend the fibres so that they are able to slide past one another easily without sticking together.

The short fibres left on the comb are called *noil* (60) and may be spun using the woollen method. They would of course have to be re-oiled to replace the natural lanolin removed by washing.

The worsted method In the worsted method, unlike woollen spinning, there is never any twist *between* the two hands. The twist, provided by spindle or wheel, follows on to the yarn behind one pair of fingers as they smooth up the fibres, before the next draft. As the fibres are straight and parallel, they meet the twist end on, there are no air-spaces between them. They lie flatly together, have little or no elasticity and therefore provide a cool yarn which is sleek and lustrous – as long as the original fibres used are suitable. In order to keep these parallel, smooth fibres together, it is necessary to put in a little more twist than into a singles woollen yarn. Singles worsted may therefore be termed 'unstable', and causes fabrics to curl at their edges, but this is overcome by *plying* two yarns together in the opposite direction to the way in which they were spun (see Pages 24 to 26).

Wheel-spinning worsted Attach some spun yarn to the bobbin, thread it, and check for winding speed as for woollen spinning. Holding the yarn in the left hand, allow fibres from the sliver in the right hand to curl into the yarn in front of the left fingers. The left fingers constantly grip the yarn, *never* allowing the twist through onto the fibres. Twist simply travels up, following the left fingers. With the left hand, draft or pull the fibres away from the right hand; these fibres should have no twist on them and may only be pulled a little way (63) or they will part company! As the fibres are drafted, the yarn travels into the wheel. At the end of each draft, the left fingers slide up

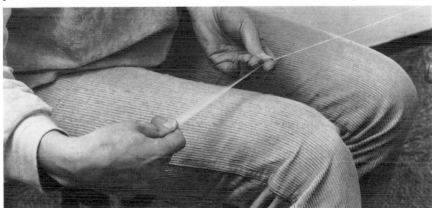

63 Worsted spinning: draft the fibres with no twist between the two hands.

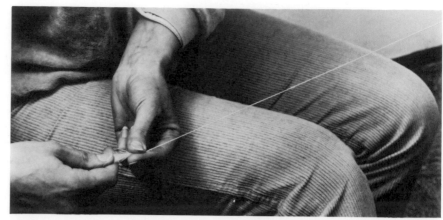

64 Smooth the left fingers up to the right hand – the twist will follow.

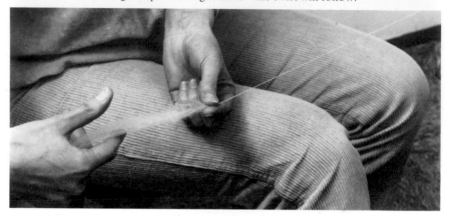

65 Re-grip the roving, or sliver, with the right hand.

towards the right hand, smoothing in any fibres and increasing the lustre of the yarn; the twist follows the left fingers (64). The right fingers re-grip the sliver ready for the next draft (65). If twist is allowed between the two hands, it is impossible to draft the long fibres as they are quickly bound together by the twist. This is an almost continuous process: the wheel has to be turning all the time, slowly and evenly to give the right amount of twist. The drafting of straight fibres, parallel with one another and the yarn, is what gives worsted-spun yarn its density, smoothness, coolness and lustre.

Other spinning methods

There are other methods of spinning which combine certain characteristics of these two distinct methods. One is the spinning of very short fibres by allowing the twist to run onto the fibres, while drafting them only a small amount; the twist catches a few fibres at a time. This is not an easy way to get an even thread. Woollen preparation is usually used.

Another method is to card the wool, then roll it from side to side instead of lengthways on the carders and to present the fibres *end on* to the twist, and then to worsted-spin them. This gives parallel alignment but uses both long and short fibres together. Try experimenting with different fibres using the same method of spinning – or try different spinning methods on one fibre – and see how different the resulting yarns can be.

Plying

Plying is the twisting together of two or more singles yarns; by plying, the weaver can increase the choice of yarn for a fabric yet again, and does this for a variety of reasons – to give a yarn added thickness, or to blend two yarns of different colours, types or twists.

Twist The easiest and most widely known way of expressing which way a yarn is twisted is to call it S spun or Z spun. The diagonal of the twist follows the diagonal in the centre of the letters S and Z (66). Most weavers begin

66 Single S and Z spun yarn.

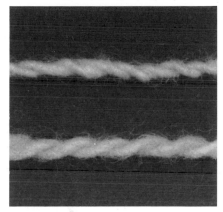

67 Two single Z spun yarns plied S.

68 *Top:* Z spun yarn plied Z, *hard.*
Bottom: Z spun yarn plied S, *soft.*

by turning the wheel clockwise, which gives a Z twist. Choose whichever twist you prefer, as long as you stay consistent for that batch of yarn. You can get some interesting effects from using S and Z twist, for instance, the appearance of subtle stripes by using the same yarn with different twists, and it can influence the handle of the cloth after *wet finishing* (see Page 99.)

Worsted yarn is usually plied to stabilise it, that is, two singles yarns *spun* Z are *plied* together S (67). This reduces the initial twist, and the fibres within the two yarns tend to run up and down the resulting plied yarn lying parallel to its long axis. Stable yarns such as these are particularly required for knitting as it is an unstable single-element fabric. Woven structures are more stable, and you may get away with a less stable yarn.

In theory half as many twists should be put into the plying of two yarns as are put into the singles that go to make them up. In fact, for weaving, particularly warp yarns, you may want to use the same number; it is a matter of experimenting until it looks and feels right.

Yarns are often termed *hard* or *soft* twist: a *hard* twist yarn is obtained by spinning and then plying Z (which adds twist); whereas a *soft* yarn is made by spinning Z and then plying S (reducing twist) (68).

Try plying S + Z yarns together, taking twist off one yarn and putting it on to the other. This may be exaggerated if one yarn is thick and the other one thin, and also if one yarn is held back and the other allowed to fold round it. All sorts of complicated fancy yarns may be built up by twisting two different yarns together, twisting them again with another yarn, and so on (21). Many of the bouclés and fluffy mohairs are produced in this way. Variation in shrinkage when the yarn is washed may also have an effect.

How to ply Plying is most easily done on a wheel, and one with a fairly large hole if thick yarn is used. The tension must be adjusted to draw the yarn in at the required speed.

Method 1 Hold the two (or more) yarns out at arm's length, count the beats of the treadle needed to give the required amount of twist, then let the yarn in, also counting (69, 70). Repeat these counts, drawing the yarn out to the same length, to get a consistent twist.

69 Count the beats of the treadle while the arm is extended.

70 Count the beats of the treadle as the yarn is allowed into the wheel.

71 Allow your fingers to act as a brake and regulate the amount of twist.

Method 2 Adjust the wheel so that it draws the yarn in at the right speed, using your fingers as a partial brake to regulate the amount of yarn passing through them, to allow the correct twist to build up on the yarn (71). This is more difficult, as the drawing-in speed will change as the bobbin fills, so the band tension will have to be adjusted constantly.

The yarn used for plying must be packaged in the same way – for example, all on cones, or all on spinning-wheel bobbins or all in balls. They should ideally be of the same size, otherwise there may also be variation in drag, unintentionally producing fancy yarns. If the yarn is very highly twisted, either by accident or by design, it may be passed between a set of bars to help straighten it out, preventing snarls occurring. Method 2 of plying will help overcome this as well.

After plying, yarn should be washed, so that it settles into itself. Washing will also cause any unexpected uneven shrinkage to make itself known *before* weaving, rather than when the cloth is wet finished after weaving. Don't stretch it at this stage, as fibres may be damaged. If you want kinks, bumps or curls, design them into the yarn in the spinning and plying stages; if you don't want them, make sure you spin and ply the yarn you want, as you won't be able to get rid of them later.

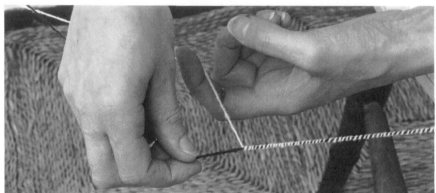

72 Plying a fancy yarn, by retarding the black yarn and allowing the white yarn to fold round it.

Using these basic techniques it is possible to spin a wide variety of fibres into a huge range of yarns. Of course once you have learnt and mastered the rules, you can learn how to break them to produce certain effects.

73 'Merrivale', by Bobbie Cox.

74 Bobbie Cox spinning, direct from the fleece, on her electric machine.

Chapter Three

Dyeing

by Geraldine St. Aubyn Hubbard

The use of colour is one of the main pleasures of weaving, and although you can buy yarn ready dyed, many weavers find that dyeing their own yarn is one of the most exciting and satisfying parts of the weaving process. It need not be difficult, and experimenting with different dyes on different fibres in a variety of combinations can give fascinating results. You have the choice of buying the dyestuffs from a supplier, or collecting your own from the countryside around. Above all, dyeing your own yarn can give you the colour you want on the fibre of your choice – not always possible when dealing with smaller quantities unless you do it yourself.

Take care

A word of warning: many dyestuffs are poisonous; always keep them separate from food and its preparation. If you are dyeing at home in the kitchen, keep separate cleaning equipment for dyebaths, etc. in the dye-cupboard – not to be used inadvertently by guests helping to wash up. Dye-cupboards should be locked, or certainly out of the reach of children.

Be especially careful of ingesting fine particle dyestuffs or chemicals; some can be harmful if used frequently. Always use rubber gloves and wear a protective apron (colour 2). In the case of substances such as ferrous sulphate, caustic soda, sodium dithionite, copper sulphate and potassium dichromate you should wear a mouth mask, and if you are using very fine powders, then you should wear an organic vapour mask.

Types of dyestuff

Dyes are of two types: *natural* dyes derived from plants and animals; and *synthetic* dyes, obtained as concentrated powders from chemical companies. Both types include dyes which are suitable for protein fibres such as wool, hair and silk, and those suitable for cellulose fibres such as cotton, linen, hemp, jute and viscose rayon.

As wool is the yarn that you are most likely to use, especially to begin with, the dyes and processes I shall describe will be suitable for wool unless otherwise stated. See Booklist for books dealing with other yarns.

In certain cases, one dyestuff will be effective on both protein and cellulose – but the resulting colours usually vary in intensity and hue, and in many cases the associated chemicals may harm one or other fibre. As a general rule protein fibres will stand a slightly acidic solution but will be destroyed by alkali, whereas cellulose fibres stand up better to alkaline substances than to acidic ones.

In the recipes in this chapter we will give metric measures, followed by the approximate imperial equivalent, and the percentage – that is, taking the dry weight of yarn as 100 per cent. If you are dyeing in large quantities, you may find the percentage amount of each substance useful for calculating how much you need to use.

The dyestuffs and chemicals can be obtained from suppliers, such as those listed by the Association of Guilds of Weavers, Spinners and Dyers, (see Page 152).

However, before beginning to dye, the weaver must prepare the yarn.

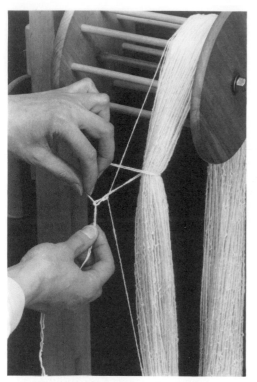

75 The double end is taken loosely round the skein and tied to itself.

76 Make four cotton ties to prevent the skein tangling.

Preparation of yarn

Yarn must be in *skein* or *hank* form for *level*, that is, even dyeing; and the skeins must be tied up, to prevent them tangling and so that they may be easily unwound. Tie the two loose ends from the beginning and the end to each other, take the resulting double end loosely round the skein and tie it firmly back on itself (75). This is more easily done if the skein is stretched out in some way round a chair, or on a *rice*. It should be flat and not twisted. Then make three or four ties at equal intervals around the skein; these should if possible be cotton (undyed – otherwise it may affect the final colour of the yarn). Cotton is strong when wet, so that if the skein is picked up by the ties from the dye-bath they will not break. Moreover, if cotton is used on wool skeins, the ties will be more visible, as they will take the dye differently from the wool.

When tying up wool divide the skein arbitrarily into two in the following manner: make a loop around part of the skein, tie an overhand knot (76), and then form a second loop round the other half and tie another knot. Make the divisions in a different place, so as not to make two separate skeins, as all the ties would slip round to one place and allow the yarn to tangle. Wool expands when wet, so ties must be loose to allow for this; if they are too tight the dye will be *resisted*, resulting in patchy colour.

However, this resist effect may be exploited by tying up certain parts of the skein very tightly, so resisting the dye completely in certain areas. This produces best results when done in a very controlled way. The method can be developed to produce very complicated patterns – using either warp or weft yarns, and is called *ikat* or *kasuri* (78, 79, colour 1, colour 3). See the Booklist for books on these techniques.

Cotton, silk and linen don't need such loose ties, and indeed the ties should be crossed several times across the skein to prevent tangling of these often much finer threads. But take care not to restrict the yarn. It may depend a little on the dye itself, as these vary in their penetration. Indigo for instance, penetrates unevenly; most synthetic dyes, particularly fibre-reactive ones, penetrate well.

Scouring

Before dyeing, the yarn must be properly cleaned so that the dye penetrates completely, otherwise colours will be very patchy. This cleaning is called *scouring*. Obviously greasy handspun wool yarn will need more scouring than yarn from a mill which may be *in the grease* or partially scoured. But even if you buy yarns ready-spun, very few arrive completely clean, as even after partial scouring some spinning oil may remain; so it is always a good plan to scour yarn. Wool should be soaked for ten minutes in hand-hot water, then for another ten minutes in a fresh lot of water with good quality soap-flakes or liquid soap. Do not use detergents, as these contain bleaching agents which will damage wool fibres, impairing their soft handle. Make sure that the soap is fully dissolved before putting in the yarn. Then give two rinses to remove all the soap.

The water should be at the same temperature all the time: wool doesn't like temperature shocks, either hot to cold or cold to hot; any temperature change should happen gradually. Handle the wool as little as possible, because it will shrink and felt if handled too much with great temperature changes in wet soapy conditions. For this reason, never run water from the tap on to yarn: always fill a bath or bucket first, and then put in the yarn. If you have one, a spin-dryer may be better than endless squeezing and wringing by hand, but don't use it for too long.

If yarn is exceptionally dirty this scouring process may have to be repeated until the yarn is clean. Silk, cotton and linen all need scouring. This entails boiling in soap, to remove gum from silk, wax from cotton and general

77 Dairy thermometer floating
in a dye-bath on a low-level gas ring.

impurities from linen. The latter may require bleaching if clear pale colours are required.

Clean yarn may be dried if there is a delay before dyeing, but should always be properly wetted out again, in water of the same temperature as the dyebath, before immersion in the dye.

Containers and utensils

To dye small amounts of yarn – 25 to 50 g (2 to 3 oz) – a saucepan may be big enough; to dye 450 g (1 lb) of wool, use a 15-litre (3-gallon) bucket. For any sort of dyeing it is most important to have clean vessels and utensils, made out of substances which will not affect the chemicals used in the dyeing process. Stainless steel is obviously the best and, although the most expensive, well worth the money. Enamel is good, but unusable when chipped, as the underlying metal and rust will contaminate the dye. Containers made of aluminium or copper are unsuitable, particularly if used for natural dyeing, unless they are kept for one specific dye only.

To heat the dye in buckets I find a bottled-gas ring the most convenient. It is easier and safer to cope with hot, heavy buckets of liquid at low level For stirring you can use a stick, such as wooden dowel, but one for each colour. For testing the temperature, you need a thermometer that goes up to boiling point – a dairy thermometer is easy to use as it floats upright in the liquid (77).

All utensils must be cleaned thoroughly between each process. Only by doing this can you ensure clear, bright colours, and any accuracy in matching them.

You will need scales for weighing quantities of yarn and dyestuffs. Dye recipes always relate directly to *dry* weight of yarn; it is not simply a matter of adding more water for paler shades, as with water-colour paint. Always place a piece of thin paper, such as kitchen towel, on the scales before weighing a chemical: it saves washing the pan each time; it can easily be transferred to the dyebath and then thrown away, and a fresh one used for a different chemical. This will also enable you to weigh out several substances and line them up for use in quick succession. Kitchen scales may be suitable for most natural dyes, as they are generally measured in relatively large amounts, but synthetic dyeing deals with very small amounts, and fine gramme scales may be used, especially if any accurate colour-matching is required.

Water

Water is an important consideration in the dyeing of yarn, as in certain cases it can affect colour. Soft water is preferable for scouring, and in most cases for dyeing, which is why much of the textile industry is based in soft-water areas. However, certain natural dyes, such as weld and madder, prefer chalky water. Water that has a lot of iron in it will tend to darken or *sadden* natural dye colours, making it difficult to obtain really bright colours. Rain-water is good, provided it is not transported in rusty drain-pipes. Certainly, I use chalky water from the South Downs area, hard though it is. Just bear in mind that water from different areas will have different trace elements, and that these alter the colours slightly.

Natural dyes

Natural dyes work most successfully with wool and silk; only a few are good for cellulose fibres, which usually need lengthy processing. (If you want to dye linen and cotton, see the Booklist.) Natural dyes can be divided into two

78 A Balinese geringsing, double ikat on cotton, early twentieth century.

main groups: *substantive dyes* need only to be boiled up with the wool to give fast colours; *adjective dyes* need the yarn to be impregnated with another chemical first. These chemicals that have to be boiled into the wool are called *mordants* (the word comes from the French *mordre*, 'to bite'), and they prepare the fibres to receive the dyestuff, to combine with it chemically; without them the dye would wash out.

Most plants will give some sort of colour if the yarn is first mordanted, but even then very few of them are really fast to light and washing. I shall describe the few dyes that are fast and well tried. Many people will want to try all sorts of plants and fruits, but care should be taken in choosing the right dye for the article. Rugs, cushions, upholstery and particularly curtains should be as light-fast as possible – sunlight is the best bleaching agent! Clothes will probably not get such long exposure to bright light, especially if kept in a dark wardrobe or drawer most of the time, but will need washing. So these colours should be fast to washing, and if possible to boiling and steaming and milling, without bleeding into one another, otherwise a fabric may be ruined when it is wet-finished after weaving. It is always a good idea to make samples and carry out tests; this saves time, money and heartbreak.

In all cases, you will probably get a better colour by boiling the yarn up *with* the dyestuff than by straining off the liquor and dyeing without the dyestuff actually present with the yarn – because the yarn helps to draw the colour out of the dyestuff.

Substantive dyes The dyes that fall into this category are mainly lichens and woods, the heartwood of trees. Certain types of lichen will give browns or yellows. The lichen is boiled up with the yarn – 100 per cent weight of lichen to dry yarn – and left to steep for 3 to 4 hours, the longer the better. However, lichens grow very slowly, some only about 1 mm per year, and most grow only in unpolluted atmospheres. As their availability is limited there are certain conservation rules about collecting them, so don't pick them unless they are growing on branches that are to be burnt anyway, or unless your roof is too thickly encrusted!

More easily available are wood-shavings from a friendly carpenter, or even sawdust, if different types are kept separately. Pale woods, such as beech or elm, produce very little colour; dark hardwoods, such as oak, walnut and mahogany, produce more interesting colours. These are also used 100 per cent of wood to dry weight of yarn, and should be boiled up with it and left to steep for at least 2 hours – the longer the darker the colour. Woods may also be used with mordants; colours will vary depending on whether the yarn is mordanted before or after dyeing.

After all dyeing, the yarn should be rinsed in fresh water several times until all surplus dye is removed and the water runs clear. With insoluble dyestuffs such as these, bits of matter should be shaken off the yarn out of doors. If a very fine yarn is used, the dyestuff should be put loosely into a muslin bag (rather than putting the yarn in a muslin bag) and the yarn left to float freely in the water, ensuring even penetration.

Adjective dyeing These dyes always need a *mordant* to make them fast. There are three basic mordants: *alum, chrome* and *iron*; *tin* and *copper* may also be used. There are a few ancillary chemicals which are sometimes used with these three – for example *cream of tartar* and *oxalic acid.*

Yarns dyed with adjective dyes require two boilings, first with the mordant and then in a separate dye solution. Occasionally these processes can take place together in a single boiling, but the results are not usually as good or as fast, especially with the chrome mordant. In certain cases it is possible to mordant after dyeing, and it is usual to do this with iron. Very often a colour is spoken of in the order in which it is dyed: *alum cochineal*, or *weld iron*, or *chrome oak chrome.*

All recipes are given for 450 g (1 lb) yarn.
Usual water ratio: 450 g to 15 litres (approximately 1 lb yarn to 3 gallons).

Where a dyestuff is bulky and is not dissolved, allow more water so that the yarn can move freely.

Mordants

Alum *Aluminium potassium sulphate; potash alum* (colour 5). Alum is one of the oldest and most commonly used mordants, and it produces the clearest colours. Too much alum can make the wool sticky, and this is impossible to wash out. Amounts to use vary from 7 to 112 g per 450 g yarn (or $\frac{1}{4}$ to 4 oz per lb; 1·5 to 25%) but 84 g per 450 g yarn (3oz; 18%) is usually plenty for full-strength colours.

Cover the bottom of the bath with 2 cm ($\frac{3}{4}$ in) of water and bring to the boil. Throw in the alum. Stir until dissolved. Add warm water, and enter the previously wetted-out yarn. Bring to the boil and simmer for 1 hour at least. It may then be switched off and left to steep. Give three hot rinses.

Chrome *Potassium bichromate or dichromate; bichromate of potash* (colour 5). Gives rich deep colours. A relatively recent mordant, in use since the beginning of the nineteenth century. This mordant is light-sensitive, so it and the yarn should be kept away from bright light while awaiting dyeing – and take care to keep the lid on the mordant bath while boiling and simmering. Chrome imparts a soft handle to wool, but too much destroys dye in the wool. Use 7 to 14 g per 450 g wool ($\frac{1}{4}$ to $\frac{5}{8}$ oz per lb of wool; 1·5 to 3%). Dissolve the chrome in 2 cm ($\frac{3}{4}$in) boiling water in the dyebath and stir well. Fill the bath with warm water. Enter the wetted-out yarn. Bring to the boil. Simmer for 1 hour at least; leave to steep if required. Give one hot rinse.

Iron *Ferrous sulphate; green vitriol; copperas* (colour 5). Iron is used *after* dyeing the yarn, and develops, changes and fixes the colour. It is another very old mordant, and gives sad grey colours or blacks. Care must be taken not to use too much, as it may harshen the wool, and in time the wool may rot away altogether. Bare patches occurring in old textiles, which may have been black outlines, have often disappeared for this reason.

You can use 3·5 to 42 g per 450 g wool ($\frac{1}{8}$ to $1\frac{1}{2}$ oz per lb; 0·7 to 9%), though I never use more than 28 g per 450 g wool (1 oz per lb; 6%). In a glass container or saucepan kept especially for iron, pour 225 cc (8 fl oz) cold water. Sprinkle a pinch of *hydrosulphite* over the surface (to remove the oxygen); wait 10 minutes.

Put in the iron and wait until it dissolves; stir gently, not vigorously, or oxygen will re-enter causing the solution to turn brown (it should be pale green). Fill the mordant bath with hot water. Sprinkle a pinch of hydrosulphite over the mordant bath and wait 10 minutes. Put the iron solution in carefully, without disturbing the surface.

Put the dyed and wetted-out yarn into the mordant bath and bring to the boil. The yarn may be removed after a few minutes, for a lighter colour – or simmered for a $\frac{1}{2}$ hour if you want a darker colour.

Mordanting may be done cold, which is perhaps better for pale shades, in which case it takes longer. As the colour develops more slowly, you can see the yarn change colour, and you can take the yarn out when it reaches the depth of shade you want. This method may also damage the yarn less.

Remove the yarn and allow to oxidise – that is, to react with oxygen in the air. Shake the yarn slightly to expose it evenly to the air for about 10 minutes; then give the yarn a soap wash and rinse. The colour will not be fully developed until after the soap wash and rinse; it becomes a darker, bluer grey compared to the lighter, more yellow grey in the bath. If you want a darker shade, put it back into the iron bath and repeat the process.

Copper *Copper sulphate crystals.* Results are very similar to *chrome*, but slightly more green. With *weld*, you will get a greener yellow, with *cochineal*, a browner purple. Use in the same way as *chrome*. Use 7 to 14 g per 450 g of wool ($\frac{1}{4}$ to $\frac{5}{8}$ oz per lb; 1·5 to 3%).

Tin *Stannous chloride*. May be used as a mordant with *cream of tartar* (see below) in a similar way to *alum* and *chrome*, but is more often used as a *blooming agent*: it is added to the dye-bath towards the end of dyeing to modify and brighten the colour. It tends to harshen wool, making it very tender and so should be used sparingly. Use 14 to 28 g per 450 g of wool ($\frac{1}{2}$ to 1 oz per lb of wool; 3 to 6%).

Cream of tartar. May be added to the *alum* and *chrome* baths for greater depth and brilliancy of colour – but too much makes yellow dull. Use 20 g per 450 g of yarn ($\frac{3}{4}$ oz per lb of yarn; 4·5%).

Dyestuffs

Weld *Reseda luteola* (colour 5). Found on chalky and sandy soil and in waste places; biennial. One of the oldest ways of obtaining yellow. Gives bright yellow with alum. Gives gold with chrome. Gives khaki with iron. Use between 7 and 450 g per 450 g wool ($\frac{1}{4}$ to 16 oz per lb wool; 100% equal weight). 336 g (12 oz; 75%) gives a strong colour. $\frac{1}{2}$ oz of chalk may be added to the dyebath; this gives greater intensity, but less purity of colour. A little salt may be added to make the colour richer and deeper.

Gather weld in July/August, just after flowering time; scatter the seeds widely to promote further growth. It may be used fresh or dried. All the plant is used except the root; use stalks and leaves together for the best results. Break it up into small pieces, and either put it into a plastic net bag with large holes (such as a potato sack), or leave it to float freely. Just cover the weld with a little water, bring to the boil for a few minutes and add cold water to fill up the dyebath; this cools the liquid ready for the yarn. Put in the wetted-out yarn. Bring back to the boil and simmer for 1 hour. Remember you will get a better colour by boiling the yarn up *with* the dyestuff present than by only using the liquor. Rinse till clear.

Madder *Rubia tinctoria* (colour 5). Gives rosy brick reds with alum. Gives pinky-browns with chrome. Gives brown with iron.

Use 84 to 336 g per 450 g wool (3 oz to 12 oz madder per lb yarn; 18 to 75%) – if of good quality, 227 g (8 oz; 50%) should produce a good colour.

Madder used to be grown in this country, but now comes mostly from the countries bordering the Mediterranean and the Middle East. The dye is obtained from the root, which is dried and ground – the more finely it is ground the more colour it gives. Quality varies: the root should be between 5 and 9 years old before being dug up; some do not produce red, possibly because they have been dug up too soon. A batch of madder should be tested first before buying in quantity.

Dissolve the madder in a little cold water at the bottom of the dyebath, mixing it into a smooth paste first, if it is a fine powder. Fill the dyebath to the correct level with warm water and enter the wetted-out yarn. Bring the liquid to 85°C (185°F), and maintain it at this temperature for at least 1 hour, the longer the better. Steeping overnight with the heat switched off is a good idea. If this temperature is exceeded – particularly with alum madder – the red colour will become browner and less bright. It should not be boiled. Rinse the yarn well; bits of dye particle may be shaken out.

Cochineal *Coccus cacti* (colour 5). A dried insect that lives on the prickly pear and is mainly obtained from South America. Gives crimson with alum. Gives purple with chrome. Gives blacks and greys with iron. Use 28 to 227 g cochineal per 450 g wool (1 to 8 oz per lb; 6 to 50%). 113 g (4 oz; 25%) gives a good strong colour.

Grind the cochineal up as finely as possible. Boil a little water in the bottom of the dyebath and throw in the cochineal. Add 1 teaspoonful of *acetic acid*

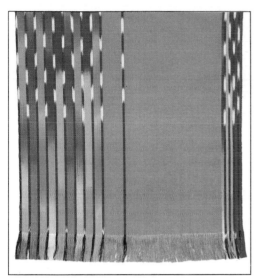

1 Silk scarf by Mary Restieaux.
The warp is part tie-dyed, part dip-dyed.

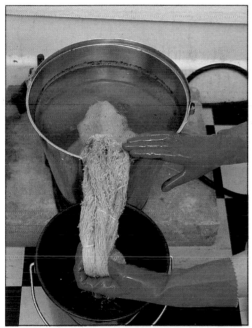

2 Woollen yarn turning blue on contact with air, as it leaves the indigo dyebath.

3 Detail from a patola, a silk double ikat textile from Gujurat, India.
The warp and weft threads have been bound up in places to resist the dye, to give an elaborate pattern when woven.

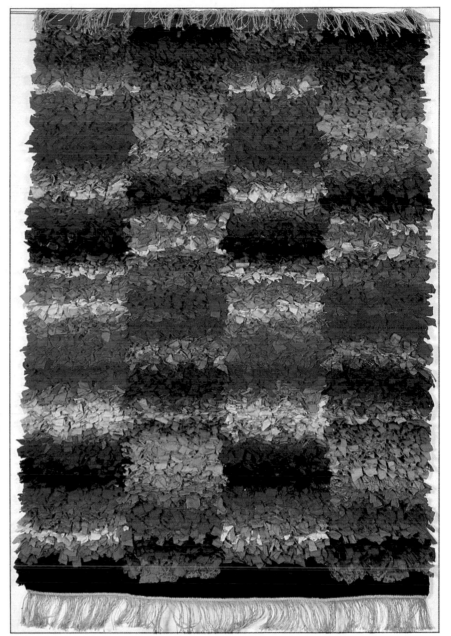

4 Rug by John Hinchcliffe;
the pile is dyed rags, woven in four separate strips.

5 *Left*: Alum weld, chrome weld and chrome weld exhaust, weld iron and weld iron exhaust; *centre*: Alum madder and alum madder exhaust, alum cochineal and alum cochineal exhaust, chrome cochineal and chrome cochineal exhaust; *right*: Alum weld with an indigo overdye, range of indigos.

6 Plain weave, weft-faced rug
by Mary Farmer, with cross stripes.

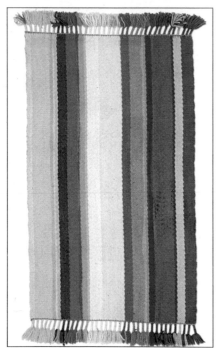

7 Warp-faced rug by Margaret Bristow
in a twill weave, with length-ways stripes.

8 Three samples, all plain weave,
identical red warp and green weft.
The colour of the cloth is altered
by the sett; *left to right*: weft-faced,
balanced and warp-faced.

9 Bobbie Cox in her studio, with one completed work and one in the making
on her large vertical frame loom. A pin-board holds images to remind her
of the Dartmoor countryside which provides much of the inspiration for her work.

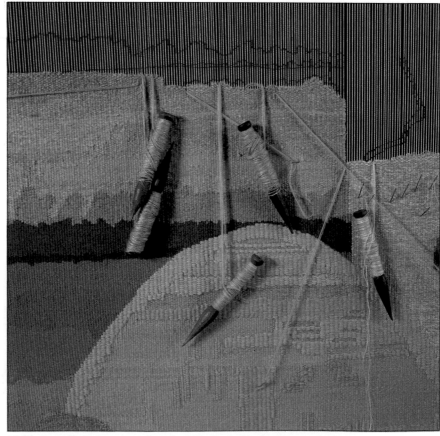

10 Tapestry from a water colour by Elizabeth Blackadder on the loom
at the Dovecot; different shades are used on the same bobbin for a subtle colour
mixture; a coarser weave is used for the raised texture of the fan.

($33\frac{1}{3}\%$ strength) and boil for 5 minutes. Fill the dyebath with warm water and enter the wetted-out yarn. Bring to the boil and simmer for at least 1 hour. Rinse yarn until clear – it may take many rinses.

Cochineal: one-bath scarlet This process uses mordant and dye all in one bath, so clean, unmordanted yarn may be used. It produces a bright scarlet, as in Guards' uniforms. Uses 28 to 227 g cochineal per 450 g yarn (1 to 8 oz per lb yarn; 6 to 50%) with 14 g ($\frac{1}{2}$ oz; 3%) oxalic acid and 14 to 28 g ($\frac{1}{2}$ to 1 oz; 3 to 6% tin – stannous chloride). 113 g (4 oz; 25%) cochineal and 14 g ($\frac{1}{2}$ oz; 3%) tin gives a good scarlet.

Boil a little water in the bottom of the dyebath. Throw in the cochineal. Add 1 teaspoonful of acetic acid ($33\frac{1}{3}\%$ strength). Dissolve the oxalic acid in hot water. Dissolve the tin (stannous chloride) in hot water. Add these to the dyebath. Fill with warm water. Enter wetted-out yarn. Bring to the boil and simmer for 1 hour at least. Rinse yarn, soap wash and rinse until clear.

Cutch *Catechu.* The sap from certain species of acacia trees growing in Indonesia. Will dye linen and cotton and wool, although it may harshen wool if used to excess. Gives yellow-brown with alum. Gives red-brown with chrome. Gives black with iron. Use 28 to 113 g per 450 g wool (1 to 4 oz per lb wool; 6 to 25%).

Check that all the cutch is well dissolved, as undissolved pieces will cause stains. Grind finely and mix with a little water in a small pan. Strain this liquor carefully into the dyebath and fill with warm water. Enter wetted out yarn and bring to the boil. Simmer for at least 1 hour. Rinse yarn until clear.

Exhausts

It is possible that with many natural dyestuffs not all the colouring matter is absorbed into the yarn during the full-strength bath. After the yarn has been removed, it is possible to obtain a paler colour – sometimes a slightly different type of colour by entering another batch of yarn that has previously been mordanted. The dyebath should be filled up again with cold water (replacing the liquor removed by the previous yarn) thus cooling the bath, and the new yarn entered and brought to the boil or treated in the same way as the first batch. This means that approximately 1 kilo (2 lb) of yarn may be dyed out of a dyebath and an amount of dyestuff designed for 450 g (1 lb) of yarn, thus saving money. This method often gives colours that relate well to each other. However natural dyes are less fast when very pale, (colour 5). Note, however, that you can't use a mordant bath for more than one batch of yarn.

Indigo on wool and silk

Indigofera tinctoria (colour 5) A plant growing widely in South America, Africa and India. The leaves yield the dye, and are prepared to form a powder. This powder is insoluble in water and in this recipe is converted into indigo white, which on oxidising in the air, turns blue. Great care must be taken, especially when dyeing wool, as too much strong alkali, such as caustic soda, in hot conditions will irrevocably make wool tender. There are two processes: making the stock and then dyeing.

Use 28 g (1 oz) indigo with 28 g (1 oz) caustic soda and 56 g (2 oz) sodium dithionite/hydrosulphite. An indigo stock will dye many kilos of yarn, depending on the strength of colour required; so as long as the proportions of the ingredients are kept the same, you can make less stock if you wish.

Remember that caustic soda burns animal substances – that means your skin! Always treat with great care, and **always add caustic soda solution to cold water, never water to caustic soda**. Keep it away from your eyes – and wear a mask.

Making the stock Keep a special saucepan for the indigo stock, a double boiler if possible; if not, a smaller inside a large one containing water. In the stock container (saucepan) mix the indigo powder with a little hot water and stir until dissolved – it will take about ten minutes. Into a glass measure pour 450 cc (16 fl oz) cold water, then add the caustic soda, stirring well. Wait until clear. Fill the stock container with cold water, leaving enough room to add 280 cc (10 fl oz) of the caustic soda solution. The remaining 170 cc (6 fl oz) of caustic soda solution will not usually be needed but may be kept in case you need to make an adjustment to the dyebath (out of the reach of children, and labelled). Add the 280 cc (10 fl oz) caustic soda to the stock. Sprinkle the hydrosulphite onto the surface of the stock. **Do not stir after this.** Hydrosulphite removes oxygen from the water, and stirring or drips would re-introduce it. Heat the stock (in the pan of water) to 60°C (140°F) and maintain for 20 minutes. Do not allow it to go over this temperature.

Test with a glass rod – it should show a clear yellow turning through green to blue within 10 seconds of exposure to the air.

Dyeing Fill the dyebath with hot water, 50°C (120°F). Sprinkle some hydrosulphite over the surface, 1 teaspoon to 15 litres (3 gallons) of water. Wait 10 minutes. Do not stir.

Carefully, without disturbing the surface or causing drips, add small amounts of the stock – a dessertspoonful or so – to the dyebath. Ensure that it is evenly distributed by stirring very gently and not breaking the surface. Wet the yarn – it is better if the yarn is wetted in water with the oxygen removed by sprinkling hydrosulphite over the surface.

Carefully enter the yarn into the dyebath, with as few drips as possible.

Wait 10 minutes. Remove the yarn carefully – wear rubber gloves, or your hands will turn blue – and oxidise by holding the skeins up in the air. Don't hold them over the dyebath, or drips will re-introduce oxygen to the bath. Open them out to ensure penetration of oxygen (colour 2).

Oxidise for 10 minutes at least. Continue to add small amounts of stock to the dyebath, and dip the yarn repeatedly, as above, to build up the colour. It is better to build up the colour with many dips than to have one or two dips into a strong bath: even pale colours need at least two dips, both for fastness, and to even out the penetration of the dye, which always tends to be patchy.

When you have the required depth of colour, soak the yarn in a bath of water, as hot as your hand can bear, to which a teaspoon of *acetic acid* ($33\frac{1}{3}\%$ strength) has been added, for 20 minutes. Rinse well in clear water.

Indigo on linen and cotton

This is a much stronger dye bath than the wool version; for paler colours wait until towards the end of the life of the dyebath, as it weakens gradually.

The stock Make a stock solution for 30 litres (6 gallons) dyebath. $1\frac{1}{2}$ cups salt; $\frac{1}{2}$ cup caustic soda; $\frac{3}{4}$ cup hydrosulphite; 1 cup indigo grains (note that indigo grains are different from indigo powder).

Put salt in stock container.
In glass measure pour 280 cc (10 fl oz) cold water, add caustic soda, stirring continuously until flakes are dissolved. Wait until solution becomes clear.

Add caustic soda solution.

Sprinkle the hydrosulphite over the surface of the stock solution.

Add indigo grains, stirring.

Add 1 cup warm water.

After standing for 5 minutes there should be a dark blue iridescent scum with a clear yellow liquid below.

79 Japanese kasuri 'The tiger and the bamboo': *top*, tie-dyed cotton weft; *below*, tie-dyed warp and weft; nineteenth century.

The dye bath Fill the container (medium dustbin size) to within 10 cm (4 in) of the rim with water at about 15°C (60°F).

Sprinkle a dessertspoonful of hydrosulphite over the surface and wait for ten minutes.

Lower the basin of stock solution gently into the dyebath so that it can be poured without splashing, to avoid introducing air into the dyebath. Stir gently with a stick that reaches the bottom of the container.

Dip out a small quantity of the dye in a glass and look through it: if the liquid is yellow, without any specks of blue below the surface, the bath is ready for use. There will be a blue scum on top.

Dyeing can begin. First dip, $1\frac{1}{2}$ minutes in the dyebath, 3 minutes oxidising in the air. Second dip, 1 minute in the dyebath, 1 minute in the air.

Rinse in warm water.

Synthetic dyes

Synthetic dyes extend the range of colours available to the weaver, making it possible to obtain some extremely bright colours, as well as subtle shades, impossible to obtain with natural dyes (colour 1, colour 6, colour 19). Synthetic dyes may be easier and quicker to use – most of them need the yarn to be immersed only once, although they then need very vigorous and prolonged stirring at an early stage to get even results. Also, certain synthetic dyes make the dyeing of cellulose fibres, such as cotton and linen, much easier, with a wide range of colours.

Like natural dyes, some synthetic dyes are best suited to protein fibres, others to cellulose fibres, though occasionally one type may be used for both – though the resulting colours will be different: although colour may take on the yarn, it may not be fast if the dyes were not specifically designed for it.

Certain synthetic dyes have greater fastness to light and/or washing than others, so take care again to choose the one most suitable for the purpose. The colour ranges within the dyestuffs vary enormously – so that this makes the choice difficult. It really depends on the type of colour that you want, the use to which the yarn or fabric will later be put, and the facilities available.

All the information about preparation, scouring, containers and utensils applies equally to synthetic dyes, although water seems to affect the colour value less than when using natural dyes.

The synthetic dyes available from suppliers which are easy to apply, and which provide reasonable fastness to both light and washing are *acid dyes, direct dyes* and *fibre-reactive dyes*. There are others which are less fast or more difficult to use. *Acid dyes* are particularly good for bright colours on silk and wool. *Direct dyes* are best for cotton, linen and viscose rayon, and some are suitable for silk and wool. *Fibre-reactive dyes* are of two types, some very good for silk and wool, the others for cotton, linen and other cellulose fibres. Dyes are sold under a variety of trade-names: try to find out from their brochures or from the manufacturer whether they are acid, direct or fibre-reactive.

Bear in mind that not all colours from a particular range of dyes will have the same properties of fastness to light and washing: some colours will be better or worse than others in this respect.

You can use the multi-purpose dyes commonly available from non-specialist shops, but because they are a mixture of dyestuffs suitable for a wide range of fibres they are likely to be less fast and less economic than the types of dye mentioned above designed for specific fibres. There is a range of wool dyes supplied in small quantities for home use.

Most brands of synthetic dyes have their own particular recipes for chemicals and treatment; follow these closely, and keep notes of the results.

Chapter Four

The frame loom

A frame loom is one of the most basic looms, useful for both beginners and professional weavers, who like its simplicity and portability: it can be used flat on a table or propped up, indoors or out; it can be any size – or even shape – and is inexpensive to buy or easy to make (back cover 3).

The frame loom is generally used for tapestry-weaving (see Chapter Five), but it can also be used for other types of weaving such as short lengths of fabric suitable for a small mat, bag, or panel. Although you can use a frame loom to make a balanced cloth, it is impractical, slow, and difficult to achieve an even result without a lot of practice; you will get better results on a frame loom if you use it for weft-faced fabrics.

You can buy frame looms from weavers' shops ready assembled, or assemble some of them yourself. Or you can buy an artist's canvas stretcher frame, complete with wedges, two to a corner, which strengthen the assembled frame (81). The sides come in various sizes, and are interchangeable, so you can learn to weave on a smaller frame, then buy larger sides later on. The smallest practical frame would be about 40 × 50 cm (15 × 20 in), but a larger one 45 × 60 cm (18 × 24 in) up to 50 × 75 cm (20 × 30 in) would be more versatile. The main requirement is that the frame should be steady and rigid with smooth edges: use timber around 5 × 1·5 cm (2 × ¾ in) – for larger frames use thicker timber, with corner braces. Very big frames, like the ones used by Bobbie Cox, are often made of scaffolding (colour 9).

There are many variations on the frame loom; it is probably best to start with the simplest type, and then adapt it for any later work, depending on the sort of weaving you then want to do. Its main *disadvantages* are that it is slow to work on, and the length of the finished work is restricted by the size of the loom – generally about three quarters of its length. The *advantages* are that it is quick to warp and the thickness of the frame causes a natural shed to form.

Warping a simple frame

A quick and easy way of spacing the warp threads evenly is to mark off the top and bottom bars of the frame in centimetres or inches. Mark the centre of the bar 0, then mark off the centimetres or inches, from the centre outwards, 1, 2, 3, etc (80). When you have marked one bar of the frame, mark the other end in the same way, taking care to keep the marks in line so the warp will be straight. These marks will help you warp to the *sett* you have decided (see Page 60) and the width of fabric you want.

You may want to clamp or weight one side of the loom to the edge of a table while warping. Tie one end of the warp yarn (wound on a ball or spool) around the bottom bar of the frame on the first mark on the left that you want to use – but not closer than 2·5 cm (1 in) to the inside edge of the frame. Use a knot or a bow – a bow can be undone if you want to adjust the tension later. Wind it across the length of the frame in a figure-of-eight, keeping the spacing and tension as even as possible (81).

If you have calculated the sett, remember that each turn of the warp over the end bar represents two warp ends – one over, the other back under. If you haven't calculated the sett, a rule of thumb for spacing the warp threads for balanced plain weave is to leave just enough gap between each thread for another of equal thickness; if you are planning a weft-faced fabric, like a tapestry, then double this spacing. Keep the number of warp

80 Mark off the top of the frame in centimetres, counting from the centre to each side.

81 Wind on the warp in a figure-of-eight to make a cross.

threads between your marks consistent, and make sure you go over-and-under each time. This crossing over of the threads keeps them in order. A *natural* or *open* shed is formed by the thickness of the frame (82).

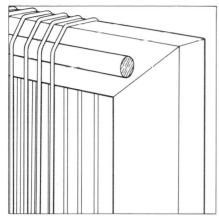

83 A rod taped to the frame during warping can be removed later to ease the tension; or add a rod later in the weaving to increase tension.

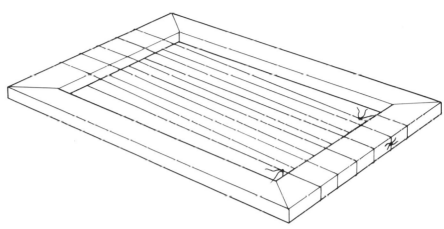

82 The thickness of the frame gives a natural shed. When changing yarn, keep the knots at either end of the frame.

Keep any knots in the warp to one end or the other. If a knot occurs in the middle of the thread being used for warping, as it sometimes does even in the best yarn, then it must be broken and re-tied so that it falls at the end, out of the way of the weaving. This applies to any warping process.

Keep the tension reasonably tight: if it is too slack, it is difficult to maintain an even tension, and the weaving will distort; if it is too taut, weaving will be difficult and may give you sore fingers.

If you intend to weave a balanced or warp-faced cloth, the warp will tighten during weaving. Allow for this by fastening a stick to the top and/or bottom of the frame before warping; these sticks can be removed to ease the warp tension as required (83).

Finish the warp by tying onto the bottom bar, and use this as the base of the frame when you begin to weave.

Adjust the tension if required by pulling any slack gradually across to one end, and retie.

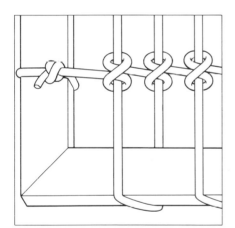

84 A heading cord tied in a clove hitch round each warp will make a firm foundation for the weaving.

If the warp slackens off during weaving you can tighten the whole thing by inserting a smooth stick, such as a piece of dowelling, between the warp threads and the top bar of the frame.

Spread the warp by sliding the warp threads into their correct positions, evenly spaced between the marks. Do this at both ends, on both sides, then fix them down by sticking them in position on the frame with adhesive tape.

Heading cords

Begin by making a *heading cord*: this provides a firm horizontal base for the weaving and helps to keep the warp evenly spaced. Take a length of warp thread and tie it to the side of the frame, near the bottom, at the height you want to begin weaving. Pass the thread in a clove hitch round each warp, and tie it to the other side of the frame (84). Alternatively you can weave two or three picks in the warp yarn – weave the first across the warp in the *natural* or *open* shed (the space between the warp threads formed by the frame); pull it tight and tie it firmly onto the other side of the frame. Tie on a second piece of warp yarn just above it and weave it into the *picked-up* or *leash* shed – the lower layer. Beat it down close to the first thread with your fingers or a fork, and tie it onto the frame (85, back cover 3). Adjust the warp spacing if it is necessary.

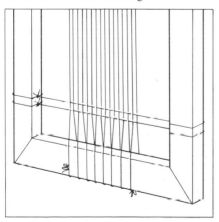

85 Heading cords made by weaving two picks in the warp yarn, and tying them to each side of the frame.

Packaging the yarn

Although it is likely that you will be using only short lengths of weft in a frame loom, it is helpful to package the weft yarn into a neat bundle so that it is tangle-free and easy to insert through the warp. The most common way of doing this is to make a *finger-skein*, also called a *finger-hank*, or *butterfly*: this is a hank wound round the fingers in a figure-of-eight, rather like an embroidery skein, which releases the yarn without tangling (86).

To make a finger-skein, take 1·5 to 2 metres (5 to 7 ft) of weft yarn: place the first end of the yarn so that it hangs down the palm of the left hand, at least as far as the wrist. This is the end with which you will start to weave.

Pass the yarn round the thumb and wind in a figure-of-eight movement between the thumb and the little finger. When the skein is wound, and before taking it off your hand, wrap the final end tightly a few times round the centre of the bundle, and tie it in a half hitch. Slip the hank off the fingers.

It is now ready to use, starting with the original end hanging down from the palm, and should run freely – although as it empties you may want to tighten the centre hitch.

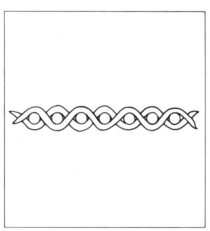

86 A finger-skein is a useful way of handling a short length of yarn so that it does not tangle.

Weaving on a frame loom

Now you can begin plain weaving. Pass the weft yarn through the open shed one way, then back through the picked-up shed the other way, beating it down with the fingers, or a fork or other type of beater.

In a weft-faced fabric the warp travels in a straight line, whereas the weft bends over and under it (87) so allow enough slack in the weft for this extra take-up: don't pull the weft too tight each time, but lay the weft across in a diagonal, so that when it is beaten down there will be enough slack for the full width of the cloth. Beat the weft down in the same direction as the weft is going, that is starting from the right if the weft was put in on the right. This way the weft can take up what it needs to cover the warp without pulling (88).

87 In a weft-faced fabric the warp remains straight, the weft bends over and under it.

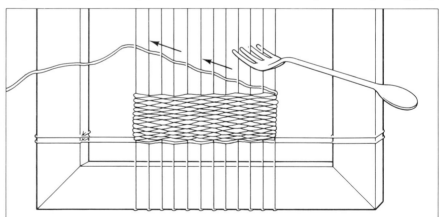

88 Place the weft in a diagonal line, and start to beat in the same direction.

If the weft doesn't have enough slack, it will gradually pull in the sides, causing *waisting*, or a gradual narrowing of the cloth, and the warp threads are also pulled closer together in the middle, altering the sett. On the other hand, if the weft is too loose it will make vertical ribs, or bubble up with loose loops on the surface. Keep the tension even and correct when you turn the weft at the edges of the cloth for the next pick.

Pick up the open shed near the top of the frame, where it is easier. Pick up the lower threads with your fingers: about four at a time is comfortable.

For more details about how to weave and for tapestry weaving, see Chapter Five.

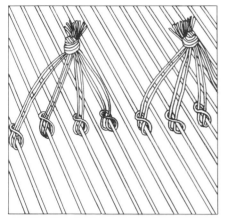

89 A leash-rod will make it easier to lift the bottom layer of warp ends.

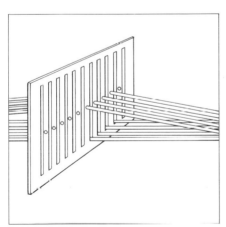

90 Or use bunches of leashes to lift the bottom layer of warp ends.

Leashes

On a small frame loom many weavers prefer to lift the picked-up shed with their fingers, but there are other ways of lifting the lower threads which may speed up the process: one is to make *leashes*, from strong cotton twine – or you can buy special *heddle twine*. You can make the leashes in several ways: tie a continuous length of twine around the lower warp threads and up around a bar (89); whenever you want to pull up the lower threads, pull up the bar. Or loop short lengths of twine around the alternate warp threads, and tie them together in bunches of four – pull up one bunch of leashes at a time (90). (For information on handling larger tapestry looms, see Page 46.)

The rigid heddle

This is an ancient and ingenious device for lifting and lowering alternate threads to make the shed when producing plain weave; it can also be used for beating the weft threads into place. It consists of a flat, generally metal, plate with alternate holes and vertical slots, through which the warp is threaded. The principle of the rigid heddle is that alternate warp threads pass through the slots – and remain static during weaving – while the other warp threads pass through the holes, and are raised or lowered as the rigid heddle is lifted or pushed down (91).

It can be used on a frame loom, providing it has clearance at the back for the heddle to move up and down, ie it may not be used on a board loom Only short lengths of yarn are needed for the warp, as they each have to be threaded through the rigid heddle. Centre the first warp thread over the top bar, thread one end through the first *hole*, the other end through the first *slot*, then tie the two ends to the bottom bar. Repeat this process, until the warping is done. Keep the tension even and correct.

Bobbie Cox uses a rigid heddle on both her big and small frame looms, and finds it a quick way of making the sheds, particularly when she is using a continuous weft (92–94).

91 Rigid heddles are threaded in both slot and hole so that a shed is formed.

92 When Bobbie Cox uses a rigid heddle on a large vertical frame it is suspended in place above the weaving.

93 Insert the weft in a gentle diagonal or curve and beat it down into place with the fingers.

94 Bobbie Cox uses a weighted tapestry beater for her heavyweight hangings.

The *disadvantage* of a rigid heddle is that each one produces only one fixed spacing for the warp: the metal ones most easily available in Britain are set at about 50 ends per 10 cm (13 ends per inch), though in America at least three different spacings are commonly available. There are some coarser, wooden ones available, or you could make them for yourself. Coarse ones can be made from flat pieces of wood – even lollipop sticks – spaced out evenly and glued to thin battens at the top and bottom; drill holes in the centre of each slat. Finer ones can be made from *reeds* (see Page 59), adding glued-in stoppers such as sticks. Make sure the holes and slots are very smooth on the inside, so the threads don't wear with the friction.

The rigid heddle can also be used on a warp which is not stretched on a rigid frame, like the *backstrap loom* (see Page 117); or it can be mounted in a specially constructed frame, the *rigid heddle loom* (see Page 44).

Finishing the work

It should be possible to weave to within about 15 to 20 cm (6 to 8 in) of the top of the frame before the sheds become too difficult to open. Cut the warps at each end of the frame to remove the work from the loom. You can either make a fringe by tying two or more warp ends together against the edge of the cloth, or by hem-stitching along the edges, or by weaving a little extra at the beginning and the end and turning over to form a hem. (For other ways of finishing see Page 42.)

A frame loom with nails

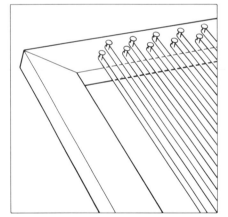

95 Frame loom with nails; stagger the nails to avoid splitting the wood.

A development of the basic frame loom is to drive small rust-proof nails into the top and bottom rails at 1 cm ($\frac{1}{2}$ in) intervals, and lace the warp threads up and down round these. Don't drive the nails in in a straight line – the wood might split – but stagger them in two or three rows. Sometimes they are best driven in at an angle, if the wood is very soft or the nails headless. Take care to line up top and bottom nails so that the warp is vertical (95).

The *advantage* of this type of frame is that weaving can, with care, go right up to the nails, so that the finished piece can be lifted off, with no fringes, and a longer piece of weaving is therefore possible. The *disadvantages* are that the spacing of the warp threads is fixed (though two or more threads can pass round each nail during warping); weft threads can catch on the nails during weaving; the warp length is still restricted to the length of the frame (though this time the full length) and no natural shed is formed. A rigid heddle could be used, but you could not then weave right up to the nails and would have to cut it off the warp.

Forming a shed

If no natural shed is formed and you are not using a rigid heddle, take a piece of stick about 1 cm (or $\frac{1}{2}$ in) thick at least 5 cm (2 in) longer than the width of the weaving, and preferably long enough to rest on the side pieces of the frame. Insert this under every other thread right across the warp, and push it up to the top of the frame where it gives a permanent shed. You may need to remove the stick as weaving gets close to it, and finish the interlacing with a needle.

A frame loom with dowels

96 Another way of warping a small frame loom, useful when using short lengths of yarn.

Another variation on the basic frame is to screw cup-hooks into the four corners, to serve as supports for dowels. Stretch the warp threads from dowel to dowel (96). Use cut lengths of thread for the warp, tied onto the top and bottom bar. Take care to get the tension of all the warp threads even.

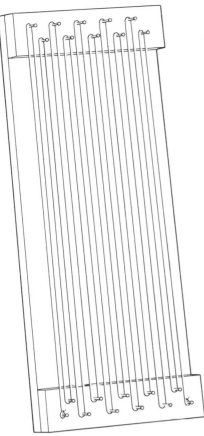

97 A board loom is a sturdy alternative to a frame.

The *advantages* of this loom are that the top rod could be left attached to the weaving as a hanging device – it could be wood, metal or perspex: when using metal or perspex, remember that tube is less likely to bend than the equivalent size of solid rod. You can use short lengths of yarn for the warp, so it is easier to plan a varied warp. The *disadvantages* are that again no natural shed is formed (but you can use a rigid heddle or make the shed, as above, with a stick); and the warp length is again restricted to that of the frame.

A board loom

Sometimes a frame loom need not be a frame at all, but a board, with bars attached at top and bottom so that the warp threads lie clear of the board. The warp can be suspended by nails or by the dowel-and-hook method (97).

The *advantages* are that this makes a firm loom; the *disadvantages* are that it is heavy to use, work is restricted to only one side, whereas one of the good things about other frame looms is that you can usually work on both sides of the warp.

The Salish loom

It is possible to weave cloth longer than the frame by a method used in many cultures – for example by the Salish Indians of North America. When warping, they carry loops of warp over the top bar and under the lower bar of the frame and catch them round a horizontal rod at the back of the frame (98).

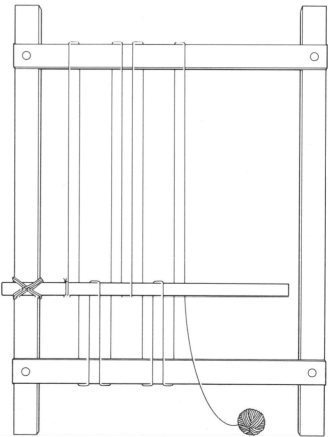

98 The Salish loom.

The weaving starts at this rod and also ends at the rod, because the whole warp and the weaving is slid around the frame as work progresses. Pulling out the rod at the completion of weaving releases a cloth nearly twice the height of the frame. With a long warp like this, it is a good idea to insert a thick stick under all the threads, and push it to the top of the frame. This can be removed to release the tension when it is necessary to pull the warp round, or it can be replaced with a thinner one if the tension gets too tight.

99 Warp threads can be tied to bars, which are then clamped to the frame.

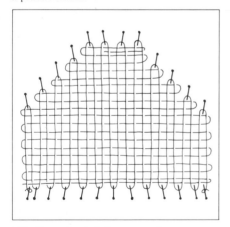

100 Looms can be circular – this is a plastic frame.

101 Complicated shapes can be woven around nails in a board.

102 A rigid-heddle loom, with storage for longer warps on rollers.

Unless the frame used is very thick – at least 7·5 cm (3 in) – you cannot use a rigid heddle with this loom, as the back layer of warp threads would impede its up-and-down movement. The warp can also be tied onto two rods, clamped to the frame (99).

Frame looms can take many shapes

Frame and board looms need not be rectangular or square: you can use a circular frame (100), or if you want a complicated shape you can drive nails into a piece of 1 cm ($\frac{1}{2}$ in) thick insulating board – not expanded polystyrene, it breaks away too easily (101). Squared paper on the board makes thread spacing easier. You can even build three-dimensional frames.

The rigid heddle loom

This loom is a half-way stage between a frame loom and a table loom: a rigid heddle is mounted in a specially constructed wooden frame (102). It has side supports designed to hold the rigid heddle in any of three positions – up, down, or central – this is useful as it frees both hands for weaving. You can buy these looms ready-made, they stand on a table, and have rollers at each end to store the warp and the cloth – which makes it possible to weave lengths of fabric much longer than the loom. These looms are more complex than the simple frame, and should be warped up differently (see Page 60).

Other looms

There are other looms which are simple to make or cheap to buy, such as the *backstrap loom, inkle* and *tablet looms*. They can be used for patterned as well as plain weave, and so are dealt with in Chapter Thirteen.

103 Navaho Indian weaving a blanket on a loom set up in Canyon de Chelly, Arizona; early twentieth century.

Chapter Five

Tapestry weaving

Tapestry is the principal form of pictorial weaving. Basically it is a weft-faced fabric in which the weft does not travel all the way across the warp from one selvedge to another, but is woven in small areas as the design demands. These characteristics make it possible to weave practically any image. It is much slower to do than normal weaving, but many weavers today are interested in making quite small tapestries – sometimes only a few square centimetres (inches) in area. These don't need specialised equipment: a frame loom is sufficient; warp tension adjustment is not essential, but is an advantage: the warp is usually under more tension than in cloth-weaving. Some small metal frame looms have adjustable tension; on a non-adjustable frame you can add one or more sticks to increase tension as required.

Tapestry looms

Large tapestries can be woven on two types of loom: on a big vertical one, with two beams, one to hold the warp at the top (the warp-beam) and another to take the finished tapestry at the bottom (the cloth-beam) and also on a horizontal loom. Several weavers can work side by side on either of these looms.

Tapestries woven on the vertical loom are called *haute lisse* or high warp. The Dovecot Studios in Edinburgh weave in this way (104). Tapestries woven on the horizontal loom are called *basse lisse* or low warp. The West Dean Tapestry Studio in Sussex weaves in that way (106). It is claimed that weaving on the horizontal loom is faster, because the leashes, attached to every other warp thread, are activated by the feet, leaving the hands free for weaving. Generally, however, high warp looms are preferred, partly because they occupy less space, but also because the tapestry is easier to see during the weaving. There is little difference in the finished product of the two types of loom.

Any loom, such as a normal table or floor-loom, can be used, but a frame is always preferable, no matter how simple.

Tapestries are sometimes woven back to front, with the ends of the weft threads hanging on the surface facing the weaver. In this case a mirror is placed behind the warp so that the weaver can keep an eye on the progress of the right side; this way the surface of the tapestry is easily kept clean during

104 A large vertical tapestry loom at the Dovecot Studios in Edinburgh; several weavers can work side by side.

105 Fiona Mathison sometimes uses a smaller frame for her own tapestries. Note the leashing rod at the top.

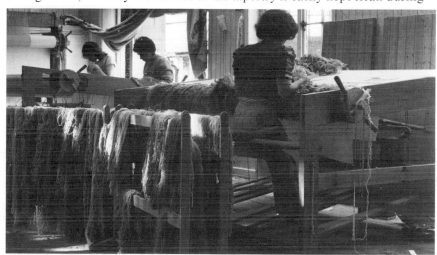

106 Weavers at the West Dean Tapestry Studio in Sussex use horizontal, or low warp, looms.

45

working and bobbins can be carried from one area to another without cutting the thread. *Basse lisse* tapestry is almost always woven back to front. Many individual weavers today prefer to work on the right side, often covering the woven surface with a cloth pinned over to protect it.

The warp

The choice of warp yarn for tapestry weaving is very important. Traditionally, yarns made of wool, linen, silk or cotton have always been used; these fibres are spun tightly into very smooth yarns, plied, and often several plies are *folded* together into a strong cord. It is difficult to obtain suitable wool and silk yarns for this purpose, and linen yarns, although strong and smooth, are not suitable for warp used by a beginner, as they fluctuate in tension according to the atmospheric humidity. A strong corded cotton, made for use in netting, is used by most tapestry weavers, and it should be set at 24 or 32 warp ends per 10 cm (6 or 8 warp ends per in). In tapestry weaving these ends are often referred to as *warps*. The colour of this warp yarn is immaterial, as it will be covered by the weft.

Warping the frame loom is as usual (see Page 38) laying the warp in a figure-of-eight course with a medium, even tension. Once the warp is complete, make heading cords (see Page 39) or weave two or three picks and take them tightly round the side of the frame. This will space the warp evenly, and will give a firm basis on which to start to weave.

Leashes

On a small frame loom it is often unnecessary to have any lifting device such as leashes. On a larger tapestry frame, however, attach a horizontal bar, called a *leashing rod*, with a cord tied along its length, to hang in front of the warp near the top of the frame; then temporarily insert a smooth, heavy rod in the *natural* or open shed.

Pass the *leashing cord* – this is a cord similar to the warp thread, but usually thinner – around the first warp thread lying behind the temporary rod, then up and around the leashing rod and tie in a double hitch around the cord which stretches the length of the leashing rod (107, 105). Repeat this process for the other warp threads, working from left to right. When all the lower warps have been attached in this way, withdraw the temporary rod; the leashes will all be the same length, making them easier to select and use.

The cartoon

Many tapestries begin with the preparation of a *cartoon*, which is a simple outline of the design. For a small tapestry, the design may be the same size as the finished work; for larger tapestries, the design is often much smaller than the finished tapestry. If it needs to be enlarged, this can be done photographically, or by the traditional method of squaring up the original or its tracing and ruling correspondingly larger squares to bring it to the required size; the content of each small square is then drawn in the corresponding larger square, until the whole design is enlarged. This cartoon is then placed immediately behind the warps and the design is *inked-on*: a chisel-shaped stick acts as a nib, and is dipped in waterproof ink.

Insert a thread in the closed shed above the sections to be inked-on so that there is no natural shed. Taking each warp in turn, mark it where it crosses a line in the cartoon (108). Because the warps will revolve during weaving, each one must be inked all round, and this involves rotating the warp thread against the wooden nib. Often a section no more than 30 cm (12 in) up the warp can be inked on at a time. It is a lengthy process, but necessary if a cartoon is to be followed accurately.

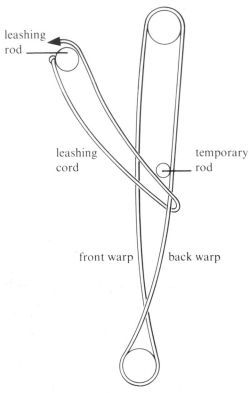

leashing rod

leashing cord

temporary rod

front warp   back warp

107 Fix the leashing rod 15 cm approximately from the frame face; the temporary rod suspended between the top and bottom bars in the open shed keeps the leashes of even length.

108 The cartoon is placed behind the warp, and each thread is rotated and inked-on as a guide.

109 A tapestry bobbin filled with yarn and secured with a half-hitch.

The weft

Wool yarns are traditionally used for the weft in tapestry, because they cover the warps so well. Worsted-spun wool gives a smooth surface which will resist dirt: the Dovecot Studios' weavers use several strands of very fine worsted together as one yarn (colour 10). This not only gives possibilities of fine colour mixing, but also makes sure of good warp coverage, as many fine threads will pack down more easily than one thick one. Often other fibres can be used in the weft for various effects, such as linens, cotton, silks and even metallic yarns.

Wind the weft yarn on a *tapestry bobbin*, and secure it with a half-hitch. If this is done in the correct way (109) the yarn can be drawn from the bobbin without the need ever to undo the half-hitch. The point of the bobbin is used to beat the weft into place (123). A finger skein can also be used (see Page 40) and the weft beaten down with a fork.

Weaving

Tapestry is woven in plain weave, and so needs only two sheds, called the *natural* shed, formed by a rod or the thickness of the frame loom, and the *leash* shed, formed by bringing forward some of the back threads either with the fingers (110–114), or by reaching up and pulling on a small handful of leashes (115, 116). It is important to realise that even though the design may dictate a large area of one colour, stretching right across the warp, tapestry is never woven right across the warp, but in small areas; only in this way can tension be maintained between plain and detailed areas (117).

The terminology used by tapestry weavers is slightly different from that used by other weavers. What would be called *two picks* – a weft shot there and back across an area of warp – a tapestry weaver calls a *pass*; so one pick is

110 Start with a half-hitch round the first warp end; then, using the natural shed, insert the thread from left to right.

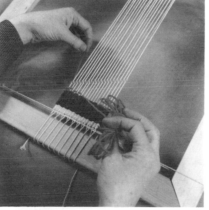

111 A half-pass is complete; you can stop at any warp to begin a shape.

112 Bring forward the back threads with the fingers and insert the weft from right to left.

113 This completes the pass.

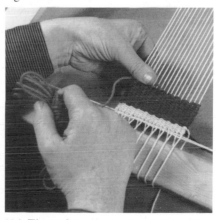

114 The weft can be pushed down with the fingers, or with the point of a bobbin.

115 Using leashes: select the group of warps you need, run your fingers up to the corresponding leashes and pull these forward.

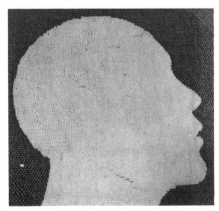

116 Use the hand to hold the shed open for the bobbin.

118 Detail of 'In the shadow of Man' by Fiona Mathison; slits are used deliberately to create the jaw-line; the hair is woven in soumak.

117 Even large areas of plain colour are woven in small sections. Leave weft tails about 4 cm long hanging at the back.

called a *half-pass*. Each half-pass must be placed in the shed with a degree of slackness; judging this amount will improve with practice. The weft must cover the warp exactly: but with too much slack the weft will make vertical ribs on the surface, or, worse, will bubble up; and with insufficient slack the warp will not be covered, or the edge will be pulled in.

In *Gobelins* tapestry the weft lies at right angles to the warp; this means that in any design many bobbins of various colours will be in use right across the warp (colour 10). Sometimes, depending on the design being woven, one area can be concentrated on and woven up so that it grows ahead of the rest of the design. If you are a beginner you must watch this very carefully, as you must not leave areas *undercut*, so that they cannot be woven using the sheds (119 and 128).

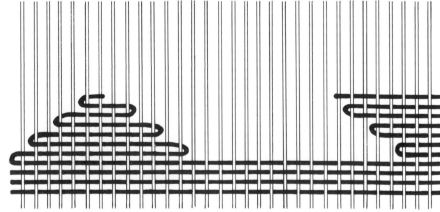

119 Building up areas: *left*, correct; *right*, an undercut – it would be impossible to use the shed to weave under it.

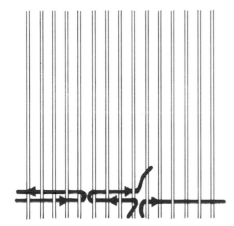

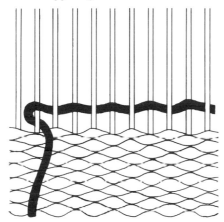

120 Weave adjacent wefts in the same shed in opposing directions.

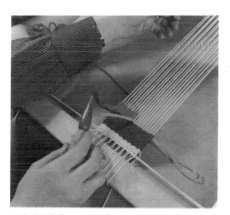

121 Start a new colour with a half-hitch around a warp.

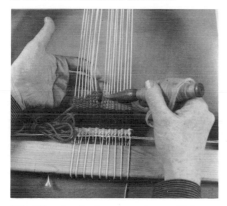

122 Building up colours separately: take care to meet and part the weft in the correct direction and shed.

123 Weaving in the next colour will leave a slit, which can be left open or stitched up.

When using more than one weft in the same shed, always work adjacent wefts in opposing directions, so that the sheds don't conflict. On starting a new weft it is vital to check the shed and the direction of the weft it will meet or leave (120). Each area being woven will need a separate bobbin.

When a colour, or a bobbin is started and finished, don't cut the end off flush with the weaving or it will work through to the front of the tapestry. Tie the thread in a half-hitch and leave about 4 cm (1½ in) hanging permanently on the wrong side of the work (117) – it doesn't need to be darned in as it will be held by the firm weaving. If you are starting a new colour, leave a similar end hanging at the back, one warp in from the edge of the area, so that the resulting half-hitch gives added security (121).

In order to prevent the selvedges getting thin or uneven, occasionally wrap the weft around the outermost thread to give strength.

Slits and joins

The meeting of two areas of weaving, often two separate colours, is the most skilled part of tapestry weaving. Where the design demands a vertical join, there are several ways of handling this problem. Possibly the easiest way is to weave up to the junction line from either side, and return, which will of course leave a *slit* after a few passes have been woven (122, 123). This slit can be left as such – it can give a lively surface to the tapestry, or can be used in various ways; for example, to make a subtle line in an area of solid colour without using a definite line of a different colour. Fiona Mathison makes a feature of the tapestry slit in several of her pieces (118, colour 13). The slit can also be stitched up preferably during, otherwise immediately after weaving, with a fine strand of matching weft; this is a traditional solution. Slits at

124 'A hill for my friend', a tapestry by Maureen Hodge.

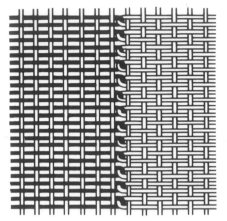

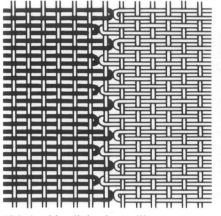

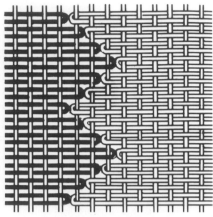

125 Slits can be overcome by interlocking the adjoining passes.

126 Avoid a slit by dovetailing the passes.

127 Diagonal joints avoid the formation of slits, although this can limit design possibilities.

vertical joins can be avoided during the weaving process by several methods – two of the most commonly used are interlocking (125) and dove-tailing (126). When these are used for a long join, however, they can get bulky and unsightly, and are time-consuming. So the ideal design for tapestry has plenty of diagonal joins, in which the slits are so small that they can be ignored (127).

Weaving shapes

By varying the number of passes in the steps of a diagonal progression any angle can be woven, no matter how steep or flat (128–132). Curves are just combinations of angles (133) but it does take practice to get the combinations right and to make a smooth curve. Inking-on helps here.

128 Steep or shallow angles can be formed by varying the number of passes in a step. Finish off the point with three passes and a half-hitch round one warp.

129 After weaving in the surrounding shapes, you should be able to weave straight across the tapestry; that is, the shed should be the same across the warp.

130 Weave shallow diagonals using deep steps over several warps.

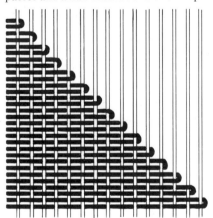

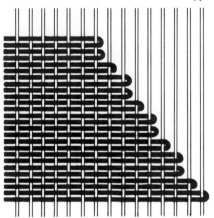

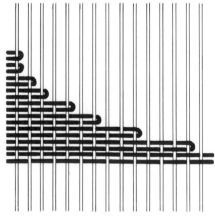

131 Weave a steeper diagonal using one-warp steps.

132 Combine different steps to get the diagonal required.

133 Curves are made with a combination of shallow and steep steps.

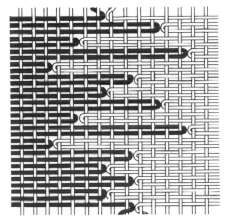

134 Hatching: two weft colours are dovetailed over several warps to create a blend of the colours.

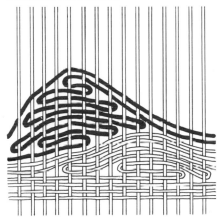

135 Using an angled weft to weave curves.

136 Fine detail on this large unfinished tapestry at Edinburgh was possible because of its close sett; it was being woven on its side.

The detail in any design is determined by the sett of the warp: the closer the sett, with a correspondingly finer warp, the more detail can be included (136, 138, colour 10, back cover 2). But tapestry weaving is a slow process, and today fine warps are usually only used for small tapestries.

Hatching is a traditional way of shading or graduating from one colour to another (134). Old tapestries show how this technique has been used to create light and shade or folds in clothing (136, colour 11).

Tapestry can also be woven with a *curving* or *eccentric* weft – where the weft is not necessarily placed at right angles to the warp, but builds up in a lively manner, with passes often curving right over a built-up shape (135). This technique seems to lend itself to leafy and organic designs, and gives movement to the surface. Many Coptic tapestries are woven in this way (138). It is not a good idea to weave at a steep angle, as this causes severe buckling.

Weaving upright or sideways

Large tapestries are often woven sideways, so that when they hang, the weft is vertical (136). This is done because the main outlines in pictorial tapestry are vertical, and it is easier to weave vertical lines sideways, along the weft. Tapestry is also stronger along its weft thread.

137 The same design woven upright, and sideways; the legs and the horizon present different problems in each method.

In Figure 137, one camel has been woven upright, and the steep diagonals of the legs have come out rather jagged; when woven sideways these steep vertical curves become shallow horizontal curves, and are much smoother. The horizon line has become a slit.

When designing a tapestry, look at the outlines: if the majority of the lines are vertical or steep angles, it may be preferable to turn them into shallow angles by weaving the piece sideways.

Taking the tapestry off the loom

There are several ways of finishing off a tapestry when it is cut from the frame. Warp ends at the top and bottom can be knotted into fringes, but a neater solution is to weave a little extra in a plain colour at the beginning

51

and the end, which can then be folded to the back and sewn down as a hem. Remember not to shorten the many loose weft ends at the back to less than 2·5 cm (1in).

138 Tapestry panel woven in purple and natural wool, Egypt, fourth to fifth century; the weft is not always at right angles to the warp.

139 Detail of Fiona Mathison's 'In the shadow of Man'; the bodies of some of the insects are whipped, and wings are made from extra warps, some with cellophane weft.

Designing tapestries

Fiona Mathison, Art Director of the Dovecot Studios in Edinburgh, also weaves smaller tapestries of her own. She says, 'Although there is a basic set of rules, the thing about tapestry is that the equipment is so simple that it offers the weaver the greatest possible freedom. You can change almost everything as you weave – even the warp can be changed: weaving two warps together changes 24 warps per 10 cm to 12 warps per 10 cm (6 warps per in to 3 warps per in). This can be used to create texture, or as a means of weaving finer detailed areas in a broader design (colour 10). It is a good idea to make a lot of sample strips to begin with: this will build up experience of warp settings and the effect of various weft threads at different thicknesses, while helping you to gain valuable experience in making the different shapes you may wish to use in a design. There are so many avenues to explore.

Materials themselves can give an enormous variety of surface, and using them as a thick or thin weft can multiply the possibilities two-fold. You can weave with anything pliable enough to pass through the warps; try a variety of wefts from grasses to silver paper, as well as the many yarns available (139, colour 12, colour 13).

In addition to the textures created by the materials themselves there are knotting and tufting techniques employed in rug-making; or for a really three-dimensional effect you can weave extra pieces and add these to your tapestry (140, 141). *Whipping*, that is, binding a thick core with weft, is also frequently found in tapestries today.

140 Fiona starts to whip an insect body.

141 Extra warp loops are controlled by the fingers, and become the wings of the insects, free-woven with a needle.

Although it is easier to weave a rectangular tapestry, you can weave almost any shape – although undercutting is not recommended. You can pull in and push out edges, or cut the warps and weave them in to create a shaped selvedge (142).

In the end, like any other technique, it is the designer's imagination which makes it come to life, and once the basic rules are understood tapestry allows an enormous freedom of expression.'

For more details of some contemporary tapestries see Chapter Fourteen; historical tapestries are discussed in Chapter Fifteen.

142 'Camel' by Fiona Mathison; tapestries can be woven in many shapes. The saddlebag is woven with soumak, tufts and tassels.

Chapter Six

Looms and equipment

All the weaving techniques described so far relate to frame looms;
they are ideally suited for weaving such as tapestry, but have limitations
for other types of weaving. If you want to weave lengths of fabric, most rugs
and patterned cloth, you will want more elaborate equipment – a table or
floor loom of some kind, because they have devices for making the shed,
storing the cloth, producing patterns, and keeping the work consistently
even. Their main advantage is speed.

Looms

Looms vary greatly in size and complexity, but there are some basic features
that are common to all these looms (143, 144):

The frame This must look stronger than necessary.

The beam The warp-beam at the back stores the warp; the cloth-beam near
the front stores the finished weaving. The larger the diameter the better,
especially for the warp-beam.

The shafts These consist of an upper and lower bar carrying the heddles.
They control the rise and fall of the warp threads, thus forming the shed.
There are often four or eight, occasionally twelve or sixteen shafts. Four-
shaft looms are perfectly adequate for beginners – and some four shaft
looms can easily be converted to eight shafts.

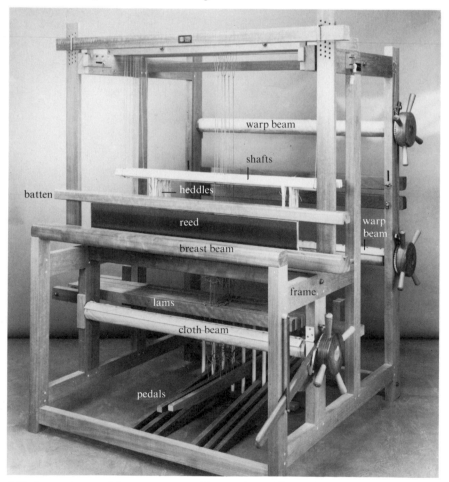

143 A countermarch loom: two sets of lams raise and lower the shafts to give
a perfect shed.

The heddles The warp is threaded through heddles. They can be made of twine which is kinder to the threads, or wire which is easier to thread.

The batten This is a pivoted frame holding the reed. It can hang from the top of the loom (overslung) or be pivoted at floor level (underslung).

The reed The reed is used for spacing the warp and beating the weft; ideally, it should be made of stainless steel to avoid rusting.

The levers (table loom), and **the pedals** (floor loom). These raise and lower the shafts. Pedals may be pivoted from the front, in which case they are easier to select, or from the back, when they provide more leverage.

Before buying a loom of any sort, it is a good idea to join a class and get advice from an experienced weaver about the best loom for you. There are not many places where it is possible to see more than one make of new loom to make comparisons, and most looms have to be bought from catalogues.

The amount of space available in your house will probably have a great deal of influence on your decision. Remember that you will require more than the space needed to house the loom itself: unless your loom has warping posts built in you will need to buy and store equipment for warping as well – and you will certainly need space to move around the loom easily.

There are various different sizes and types of loom, and it is useful to know what is available.

The table loom

A table loom (144) usually weaves cloth up to about 60 cm (24 in) wide, and has four shafts, which means that you can weave many interesting patterns. You raise and lower the shafts by hand, using the levers, each time you insert a weft thread. (Some table looms are made wider, but it is better to weave wider cloth on a floor loom.)

It must sit on a firm table, or on its own stand, and it does not fold up for storage. Not all fabrics should be woven on a table loom: it is almost impossible to weave a good rug (although there are models on the market which claim to do so), and long lengths of fabric are very slow and boring to produce. It should be useful for scarves, cushion covers and samplers (but see next page, *Floor looms*).

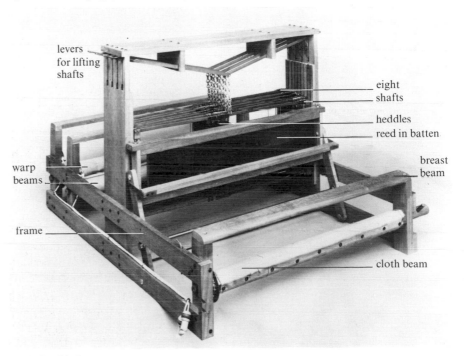

levers for lifting shafts

eight shafts

heddles

reed in batten

breast beam

warp beams

frame

cloth beam

144 A table loom.

Floor looms

Table looms are excellent for trying out weaves, and for weaving small articles, but for any speed of production, or just to be able to weave with a satisfying rhythm – which also affects the look of the cloth – some form of floor loom is essential. Floor looms have pedals, whose main advantage is that they enable you to lift the shafts by foot-power, so leaving your hands free to throw the shuttle.

When using a four-shaft table loom, for most weaving two or more shafts have to be lifted at once by hand for each shed, whereas on a floor loom the pedals can be connected to one, two or three shafts and will therefore raise them all simultaneously. They are not connected directly to the shafts, however, as this would make it impossible to lift the shafts evenly, but to *lams* (or *marches*), which are supported a little way under the shafts: they centralise the lifting, and, except on a *countermarch loom* (see below) there are the same number of lams as shafts. Many learner weavers are puzzled by the appearance of *six* pedals on a four-shaft loom, but in fact the shafts are lifted in six common combinations, and so six pedals are provided. (For how to tie up the pedals, see Page 74 and Pages 89–90.)

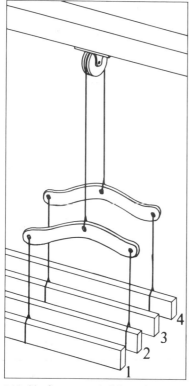

145 Shafts suspended from horses.

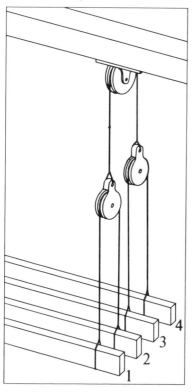

146 Shafts suspended from pulleys.

The folding loom

The most popular floor loom for beginners is the *folding loom*, which weaves cloth up to 86 cm (34 in) wide and has four shafts. As its name implies, it can be folded flat with the warp on, either to move around the house or garden, or to store away – for example, behind a sofa. It will cost little more than a table-loom, but it has many advantages. It won't be suitable for weaving heavy rugs, but it will weave satisfactory lengths of cloth. For really long lengths, you will need a larger floor loom, which is capable of holding warps up to 36 m (40 yds) long (depending, of course, on the thickness of the yarn to be used).

Choosing a larger floor loom

The serious weaver wishing to weave rugs, longer lengths of cloth, large hangings – as well as light-weight or small pieces – will need a good, solid floor loom. When buying a floor loom, the sturdier it is, the better; it certainly must not sway or flex in any direction when erected. These looms are supplied in pieces for simple assembly.

Big looms are no more difficult to use than small looms – in fact most weavers think they're easier, because you can get inside them more easily for threading. They have the great advantage that they will weave anything, large or small, thick or thin. Although looms most commonly have four shafts, eight shafts (and eight pedals) will broaden the eventual scope of the weaving considerably, and looms can have twelve or sixteen shafts. Looms with two back beams are especially useful for dealing with two different types of warp thread. Occasionally looms will be fitted with pegs for making warps on the side or back of the structure – this will save the cost of a separate warping frame.

Sometimes second-hand looms are advertised – for example, in the *Weaver's Journal*, and in *Crafts* magazine, and, like anything second-hand, can be a bargain or a waste of money. Beginners should beware of the home-made loom being offered, often described as 'unique', and should buy only reputable makes. Age doesn't often matter: some of the best looms are very old indeed. Sometimes parts will be missing: their replacement is fairly easy if they are made of wood, but any missing metal parts can be expensive or impossible to replace.

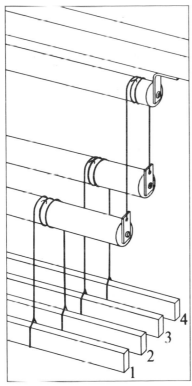

147 Shafts suspended from rollers.

The counterbalanced loom

This very common type of loom is usually limited to four shafts which are suspended by cords passing to horses, pulleys or rollers attached to the loom frame above (145–147). There is one lam, or march, connected to the bottom of each shaft and the pedals are tied to a selection of these lams. Pressing a pedal therefore lowers the shafts to whose lams ties have been made and, through the system of pulleys, automatically raises all the other shafts – hence the name, *counterbalanced*. So to raise shafts 1 and 3, a pedal has to be tied to the lams of shafts 2 and 4.

A good shed results when any two shafts are lowered and the other two raised – that is when weaving 2/2 twill and plain weave – but there are difficulties, both with the depth of shed and its level relative to the beater, with the 3 up, 1 down and the 1 up, 3 down sheds. Another disadvantage on a loom fitted with horses or pulleys is that the shafts tilt unless there is a full-width warp to steady them. This can be very annoying when weaving a narrow sample. But if on a loom with rollers, each cord is wrapped around the roller several times and then the central wrap stapled to the roller itself, this tilting is impossible and the shafts always stay parallel.

But the main disadvantage of a counterbalanced loom is that extra shafts cannot be added to the original four. It is therefore not the loom for a weaver interested in complex weaves, like eight-shaft twills, patterned double cloths and so on. However many weavers, content with the almost endless possibilities of four shaft weaving, find it a very pleasant loom to work, especially liking its simple pedal-to-lam ties.

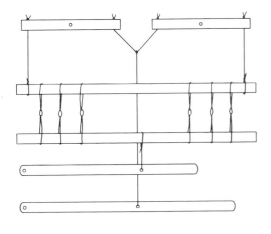

148 The principle of the counter-march loom.

The countermarch loom

This loom (143) is the one preferred by most professional weavers in Europe because it will give a perfect shed with any number of shafts. This is possible because each shaft works as an independent unit and so its rising and falling is controlled only by the pedals, not by the movement of the other shafts, as in the counterbalanced loom. To achieve this, each shaft needs two lams, a *march* and a *countermarch*, hence the name. One lies directly below the shaft and is attached to it, so by lowering this lam the shaft is lowered. The other lam is connected by means of cords, passing over pulleys or up to levers in the top of the loom, to the top of the shaft, and so lowering this lam raises the shaft (148).

These two sets of lams are either mounted on separate rods, one above the other, or they are interleaved alternately on a single rod. Each pedal has to be tied to either the lowering or the raising lam of *every* shaft in use. In other words, whereas with a counterbalanced loom you only tie the pedals to the lams of the shafts you want to lower, here you have to tie the pedals both to those you want to raise and the ones you want to lower. This doubled amount of tying often puts weavers off the countermarch loom, but the extra work is offset by the complete control the weaver has over the depth of shed, no matter how many shafts are in use. So, for example, shaft no. 12 can be made to rise and fall slightly more than shaft no. 1 and so give a perfect shed. The other advantage of the system is that it can be used for any number of shafts, odd or even; countermarch looms are usually supplied with extra space to take up to 12 or 16 shafts.

The dobby loom

If a weaver wishes to use 16 or more shafts and maybe change at frequent intervals the combination of those lifted, as when weaving samples, it is very tedious to keep on re-tying the pedals of a countermarch loom. After all, 16 shafts connected to, say, 8 pedals means $16 \times 8 = 128$ ties. In circumstances such as these a dobby mechanism proves its worth (149, 150). It is a device

149 Fay Morgan using a sixteen-shaft dobby loom. One pedal lifts pre-set combinations of shafts.

150 Pegs are driven into lags according to the liftings required.

fitted to the top of the loom which is worked by a single pedal. The required lifts for each pick are programmed by putting pegs into short wooden bars, known as *lags*, which are then chained together to make a closed loop. So if the pattern repeats every 40 picks, the loop consists of 40 lags chained together. Pressing the pedal not only raises the shafts indicated by the pegs on the one lag in the critical position, but also moves the whole chain round so that the next lag is presented to the dobby.

Weavers often keep sets of lags giving plain weave, twills and so on, so they can quickly try these common lifts on whatever warp is being used. The dobby has a rising shed only, so one of its disadvantages is the heavy lifting of the shafts which are held in the down position by weights or springs. The weaver therefore works standing up to exert more pressure on the pedal. Another disadvantage is that a pattern with a very long repeat needs a cumbersomely long chain of lags; however most dobbies have a lever which reverses the direction in which the lags move, in this way increasing the size of the woven repeat. Dobbies are therefore most suited for weaves which require many shafts but have fairly small repeats; they are often used by weavers designing for industry.

Rug looms

Rug weaving is covered in Chapter Twelve (see Page 104).

Other equipment

Having chosen a loom and a means of making a warp (see Pages 61 and 62) there are still other items to allow for in the budget. Their use will be described later in more detail:

A **temple** (289) is used to maintain consistent width of the fabric, especially rugs.

The raddle (165–167) is used for spreading the warp onto the warp beam during beaming. It looks like a coarse reed, with commonly 8 dents to 10 cm (2 dents to 1 in) and a removable top. You can make your own with board, nails and masking tape.

The reed (176, see below), is sometimes supplied with the loom. Say what dentage you want. Most weavers will eventually need at least six reeds in different dentages. Sometimes you can get hold of these second hand (brass or stainless steel are best, but expensive). Use a very sturdy one for rug weaving, or it will bow under the strain.

A threading hook for threading the warp through the heddles.

A reed hook (176) for threading the warp through the reed.

A stick shuttle (250) for holding the weft for simple weaving.

A boat shuttle or **a roller shuttle** for holding a bobbin of weft, used on table and floor looms (193, 205).

A bobbin winder (191), hand or electric; this is essential for use with either boat or roller shuttles.

A stool is often designed to go with the loom; this can be useful as it will be the right height to avoid backstrain; some have useful spool-holding rods and a shelf underneath, some are adjustable in height.

Most looms come supplied with **shed sticks** (169), and **cross-sticks** (171).

Choosing a reed

Later on, when you come to threading up the loom, you will want a reed which is compatible with the *sett* you have chosen (see Page 60). Reeds are made with a certain number of dents per centimetre (or per inch); they are marked down one end with the number of dents per 10 centimetres (or per inch): if in doubt, check with a ruler.

Many weavers still use reeds in imperial measurements, but they are also obtainable in metric measurements which are similar but do not correspond exactly to the imperial equivalents. If you calculate the sett in metric measurements, use a metric reed.

Most weavers use a reed not with the same dentage as the sett, but a lower one with *half* the number of dents per cm (in); for example, they would use a 6 dent reed for a 12 epi warp, sleying 2 ends per dent. This is to reduce friction on the yarn. For a very fluffy yarn you may need to use one thread per dent to keep the warp ends separated. (For rugs see Chapter Twelve.)

You may well find that the sett you want for your next piece of weaving doesn't coincide with a reed in your possession, but you can in fact obtain many different setts from a limited number of reeds. Suppose the number required is *15 ends per inch*, and the reeds you have available are *10, 14* and *16* to the inch: by increasing or decreasing the chosen number by one a *14* or a *16* reed could be used, with one thread per dent. But by threading the 10's reed with 2 and 1 thread alternately in the dents, the required 15 ends per inch is achieved. Reeds can also be threaded, 2, 2, 1 or 1, 1, 2 or every other dent. The table gives you an idea of the variations of sett possible from a few reeds (151).

Some suppliers stock only commonly used reeds, such as 8, 12 and 14, but reeds are obtainable in any dentage.

Reed threading – ends per inch (epi)

dents per inch	every other dent	every dent	1, 2	1, 1, 2	1, 2, 2	2 in each dent
8's	4	8	12	$10\frac{2}{3}$	$13\frac{1}{3}$	16
10's	5	10	15	$13\frac{1}{3}$	$16\frac{2}{3}$	20
12's	6	12	18	16	20	24
14s	7	14	21	$18\frac{2}{3}$	$23\frac{1}{3}$	28
16's	8	16	24	$21\frac{1}{3}$	$26\frac{2}{3}$	32

151 A 'dentage' table.

Chapter Seven

Making a warp and dressing the loom

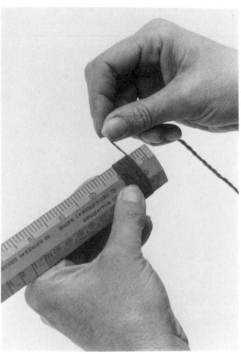

152 Wind the yarn around the ruler so that the threads are just touching.

Sett

It is important, before you begin to weave, to decide on the *sett* of the cloth. Sett means the number of threads to the centimetre (inch) of warp and weft. This is a very important decision: a well-woven cloth made of good materials can be useless for its purpose, and look poor, if the sett is wrong. It can be a complicated calculation, because a lot depends on the weave to be used, but there is a rule of thumb:

Take the warp yarn and wind it round a ruler over 3 cm (or 1 inch) so that the threads just touch one another (152). Count the number of threads: divide by three to get the number of threads per centimetre (not necessary if you are working in inches). Half this number will give you the number of warp threads per centimetre, that is, ends per cm (e/cm) or ends per inch (epi) for a balanced, plain weave cloth (colour 8).

For a warp-faced cloth, you will need more warp threads than weft threads per centimetre (inch), so increase the number by up to two-thirds when you use this method to plan your warp. For a weft-faced fabric – for example, a tapestry – you will need a greater number of weft threads than warp threads to the centimetre, so decrease the number (see Chapter Five).

The sett will have an effect on the feel of the fabric: fewer threads per centimetre (inch) will give you an open, softer, more flexible fabric; more threads to the centimetre (inch) will give you a closer, firmer, more rigid fabric, more suitable for upholstery, for example. As you become more experienced, you will be able to adjust the sett you find by wrapping round the ruler, to suit the function of the fabric you are making. Once again, making samples will help you get the correct relationship of warp to weft without wasting a whole warp.

For weaving on anything other than a frame loom the weaver must prepare the warp threads in advance in a way which will keep them tangle-free and easy to thread on the loom in the right order. You can think of a warp as a long skein of yarn, with a figure-of-eight cross in the threads at each end (153).

153 A warp is a skein of yarn of any length, with a cross at each end.

Calculating the warp

Before beginning to make the warp, you need to calculate the length you require: the length must be greater than the length of the finished fabric you are planning. Some is inevitably wasted by knots at the front, and by the fact that it isn't possible to weave all the way to the end of the warp. As a general rule, allow 1 metre extra (3 ft) 'for the loom', and then about 8 cm per metre (1 in per foot) of weaving for the take-up which occurs when a normal balanced warp is woven. (Increase this for a warp-face fabric, and ignore it for a weft-face fabric like a tapestry.)

So for example if you plan a finished fabric to measure 2 metres long, add:

2·00 m (cloth)
1·00 m (for the loom)
0·16 m (for the take-up of weave)
3·16 m warp length

This doesn't take into account any shrinkage which might occur in any wet-finishing: some weavers add another 10 centimetres per metre to allow for this when weaving a woollen cloth (4 inches per yard – ie they weave a 40-inch 'yard'). Keep records of warp length and cloth length, and you will get to know how much extra warp to allow for your particular loom.

So you can see that it is very wasteful to use short warps: the 1 metre (3 ft) for the loom applies whether the warp is short or long; and then the time spent in threading up the loom is also the same for a long or short warp.

Once you have worked out the sett, and decided on the width of the finished fabric, then the number of warp ends is just the result of a simple multiplication: ends per centimetre (inch) × centimetres (inches) of fabric width. But not quite, for the woven fabric will end up narrower than the width of the threads in the reed, usually by about 8 centimetres in one metre (1 inch in 1 foot) – this is a rule of thumb, accurate enough for most purposes. If ever it is essential to get the width exactly right, you will have to weave a sample, keeping records of width before and after weaving, and also after washing, when more shrinkage will take place. So add more warp ends to compensate for this narrowing effect, and another 4 or so ends for *selvedges*.

The selvedge

The selvedge is the edge of the woven cloth, formed down each side as the weft is woven into the warp. Hand weavers pay much attention to the selvedge: it is a traditional place to inspect good craftsmanship. Often selvedges are cut off, or hidden in seams during the making up of the weaving, and it may seem pointless to spend much time getting them neat; but if you are careless about selvedges, and allow the weft to pull them in too much, you will get broken threads on the edge, the tension will suffer generally, and the whole cloth will be affected. The quality of the selvedge is also affected by the way in which the shuttle is passed from side to side and by the way in which the bobbin is wound, but when making the warp the important thing is to strengthen it adequately for the strains which it will have to withstand.

Some weavers double the sett at each edge, *cramming* a couple of dents in the reed (154). As selvedges often present such a problem there are many other possible solutions: double the threads in the heddle, but not in the reed; or use selvedge threads separately tensioned on bobbins. So allow for extra selvedge threads when planning the warp.

In some weaves the weft does not catch the outermost warp thread, so it is a good idea to use a *floating selvedge* – (see Page 113).

When all the calculations have been made – recorded in your notebook – make sure that the yarns are packaged so that they run freely, as an even tension of the thread during warping is important (see Page 14).
Then warping can begin.

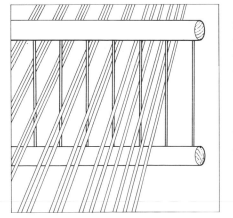

154 Extra threads crammed in the reed to strengthen the selvedge.

Warping equipment

In some countries, warps are made in one long length, with the warper (often a small energetic boy) running up and down carrying the warp thread freely revolving on a stick, taking the warp threads round 3 pegs at either end. As each thread may involve a trip of about 30 metres (30 yards), we may find it convenient to find some means of folding or spiralling up the length of the

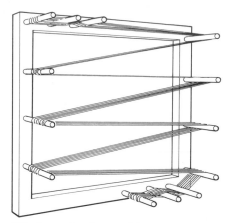

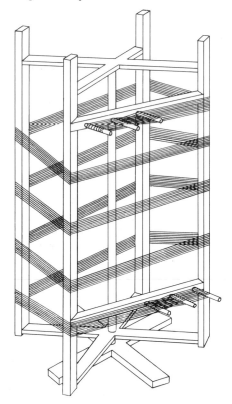

155 A warping frame with maximum length of warp on it.

156 A warping mill, with a warp on it.

warp, so that the warper can remain in one place. This is the function of warping equipment such as the *warping frame* (155) or the *warping mill* (156).

A short warp can be made by using *warping posts* clamped to a table (157). Warp length can be built up by zig-zagging across the table, around single posts. A warping frame can be made out of a stout picture-frame drilled to take thick dowels. In all warping equipment, however, make sure that the posts are securely at right angles; flimsy and unstable equipment is useless.

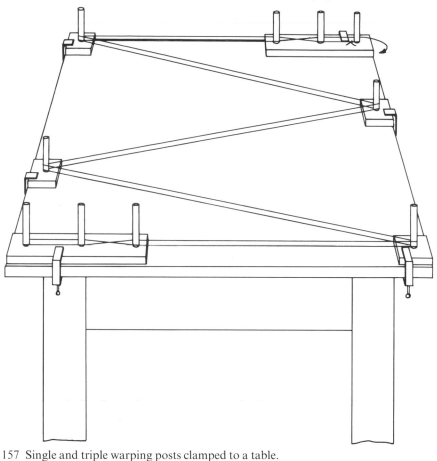

157 Single and triple warping posts clamped to a table.

Making the warp

Warping, though a simple process, must be done very carefully, to avoid waste of both materials and time. If a warp is accurately constructed, the figure-of-eight crosses automatically keep the threads in the right order for threading on the loom.

Many weavers like to make the warp in two halves across the width – that is, two warps with half the total number of warp ends in each. This prevents build-up of yarn on the warping mill or pegs, it is easier to handle, and it is easier to find the centre. If the warp has very many ends per cm (ends per inch) you can make it in several parts.

Take a piece of string, the length of the required warp – this is the guide string – and attach it to the end post. Lead it zig-zagging across the table or board, or spiralling round the mill, and place the other set of double or triple pegs so that the string reaches the furthest peg. Attach it to the peg. Make sure that all pegs are firm. Now warping can begin.

Start by tying the warp yarn loosely but securely to the end peg, and take it in and out of the pegs and on to the other end, where it goes in and out of the pegs again and returns to the beginning, weaving itself the opposite way round the pegs. Two figure-of-eight crosses are formed this way, one at each

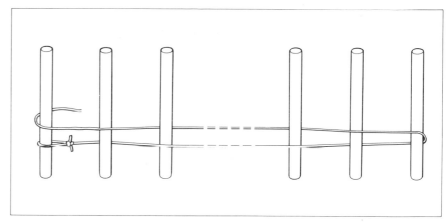

158 Whatever the equipment used, the path of the warp to form the crosses is the same. The warp can be any length.

end of the warp (158). Keep on doing this for the required number of warp threads. Remember the following points:

a) keep the tension even throughout; build up a warping rhythm;

b) be very careful to make the cross perfectly – that is, keep the yarn going round the pegs on exactly the same path each time;

c) if a knot occurs in the yarn, break it and retie the yarn so that it occurs only at one end or another. (Sometimes, if the yarn is fine, and the warp is very long, this rule can be ignored by the experienced weaver);

d) similarly, if you want a change of colour of yarn, join it by tying it at one end or the other, as required (159);

e) make sure that the ends don't overlap and build up on the posts;

f) keep careful count of the number of ends by inserting a thread of a contrasting colour in and out at 1 centimetre (or $\frac{1}{2}$ inch) intervals to correspond with the commonly used approximately 1 cm ($\frac{1}{2}$ in) spacing in the raddle. This will save re-counting all the time and will be useful when raddling later (160).

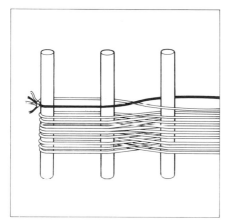

159 Tie any new yarn onto the old at either end peg.

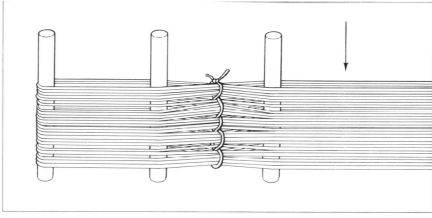

160 The counting thread can be at the cross, or near the arrow.

When the warp is completed, tie the ends of this counting thread together loosely but securely. Note – every thread counts towards the total: make sure you're not counting one side only – so count the threads at the cross. Warps can be made with two threads at once, to save time, but they should come from the same sort of package, ie both from cheeses on a rack, or both from jars or buckets (separate ones) on the floor, to maintain even tension of the threads. This is also useful if you have planned alternate colours for the warp order. (Some professional weavers make warps with many threads at once – say 12, or even 60 – but additional devices are needed to make the crosses at the ends of such warps.)

When the warp is finished, tie the last thread to the end peg.
Do not take the warp off the pegs yet – or it will be wasted.

Next, tie up the crosses: take eight threads of a contrasting colour, and tie each around one arm of the two crosses, but leaving room to get scissors in later. The reason for the contrasting colour is so that the ties can be seen and dealt with very easily and safely (161). (Don't tie in the original guide-string though, as you will leave that behind on the warping board.)

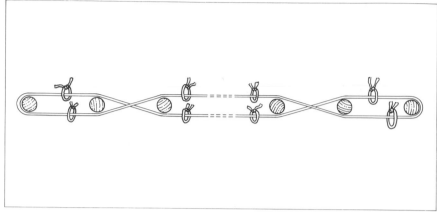

161 Tie all four arms of the cross firmly.

Then put on a *choke tie*: about one metre (yard) from the end of the warp with the counting thread, the end which is to be wound first onto the loom, tie a thread in another colour very tightly round the warp. Later on this will be useful to stop the threads shifting round while raddling, or in case you drop the raddle, catch your foot in the warp, or all the other things that can go wrong. Some weavers, when making a long warp, put several choke ties like this at intervals of a few metres (yards) or so all along the warp, as an anti-tangling safeguard and to help keep the tension.

Once all these ties have been made securely, slip the end furthest from the counting thread off the pegs and, slipping your wrist through the loop, grasp the warp and pull it through (162).

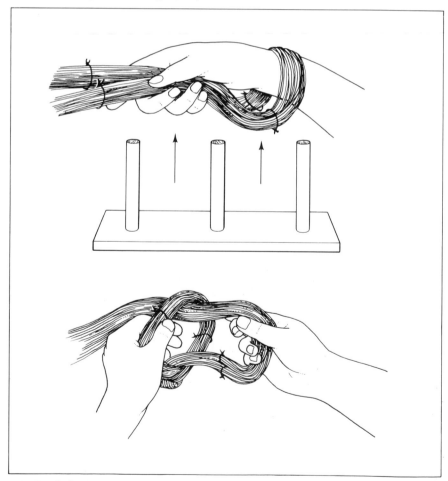

162 To chain the warp, slip your wrist through the end, and pull the warp through in a loop.

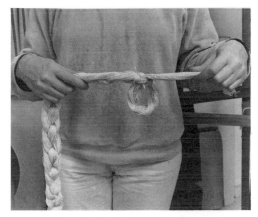

163 The chained warp should undo easily when required.

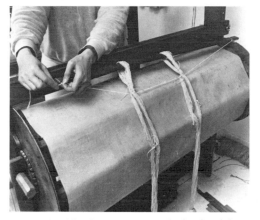

164 Slip the warps onto the back-stick of the loom, pass the cord through the other arm of the cross, and tie it to the stick securely.

Continue this action like a crochet chain until the other end is reached, and slip the end off the peg, but don't pull it through the last loop made. This chaining makes the warp convenient to handle (163). If the warp is to be left for a few days before being used, tie a luggage label to it, marked with its length, width, sett, and so on.

If you are making the warp in two or more parts, make them all before you start putting any on the loom.

Dressing the loom

The main aim of *dressing the loom* – that is, putting the warp on the loom – is to store the warp on the warp-beam in a very orderly, firm manner, so that no thread is allowed to get longer or shorter than its neighbours, and to thread the warp accurately through the shafts and reed so that it may perform the function of weaving as efficiently as possible.

There are various ways of doing this; this book describes one main method: the weaver works from the back of the loom to the front: first winding the warp onto the warp beam, then threading it through the shafts, then through the reed and finally tying it onto the front stick.

1 Inserting the back stick Take your warp (made in two or more parts) and insert the *back-stick* from the warp-beam into the end loop, pass the cord of the back-stick through the other loop of the cross and tie it to the other end of the stick (164). Now you can undo the four cross-ties at that end of the warp – but leave the choke ties. (Many weavers attach the back stick to the apron before raddling to help tension.)

2 Raddling Clamp the raddle so that it is centred onto the back cross-bar with the top off, and lay pieces of folded paper over it so that the warp can lie over it (165). Decide on the position which the centred warp will take in the raddle, undo the ends of the counting-thread and assuming that your raddle has 8 dents per 10 cm (2 dents to 1 in), slip the first 1 cm ($\frac{1}{2}$ in) bundle of warp threads carefully across and down into the correct dent (166). If you haven't used a counting thread, just count out the threads so that each dent holds the number of planned ends per centimetre or *half* the number of the planned threads per inch. Keep doing this until the raddle is loaded: then put the top on the raddle and secure it.

165 Lay the warps on folded paper over the secured raddle.

166 Slip the counted bundles of warp threads into the raddle dents.

167 Secure the top on the raddle, and tie the back-stick to the apron at several points.

3 Attaching the back-stick After distributing the loops evenly along it, attach the back-stick to the warp-beam (167). You will find that it is attached to the beam by either a canvas 'apron' or by lengths of cord; an apron is preferable, as cords can build up as the beam turns and poke through the warp, making it uneven. Many weavers remove cords from a new loom, replacing them with strong canvas aprons.

168 Pull gently on the warp, then wind it gradually and smoothly onto the beam, keeping it taut.

4 Beaming Once the warp is firmly attached to the beam, hold it at each choke-tie and give it a hearty tug. This helps all the warp threads to straighten out and helps to clear any tangles. Standing at the back of the loom take the chain of warp and undo a little, pulling gently but firmly on the whole of it. Wind it gradually, spaced through the raddle, onto the warp beam, undoing each choke tie as you reach it (168). If you are working on a floor loom it is a good idea to have a helper to do the winding, while your weight tensions the warp as you hold the chain. Wind on very carefully and evenly. Every few revolutions wind in four equally spaced *flat sticks*, or four strips of thin stiff card all of which must be wider than the warp. Make sure that the next set of four lies in between the previous set (169). These are to prevent the yarns from biting down unevenly through the layers of threads and to prevent threads at the edge of the warp from slipping off. If you have to beam single-handed, then wind on one complete turn at a time, stop to apply tension and even out the warp as it goes through the raddle, make another complete turn, and so on.

5 Putting in cross-sticks Once the warp is firmly beamed and the chain is completely undone, the second cross will appear. Wind the warp onto the beam until this cross would just reach to the other side of the shafts. Now unclamp the raddle and carry it and the remaining warp around the back bar so it is now lying in the correct position for weaving (170). Release the raddle by removing the top. Place a pair of cross-sticks through the cross and tie their strings so they cannot fall out. Suspend them on cords behind the heddles at a height convenient for threading (171).

169 Wind plenty of shed sticks, or stiff cards, in between the layers.

170 When the second cross appears, bring the raddle around the back bar; it can be reclamped to it, and remain there during weaving, or it can be removed altogether as in the photographs.

171 Insert a pair of cross-sticks through the cross, and tie a cord on each from one end to the other; suspend them at a height convenient for threading.

6 Checking the heddles Make sure that you have enough heddles on each shaft to take the total number of warp ends allotted to that shaft (see Page 88). For a *straight draft* on four shafts, as described below, this means that each shaft should have one quarter of the total number of warp ends in the warp, and these should be distributed equally on either side.

7 Threading the heddles on a four shaft loom Now you can cut through the cross-ties. If you did not make the warp in two halves, divide the threads into two parts and bring each forward between the heddles and the side of the loom. You can see that the threads lie in the correct order, because of the cross. This is the order in which they should be threaded. (If a thread has somehow missed the cross during warping, it should be put in as near as possible to its original place.)

172 Bring each half of the warp forward between the heddles and the side of the loom, cut the ends and tie to the front bar with a lark's head knot.

Holding the left-hand bunch of warp threads, cut through the loop at the end and tie this bunch to the front bar – using a *lark's head* knot (172) – this holds the warp firmly, but allows threads to be withdrawn. From the shaft nearest the back of the loom (no. 4) slide a heddle from those on the left along towards the centre. Start with the thread nearest the centre of the loom, and thread it through the heddle from the back to the front, so that it hangs down towards you (173). You can use either a threading-hook or your

11 One of the six tapestries, collectively known as 'The lady and the unicorn';
possibly a wedding gift, hence 'A mon seul desir' on the tent;
French or Flemish, fifteenth century.

12 'Picnic', Fiona Mathison; the tapestry
is mainly cotton; the 'grass' is tufted
raffia, sisal, flax and other yarns.

13 'In the shadow of Man', Fiona Mathison; the dark background is linen,
the light is wool; the insects on the shadow are woven flat, the others
are three-dimensional, the wings made with extra warps.

14 Indian silk sari, with gold thread in warp stripes.

15 'Burning moss' by Tadek Beutlich, consisting of many tightly wrapped elements springing from a woven base.

16 Blockweave rug by Roger Oates using two strands of natural dark grey and dyed 2/60's rug yarn on 6/10's linen at 6 epi.

17 Half of a Middle-Eastern saddlebag in soumak technique, nineteenth century.

18 Hanging 'Zig-Zag three', Ruth Harris, using tapestry and soumak techniques.

19 Twill-woven rug by Roger Oates, three strands 2/60's rug yarn on 6/10's linen warp set at 6 ends per inch, from a group of three linked rugs in the Crafts Council collection.

fingers. If you need more length of warp, release some extra from the warp-beam. Take the second thread and move a heddle on shaft 3 along to accept it. Thread the third one through a heddle on shaft 2, and the fourth through a heddle on shaft 1 (174). Repeat all the way along to the left until that side of the warp has been *entered* (threaded). Repeat the process for the right-hand half of the warp. But be careful here: in order to keep continuity across the warp it will be necessary to thread the shafts in the order 1, 2, 3, 4, – not 4, 3, 2, 1 as before (175).

In some weaves it is important that the selvedge thread is entered on a particular shaft. In this case, it is best to thread continuously from the right side of the warp to the left, a method preferred by some professionals.

8 Sleying Once the entering is complete, the threads are ready to be *sleyed* – that is, threaded through the reed. Another type of threading-hook is designed for this, called a *reed-hook* which is easy to slip in and out of the dents. (An 'automatic' reed-hook exists, designed so that it moves from dent to dent without having to be removed, but it is useful only for very fine warps and reeds.)

173 Selecting the first heddle, thread the first end from the right of the left-hand warp.

174 When the first four heddles are threaded tie the warp ends in a slip knot.

175 The warp is now threaded through the heddles.

176 Using the reed-hook, sley the warp through the reed, tying it in bunches for safety.

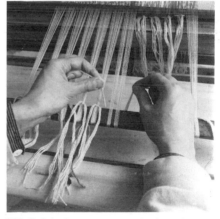

177 Bring the apron over the knee bar and around the breast beam, take a bunch of ends over the top of the front-stick, divide, and bring each half up; tie the first half of the reef knot.

Starting at the centre as before, the ends are taken in the order in which they were entered in the heddles, and as many entered in each dent of the reed as were originally planned (see Pages 59 and 90, (176). Again, many weavers sley, as they threaded, from right to left.)

9 Tying on Once the reed is sleyed, the warp can be tied onto the front beam. Again you will find an apron or strings ending with a front-stick: make sure that it comes over the knee bar and around the front bar, if these are present. Taking small bundles of warp at a time, 1 cm ($\frac{1}{2}$ in) at the selvedges, 2 cm (1 in) across the rest, bring the bundle over the front-stick, divide in two,

69

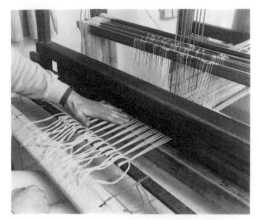

178 Pat the warp to check for even tension and adjust if necessary; then tie the second half of the reef knot.

179 You can beam the warp through from the front.

take the halves around the stick, bring them up and knot them together on top, using only the first half of a reef knot (177).

When this is completed all along the warp tighten the warp. Close your eyes (it helps to isolate the sense of touch) and pat across the warp (178) feeling for areas slacker or tighter than the rest. Adjust the tension – I find it easier to go right across making each bunch as tight as I can – and then tie the second half of the reef knot.

You are now ready to weave.

Variations of method

This method of dressing the loom has many variations, which may be learned from other books or other weavers, or you may evolve them yourself as required. For example, if there is not enough space for the weaver to work behind the loom, the warp for beaming can come through the front of the loom as follows.

Clear a space so that the warp can be unchained through the loom towards the front. Different makes of loom will vary. If you are using a narrow warp, just push the heddles to the sides; but for a wider warp, where they might get in the way, you may need to take the shafts out of the loom. Remove the batten completely, or remove the top of the batten and take out the reed, so the warp can pass straight through the loom (179).

Another method, which is my favourite for short warps, goes from front to back. Make the warp, but you only need one cross. Insert the cross-sticks and fix them firmly between the batten and the breast-beam (180). Cut the end loops, taking care not to allow the cut threads to pull back through the cross, and tie the ends into bunches. Sley through the reed from front to back (181), and then thread through the heddles (182). Collect the ends in

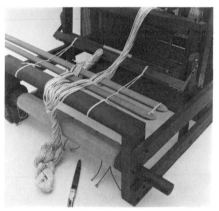

180 Sling the cross-sticks firmly at the front of the loom, and cut the warp ends (knot the left half for safety).

181 Taking the threads from the cross, sley them through the reed from front to back.

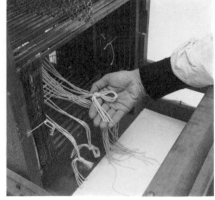

182 Enter the warp through the heddles.

183 Tie the warp in bundles *with the ends as even as possible*.

bunches, with all the threads of equal length (183) and tie to the back stick (184). Standing as far back from the front of the loom as possible, take the chain of warp and shake and pull it (185). Beam the warp as before, sliding the cross-sticks along as necessary. Continue until the last loop is about level with the front of the loom (186). Cut the end loops, remove the cross-sticks, and tie the warp to the front stick in the usual way. The warp is now ready for weaving.

184 Tie to the back-stick with reef knots.

185 Stand back from the front of the loom and pull, winding the warp on when it is smooth, using sticks or card.

186 When the end loops are level with the front of the loom, cut them across, and tie as in 177, 178.

Threading a rigid-heddle loom

When threading a loom with rollers and a rigid heddle, it is better to use the method just described, threading alternately through slot and hole in the heddle, instead of the separate threading through reed and heddles. Tying on and beaming is the same.

Correcting mistakes

Although in theory the warp is now ready for weaving to begin, it often happens that when the shafts are lifted, some threads have been wrongly threaded. Occasionally it is necessary to re-thread from the place of the mistake to the nearest selvedge, but sometimes this can be avoided.

Fault: When the first shed is made, it is not clear whether a thread is in the top layer or the bottom (187). Check first to see if this is merely a tension fault: an odd slack thread can be pulled forward and secured into the knot on the front stick. More often though, by looking behind the reed, you will see that it is crossing over an adjacent thread.

Remedy: Remove these two threads from the front knot and reed and then re-thread them through the reed in the order in which they lie in the shafts. Be careful to maintain the colour order, if there is one.

187 A threading mistake: when the first shed is made a thread is left in the middle.

71

Fault: Sometimes, after a few picks have been woven across the warp (usually in plain-weave), two threads are seen to be weaving side by side in the warp (188). A faulty threading of, say, 1, 2, 4 is discovered – you have missed out 3.

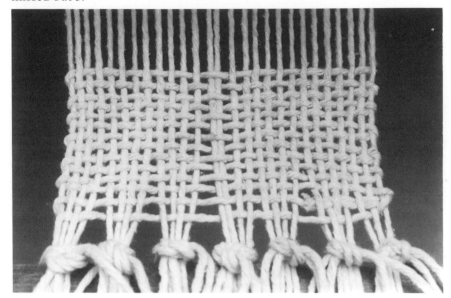

188 A threading mistake in a plain warp, two warp threads weaving together as one.

Remedy: Sometimes, if the colour order is important, you may have to re-thread to the nearest selvedge in both heddles and reed; but on a plain or random-coloured warp you can insert an extra thread on shaft 3. To do this, make an extra heddle to hold this thread: loop a length of smooth twine around the bottom bar of the shaft, tie a knot exactly level with the base of the *mail* (eye) of the standard heddles on that shaft, then another knot 1 cm ($\frac{1}{2}$ in) above it. Tie the top of the heddle to the top bar of the shaft (189). Then measure a length of the warp thread as long as the original warp, and enter it from the back – through the extra heddle, through the reed (you will almost certainly have to re-thread the warp in the reed along to the nearest selvedge) and tie into the appropriate knot on the front-stick. Wind the excess length at the back onto a cotton reel, or other spool, and weight it carefully to provide the same tension as the rest of the warp. It must of course be released as the warp is moved forward during weaving (190).

Sometimes you may find that a spare heddle and dent space already exist for that missing thread, which may have snapped during beaming, and so re-threading of a number of threads is not necessary, just the insertion of that one warp length through the heddle and reed; again wind it on a spool.

Fault: An end may be entered on the wrong shaft.
Remedy: Either break the thread and enter it into an extra heddle made of twine as above on the correct shaft, or cut away the heddle, even if made of wire, from the thread and the shaft and discard it. Make an extra heddle on the correct shaft, knotting the eye of the heddle around the thread, thus saving any re-threading.

Some looms have special shafts of an industrial type, and for these repair heddles are available which can be clipped on as required.

The best thing is to avoid these mistakes by getting into the habit of checking at all stages of threading.

189 A false heddle tied in position ready to receive the extra warp thread.

190 A wooden cotton reel will carry and weight the extra thread.

Chapter Eight

Weaving on a table or floor loom

Before beginning to weave, you need a considerable length of tangle-free weft yarn in a convenient form. If you need only small quantities of yarn for, say, inlay work or tapestry, a useful way of packaging yarn is the finger-skein which is used most often by weavers on frame looms (see Page 40). For a wider warp and larger amounts of weft, some kind of shuttle is necessary, with or without a bobbin.

Shuttles without bobbins

These shuttles are more suitable when smaller widths of warp and thicker wefts are required.

The simplest form of shuttle is the *stick shuttle* (250). This consists of a thin, flat stick, notched at each end, and can be home-made if necessary, with its edges carefully smoothed so that nothing catches on the yarns. (Cardboard is no use – the prongs will bend and catch on the warp threads.) Load this shuttle with yarn by winding the weft around it; don't be tempted to put too much weft on it, as this can slow down the weaving. You can buy stick shuttles in a variety of lengths – try to use one which is just a little longer than the width of your weaving, to avoid the possibility of straining the selvedge threads by having to put your hands into the shed.

A variation on the stick shuttle is the deservedly popular *ski shuttle* (288). This is used for rug weaving, as it can hold a lot of thick material, even rags (332). Wind the weft around the prongs. The advantage of a ski shuttle is that it can be thrown through the shed, and will skim on its smooth under-surface like a ski.

When using any of the above shuttles you need to unwind as much weft as is necessary for the next pick before passing the shuttle through the shed.

Shuttles with bobbins

As soon as you want to weave any greater width of fabric, or use finer yarns, you need a shuttle which can take a lot more yarn, and can be *thrown* through the shed. These shuttles contain bobbins which hold the yarn.

Boat shuttles (193) are specially shaped to pass easily across the warp. They are at their best when used for light-weight yarns, and run well across a spaced warp.

Roller shuttles (205), as the name suggests, have rollers underneath to help their passage through the shed. They are particularly useful for a wide warp, as the rollers are designed to steer the shuttle so that it hugs the reed. They are generally not used on table looms, but only where they can be supported by a *shuttle race* on a floor loom; this is part of the batten, a bar in front of the reed. These shuttles do not run so well across a spaced warp.

Sometimes shuttles have spaces for two bobbins: these are called *double boat shuttles* and *double roller shuttles*. This makes it possible to run two yarns, often of different colours, through the same shed, to get a streaky effect. For weft stripes, of course, you would need to use a separate shuttle for each colour, of the same type and weight to ensure evenness of throwing and therefore of result.

To wind a bobbin

As with most processes connected with weaving, the more carefully and accurately this is done, the more successful will be the piece of weaving. A badly wound bobbin will tangle in the shuttle, causing pulled threads at the selvedges, and eventual broken threads. It is also impossible to weave evenly with badly wound bobbins. You will need a bobbin winder. To wind a good bobbin the yarn must be running freely, especially when taken directly from the hank (see Page 14).

Although wooden bobbins or cardboard *quills* are available, most weavers make paper quills. Take an oval-shaped piece of paper, shorter than the gap in the shuttle by at least 2 cm ($\frac{3}{4}$ in). Even the type of paper is important: newspaper is too soft and will disintegrate at the ends – try glossy magazine paper or something with a similar life to it. Whether to cut or tear the paper shape is also a debated point – try both methods. The papers can be used over and over again. Wind the paper on to the shaft of the winder – I like to wind it diagonally, though some weavers prefer to place it at right angles. But however it is wound, feed in the end of the yarn for the last inch of the paper, to secure it firmly (191). Continuing to turn the handle, wind the yarn along the paper to within 1 cm ($\frac{1}{2}$ in) of the end – never nearer to the end or it will spill off and tangle during use. Guide the yarn rapidly backwards and forwards across the centre section, gradually reducing the travel, until the bobbin is shaped like this (192).

The bobbin should be inserted in the shuttle so that the thread emerges from the underside of the bobbin to pass through the eye, which must always face you when weaving (193).

Some shuttles have removable pins, with one end in a sprung hole, others are pivoted at one end – these are preferable as they can't go astray. Before placing a bobbin on the pin, bring the end of the thread through the eye in the side of the shuttle.

191 Winding a bobbin: start to feed in the yarn.

192 The finished bobbin, showing the ideal shape; notice the last 1 cm of paper is left showing at each end.

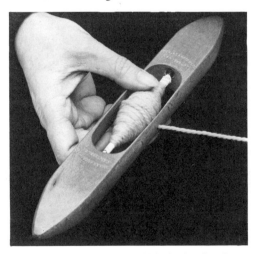

193 The finished bobbin in the shuttle, with the yarn threaded through the eye.

Tying up the pedals on a floor loom

Floor looms have a minimum of four shafts, but, as they are lifted in six common combinations, six pedals are provided. If you only want to weave plain weave, you need to tie up only two pedals. Assuming that the warp is threaded in a straight 1, 2, 3, 4 sequence, tie up one pedal so that pressing it raises shafts 1 and 3, then tie up the other pedal to raise shafts 2 and 4. Then you press these pedals alternately. (For other weaves, see pages 89–90.)

Although some looms have chains to fasten the pedals to the lams, the most common and quiet way is to use cord. Special hemp cord sold as *loom cord* must be used – it is smooth, non-stretch, and very strong. It is expensive, but lasts for a long time, and can be used over and over again.

There is a very useful knot to learn – a *snitch knot* – which is used all over a loom where cords may, at any time, need to be adjusted. To tie this knot, you will need a loop from one end and tails from the other. Make sure that the anchoring knots in the lam and pedal will never pull through the holes in the wood where you attach them (194). Fold the loop back on itself, and pass the tails through (195). Then tie an overhand knot, one tail with the other (196). Don't be tempted to add the second half of the reef (or granny) knot – this is quite strong enough as it is, provided you have tied the over-hand squarely, that is, with both ends taking equal strain in the overhand.

When this needs to be adjusted, it can be undone very easily, even if it has been under tension for years: pull on the tails and slide up the loop, and the overhand knot will loosen. This knot must be used throughout in setting up a floor loom, otherwise both patience and fingernails will be lost in later adjustments.

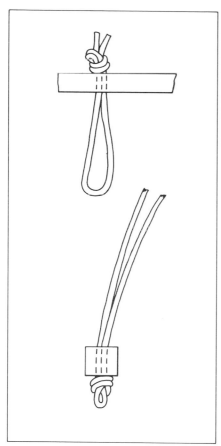

194 Make sure that the knots are big enough to stop the cords being drawn through the holes in the wood.

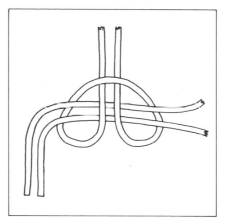

195 The snitch knot: fold the loop back on itself, and pass the tails through.

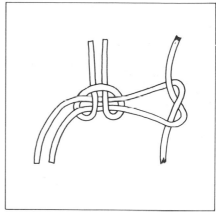

196 Tie an overhand knot, one tail with the other.

Check your loom

Before starting to weave, there are one or two things to check on the loom, which will make weaving easier.

The shafts Make sure that the shafts are hanging at the same height. But on a loom where the back bar is higher than the breast beam the eyes of the heddles should be just slightly above one another, from front to back. Tie a guide string from front to back bar, on each side, or balance a long stick through the loom, and adjust the heddle eyes to that line. (You don't need to do this on a table loom; the shafts will already be set on this line.)

The lams Make sure that the *lams*, on a foot loom, are parallel to the floor.

The pedals Make sure that the pedals are set at the right height for comfortable working. Time spent now in adjusting the tie-up cords will be saved in speed of weaving later.

Weaving

Weaving consists of three processes: raising the warp threads to make a shed (197); inserting the weft (198, 199); and beating the weft into place (200–203). Particular techniques apply to different types of weaving – for rug weaving see Page 107, and cloth weaving see Page 99.

Making a shed How the weaver does this will, of course, vary from loom to loom. It is an inherent part of each loom's action, and each is suited to certain types of weaving: on a frame or back-strap loom the weaver uses a shed stick and leashes, or finger – the raising of small groups of threads

197 Raise every alternate thread by pressing the levers; the warp must be very taut at this stage.

198 Insert the shuttle in the open shed.

199 Receive the shuttle with the left hand; the weft is now lying in the shed.

75

200 Grasp the batten in the centre.

201 Beat the weft into place; make sure that the shuttle doesn't fall to the ground.

202 Lower the raised threads, and raise the alternate ones in their place.

203 After a few inches have been woven in this way, the cloth begins to form.

in this way is suitable for some techniques; on a rigid heddle loom the weaver raises or lowers the rigid heddle itself to make a shed; on a table loom he raises or lowers the levers or knobs which operate the shafts; on a floor loom he presses down the pedals, which allows him to raise several shafts at once.

Inserting the weft Weavers usually begin by weaving a few picks of weft, often in a thicker yarn. This draws the gaps in the tied warp together, evens it out, allows you to check the threading, and provides a firm base to beat against.

Throwing the shuttle To throw a shuttle from one side of the shed to the other is a skilled operation which comes with practice, and it is a good idea to try with an empty shuttle first. Hold the shuttle in the palm of the hand, insert the tip into the shed, then throw it through the shed with a flick of the wrist (205). The shuttle, as well as being thrown, must always be *caught*, as not only is it annoying to have to pick up a dropped shuttle, but its end can be damaged in the fall, and will catch on warp threads unless repaired and smoothed down. Catch the shuttle with a finger on the bobbin to control the

204 Geraldine St. Aubyn Hubbard at her loom; it has two warp beams, which help tension control of differing yarns.

205 Throw the shuttle through with a flick of the wrist.

206 Place your finger on the bobbin when catching the shuttle. Note how the weft lies in a diagonal.

flow of yarn at the end of the *shot*, or throw. Then release the finger before beating the weft. The smooth action of throwing the shuttle and its accurate catching is important to master in order to achieve any speed and neatness of weaving (206).

When throwing the shuttle neither the hands nor the shuttle should touch the raised warp threads at either edge. When the shuttle is thrown, and caught, the thread left behind should lie at a gentle loose diagonal. Don't attempt to pull it straight: enough slack must be left to allow the yarn to pass over and under the warp threads; unless it is, the selvedges will be pulled in. On a wide cloth, keep the arms extended for both the shuttle-throwing and then the beating.

Beating the weft into place The weft is beaten into place with the batten, the shed is changed and the process repeated. Even this seemingly simple oper ation can have many variations, each suitable for different types of weaving. Basically, the beat must be controlled: usually each beat should be the same; and parallel: *always* grasp the batten by the centre if you use one hand, or equidistantly from the centre if you are using two hands for weaving a heavy fabric or rug (200, front cover).

However, the weaver can vary the moment at which he beats – sometimes it is better to change the shed, beat, throw shuttle and beat again. The first beat clears the shed, that is, it separates any warp threads which may be sticking together, and also helps to hold the previous pick in place.

If great control is needed over the placing of the weft (say in a very open fabric) then it is easier to insert the weft, then change the shed before beating it into place. The extra friction makes greater precision of placing possible. Alternatively, beat on a closed shed. You can use one or two beats: often two light ones can be more effective than one heavier beat.

When weaving a balanced cloth, the beat must be adjusted so that the number of weft picks to the cm (in) equal the number of warp ends. Weaving this sort of cloth, especially with the weft in strong colour contrast to the warp, is thought by experienced weavers to be a great test of skill, so it's an excellent exercise in learning to beat accurately.

Aim for a steady rhythm, *change shed, throw shuttle, beat* or whatever order you have chosen, with as few breaks in this routine as possible. On a floor loom, your feet will be part of this rhythm as they change the shed.

Selvedges

Selvedges are the classic inspection point for good weaving: it is no good trying to correct them by pulling them about or adjusting them after each shot. Straight selvedges come from good bobbin-winding, correct shuttle-throwing, and a sensitive reaction to the weft's tension and behaviour. Incidentally, it is very rare for both edges to be of similar quality: one is always superior to the other.

Winding on

After about 8 cm (3 in) have been woven, you should stop and wind on some fresh warp. Whether using a table or a floor loom, it is never wise to weave for more than this distance before winding on, as the difference in the shed and beat will otherwise show in the finished weaving. Before winding on always place the shuttles somewhere safe, so that they will not fall. First release the *cloth-beam* slightly; then release tension on the *warp-beam* and wind on the *cloth-beam*. Don't wind on too much or you will be weaving too close to the breast beam. The best way of winding on is 'little and often'. On many looms you will not have to go to the back of the loom to release the warp-beam; there will be some means of reaching the ratchet and pawl from

207 Join wefts by overlapping them for about 2 cm (1 in).

208 Take a new colour around the outermost warp, and tuck it back into the shed at the selvedge for about 2 cm (1 in).

the front – but *always* release the cloth-beam slightly first to avoid strain being placed on any part of the loom. Winding the woven cloth onto the cloth beam must be done as carefully as when the warp was wound onto the warp beam: no lumps or bumps of string must be allowed to poke into the cloth, and a layer of warp sticks should be wound in with the fabric.

When stopping weaving for any length of time – say, overnight – always release the warp tension slightly, to avoid straining the threads.

Starting a new weft thread

At some point the weft yarn on the bobbin will run out: when starting a new bobbin of the same colour, you can often overlap the new thread with the old end for about 2 cm (1 in), in the same shed of course (207). For most weaving any excess can be trimmed off after you have woven some more picks which hold the new ends in place but for rug-weaving the ends must be darned in down a warp thread (see Page 107).

You may want to change the weft yarn in order to start a new colour or texture. When weaving narrow stripes, where the original colour will be needed again in less than 2 cm (1 in), there is no need to break off each colour at the end of the stripe, just carry it up the selvedge, holding it in place by taking the shuttle you are using round it as it turns back for the next pick.

If you are weaving wider stripes, or if you decide to stop using a particular colour, then take the yarn round the outermost warp thread at the selvedge and then tuck it back on itself in the same shed for about 2 cm (1 in). Start the new thread in the same way in the next shed (208). You can start the new weft from the same side, or the opposite side. When weaving plain weave, I like to press the right hand pedal on my foot loom when the shuttle is about to enter from the right, and the left one when inserting from the left, so this order would be disturbed if I started the new colour from the opposite side.

Measuring

You need to measure your work in two ways: made a periodic check of the number of picks to the centimetre (inch), to make sure that the beat is accurate; and measure the length of the finished fabric as it progresses. Always release the tension before measuring the length of the cloth, and measure at the selvedge, inserting a thread marker at set intervals, say every 20 cm (8 in) with a special marker at 1 m (3 ft) intervals – so that there is no need to unwind the woven cloth to know how much you've done.

Faults in weaving

Sometimes you may weave a few centimetres (one or two inches) of cloth before you notice a faulty pick in the cloth. Although it is possible to unweave cloth back to that point, in practice it might make the cloth very fluffy, especially when weaving wool, and this will show in the finished cloth as an uneven band in the weft. A better solution is to cut the weft *very carefully* about every 25 cm (10 in) up between the warp threads, and pluck out the weft as far back as the mistake, using the point of a needle (210). Alternatively, if you do not wish to waste expensive weft yarn in this way, leave it until weaving is completed, then cut out that one pick and darn in a new one with a needle.

If a warp thread breaks, first try to find out why it has broken, so that you can prevent more breakages. If it has broken at the selvedge – near the fell, for example – this usually means that you are pulling the weft too hard against the selvedge threads, and they are being forced out at an angle by the reed, and so get worn away (209).

209 Don't pull the weft so tight that the cloth is forced out of shape, or the reed may wear the selvedge threads.

210 Cut out the weft along a warp thread with great care, and remove the cut weft with a needle.

Sometimes a knot, allowed through by mistake in the warping, will drift apart, or tangle in the heddles and break the thread. A broken thread, no matter how caused, must be repaired so that no knot passes through the heddles and reed. This means that the repair must be done in *two stages*.

Firstly, locate both ends of the broken thread. Then, taking about 1 metre (40 in) of the same yarn, pass one end through the appropriate place in the reed and shafts, to the back. Without breaking short the original end, tie it to the new thread with a non-slipping bow, positioning it as far towards the back of the loom as possible. Now take a dressmaker's pin and stick it into the woven cloth, about 2 cm (1 in) from the fell. Taking care to match the tension of the new thread with the rest of the warp, wind the near end of it round the pin (211). You will then be able to carry on weaving, for about 25 cm (9 in). The new thread becomes part of the cloth.

Secondly, remove the pin from the cloth, before it gets wound round the cloth-beam – you can darn the ends in later. Go to the back of the loom and untie the bow made of the old and new threads; you will find that the old one is now long enough to take its original place through shafts and reed. The replacement thread can now be left to lie on the surface of the cloth, and the original one fastened round a pin, as before, making sure that the tension is correct. Remember to remove this pin after a few centimetres (inches) of weaving, and certainly before the cloth goes around the beam.

211 Mend a broken thread by inserting another length with bow and pin.

Removing the finished cloth from the loom

When you have woven the length of cloth you want, or it becomes impossible to weave any more, it should be cut off the loom. You can cut the warp ends behind the shafts, if you need the ends for, say, a fringe. Or, by cutting carefully *in front* of the reed, it is possible to tie-on a new, similar warp by taking ends from its cross and tying each new thread to an old one. It is safer to do this in small amounts, using the woven cloth to support the new warp as it is gradually tied in. Beaming then takes place from front to back.

Chapter Nine

Plain weave, variations and possibilities

Any loom, no matter how simple or complicated, can weave the basic over-one, under-one interlacement of threads called plain weave. But don't be misled by the name into thinking that plain weave is dull: it is suitable for almost every purpose, and is capable of innumerable variations. Beginners and professional weavers like it for its simplicity, strength, and versatility. Although it needs only two shafts (or a rigid heddle), many weavers prefer to thread it on four shafts, especially if the yarn being used is very closely set, as the thickness of the heddles themselves, distributed on only two shafts, may be thicker than the warp threads.

Balanced, warp-faced and weft-faced cloth

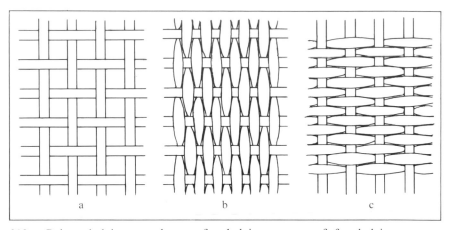

213 A table mat by Barbara Sawyer: The warp is confined to narrow bands with wide gaps between, and the cellophane weft is semi-rigid.

212 a, Balanced plain weave, b, warp-faced plain weave, c, weft-faced plain weave.

Balanced plain weave has the same number of ends and picks per centimetre (inch). This means that the warp and weft show equally (212, colour 8).

Alter the balance (the weave remains the same) so that there are more warp ends per centimetre than weft picks, and the cloth will be *warp-faced*: the warp is set very closely, and the weft hardly shows. A warp-faced cloth will often hang better (for curtains, and so on) than a balanced cloth using the same amount of yarn. It is slower to thread up, but quick to weave, because you need to thread up more warp ends but you spend less time inserting the fewer wefts. The colours come from the way in which you design the warp: the weft colour matters much less (291, colour 7).

Alter the balance the other way (still the same weave) so that the warp threads are spaced out, and the weft is beaten down to cover them, and you have a *weft-faced* cloth. Many rugs are woven like this (colour 6) and so is tapestry. Threading up is quick, because there are fewer warp threads; weaving is slower, because you use a lot of weft threads. The colour and design in a weft-faced cloth come from the weft you use.

214 The stripes in this fine silk cloth by Anna Cady are made by leaving narrow gaps in the warp.

Plain weave cloth can also be woven with warp-faced, balanced, and weft-faced bands. This is known as *cramming* and *spacing*. You can *space* the warp only, by leaving spaces between various groups of warp threads when threading up, then weaving in the weft normally (213, 214); or you can space the weft as well by weaving a few picks and beating the weft as usual, then weaving some picks beating the weft very gently, to space them out. Repeat this process to build up an interesting design (215). The reverse of this is *cramming*, where the warp is set, or the weft is beaten, more closely than normal. Cramming and spacing can occur in the same cloth (216).

215 A sample on the loom: *below*, a crammed and spaced warp; *above*, the weft is crammed and spaced as well.

216 A fine cotton cloth from India uses cramming and spacing to form a check.

Vary the yarn

Still using plain weave, the weaver can use a different thickness of yarn in the warp, weft, or both. A great difference in the thickness of the warp threads could lead to tension problems. Overcome those by using two warp beams or by putting a stick under the slacker threads and attaching weights.

Textured yarns such as mohair loops or fancy yarns can be used in the same way, to give warp or weft stripes or checks (217). Take care here, though, not to include heavily textured yarns in the warp, as the loops, knops and slubs will catch in the heddles and will break when passing through the reed.

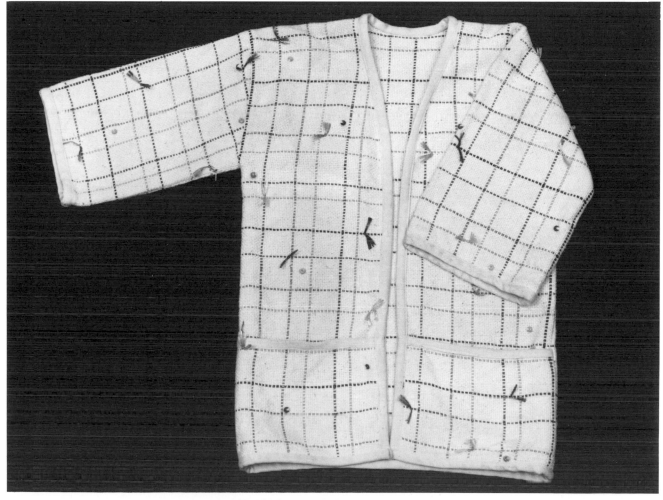

217 Thick cotton jacket by Hilary Auden, with synthetic raffia and beads woven in to form checks, and knotted in the weft.

Stripes

One of the most important design elements in a woven cloth is the stripe, in the warp or the weft (colour 7, colour 14). Stripes in both directions will produce a check. The planning of colour and proportion of stripes and checks is a fascinating part of weaving. Colours change when used in different proportions and in different juxtapositions, and when crossing one another in checks the mixings are sometimes totally unexpected to the eye.

Colour-and-weave

One fascinating family of patterns using colour variations is called *colour-and-weave*. By using careful combinations of different coloured threads, or often just black and white, in a simple weave like plain weave, the weaver can create a multitude of little repeating patterns (218). Some of these are well known from familiar traditional tweeds, such as Prince of Wales check or Glen Urquhart, but many new combinations wait to be discovered.

Before you weave, you can get an idea of how the finished combination will look by making a trial on graph paper; then you can weave the successful designs.

You will need some 2 mm ($\frac{1}{8}$ in or $\frac{1}{10}$ in) graph paper, a pencil, and a fibre-tip pen. When planning any weave on graph paper, the space between the printed line represents a thread, of whatever thickness or texture. So two sets of threads, warp and weft, would look like 219.

But drawn like this you don't get any indication of interlacing. So, where two threads cross one another, draw in only the one which is uppermost at that time. A plain weave would look like 220.

So, in order to be able to plan some colour-and-weave patterns, in pencil indicate plain weave all over, say, a 4 cm ($1\frac{1}{2}$ in) square of the graph paper.

218 A colour-and-weave sampler on the loom.

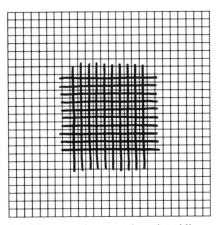

219 The space between the printed lines on the graph paper represents a thread.

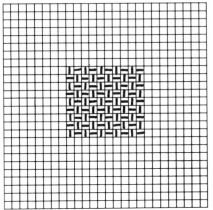

220 Plain weave: where two threads cross, draw in only the thread which comes uppermost.

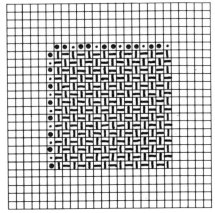

221 Indicate with spots around the edge which threads are to be dark, and which light.

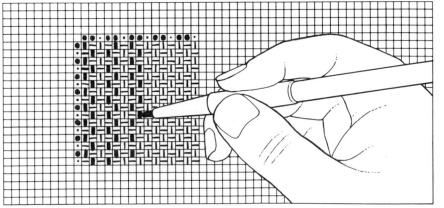

222 Black-in the dark warp threads where they are uppermost.

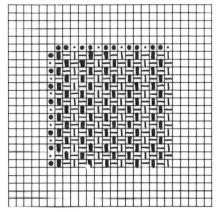

223 Repeat for all the dark warp threads.

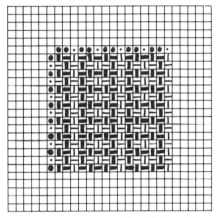

224 Black-in all the dark weft threads where they are uppermost; a pattern will appear.

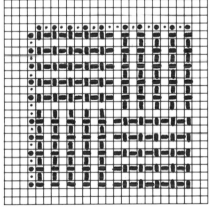

226 'Log cabin'.

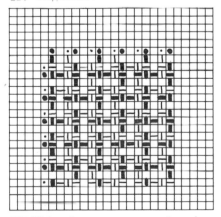

227 This colour arrangement gives a twill-like appearance.

Then, around the top and to the left hand side of the square indicate, perhaps with dark and light spots, which threads are to be dark, and which light. Keep to a simple repeated combination. You can use the same combination for both warp and weft threads, or you can make them totally different. The square will now look something like 221.

Then, with the fibre-tip pen, and starting with the first dark warp thread from the left, follow its path downwards, blacking in only where it appears on the surface of the weave – that is, each vertical mark in that row (222).

Repeat this process for each dark warp thread. Ignore the light tones (223).

Do the same weft-ways, blacking in each dark weft where it surfaces and a pattern will appear; half close your eyes if it is difficult to see at first (224).

Try out a number of variations using this graph paper method. You may find, after some practice, that you can dispense with the pencilled 'weave'.

Try 'weaving' one pattern immediately alongside another; you may find that interesting patterns will emerge by accident (225).

One very simple but effective colour-and-weave pattern is called *log cabin*. It consists of a section of warp threads coloured one end dark, one end light, followed by another section of one end light, one end dark; so at the join between one section and the next you have two warp ends the same colour. The weft colour order is the same as the warp, alternate light and dark with two the same colour at the change between sections (226).

You can of course use more than two colours in warp and weft. This is one where the colour arrangement gives a twill-like appearance (227).

This way of patterning with a combination of colour order and weave can, of course, be applied to weaves other than plain, and traditional checks which are patterned in this way are usually woven in a 2/2 twill (10) (see Page 91.)

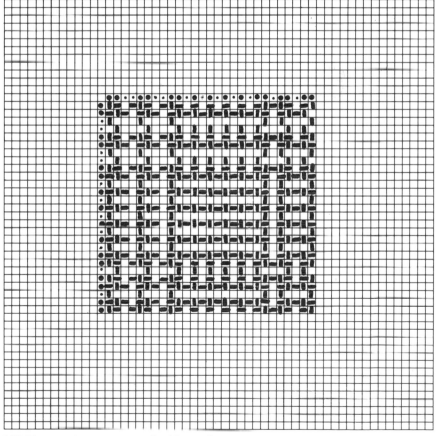

225 Try weaving one pattern beside another.

A colour-and-weave design

228 Jacket fabric in colour-and-weave by Geraldine St. Aubyn Hubbard.

The illustration (228), shows a jacket fabric woven by Geraldine St. Aubyn Hubbard. This is how to make this particular colour-and-weave design:

Warp of woollen-spun yarn 8's ysw, set at 20 epi in 2 colours, red and blue; make the warp with the two threads running together (when selecting from the pair in the cross for threading the weaver can choose which colours go onto which shaft – for example red on shaft 1, blue on 2, red on 3, blue on 4). Repeat this 8 times (ie 32 ends, 16 red, 16 blue). Then thread blue on 1, red on 2, blue on 3, red on 4. Repeat this 8 times (ie 32 ends, 16 blue, 16 red). If this alternating is continued, every time the threading order changes the same colour will have two threads side by side.

Use two wefts: a fine weft *a* of woollen-spun yarn 8's ysw natural black wool; and a thick weft *b* of 4 strands used together of woollen-spun yarn 5's ysw dyed crimson.

Weave alternate rows of plain weave with *a* and *b*, ie shafts 1 and 3 up for *a*, shafts 2 and 4 up for *b*. Repeat 8 times.

Then change the order ie after shafts 1 and 3 up with *a*, weave shafts 2 and 4 up with *a*, then 1 and 3 up with *b* and so on. Repeat 8 times.

You will begin to see elongated rectangles forming: these will become square when the tension is released and after wet finishing (see Page 99).

All sorts of stripes and rectangles of varying sizes may be woven using this very simple structure, by altering the threading order and the weft sequence. Try using two contrasting colours such as yellow and blue to see how the eye mixes the colours to produce different greens. And notice the different effects when you use colours near in hue, such as different shades of red and pink.

Manipulating threads

There are many ways in which plain weave, even on the simplest of looms, can be enriched by manipulating the threads or by adding extra ones. All these are essentially hand processes.

For making open fabrics such as a simple gauze, single or grouped warp threads can be crossed over one another and held in place by a weft pick before the next area of plain weave is woven. To do this, take a flat, pointed stick in one hand; with the other hand select the first pair of warp threads and cross them over, passing one under the other; insert the stick to hold the twist temporarily and deal with the rest of the warp pairs in the same way. Twist the stick on edge and pass the shuttle through this picked-up shed. Remove the stick and then continue to weave as usual. This will give a lacey, gauze effect, and can be done either in small areas or all over the fabric (229, 230). The Peruvians often used this technique with their back-strap looms to achieve fine and delicate designs (403).

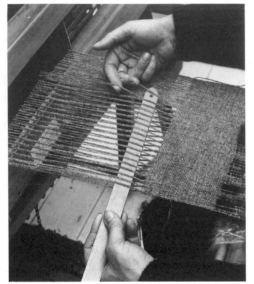

229 Making a gauze on the loom. Insert the stick to hold the twist in the warp threads, then pass the shuttle through this shed.

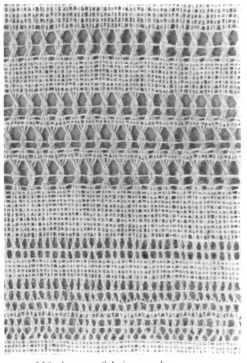

230 A gauze fabric sampler.

231 Take the shuttle around small groups of warp threads.

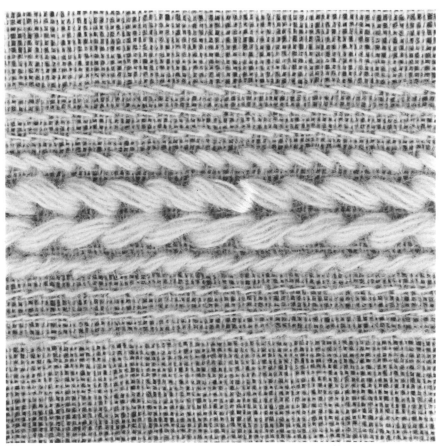

232 A Soumak sampler.

Another way of grouping threads to give a similar sort of effect is to take the shuttle around small groups of warp threads (231).

Several techniques, more commonly used in rugs, and described in more detail on Pages 108 to 112 can be used in cloth, in plain and other weaves, as follows:

Soumak is a technique which involves wrapping the weft around the warp ends to form a ridge; it also builds up a raised area if repeated (232, 312, colour 17, colour 18).

Chaining produces a similar effect (318).

Pulled-up loops produce a raised surface of weft loops on the cloth (314).

Individual bunches of weft threads can be knotted around the warp to make a **tufted pile**. The ends of the knots can be cut long or short, evenly or unevenly (306–311).

It is important to weave one or two picks between each row of all the above techniques.

Curved and angled weft

These are two rather unusual techniques used in plain weave whereby the warp and weft do not cross at the usual right angle.

Vary the warp tension The traditional ideal is for the warp to be of uniform tension; the result of an uneven tension is a waving line at the fell, usually unsightly. But if given a little thought, most faults can be used to advantage and you can get another dramatic variation on plain weave by deliberately varying the warp tension in some areas. One of the simplest ways of altering the tension of the warp is to take a smooth dowel of about 2·5 cm (1 in) diameter and insert it under the batches of threads you want to tighten, pushing the stick on to the back bar, where the tension of the threads will hold it in place.

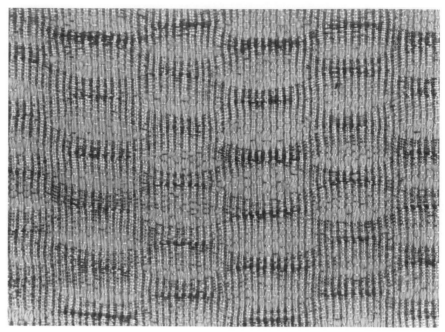

233 A fabric where the warp tension has been altered in a regular way.

The selection of groups of threads to tighten can be random or regular (233). In both cases the selection is altered after weaving about an inch of fabric, so that threads are not permanently affected.

Angle the weft There is another way in which deliberately breaking the rules can lead to interesting results. Instead of beating the weft into the fell at right angles to the warp, it can be beaten at varying angles. To do this, you will have to remove the reed from the batten, or use the pivot points on the overhead batten of a floor loom to guide the angle (234). It is perhaps easiest of all with a rigid heddle loom, where it is all too easy to beat at an angle other than 'square'.

In these ways, plain weave can give the weaver an enormous range of different effects. Combine some of the techniques we have described with the use of different colours and textures, and the possibilities are endless.

234 'Trianglefell', linen and fibreglass hanging by Peter Collingwood.

Chapter Ten

Weaving with four or more shafts

235 Double-cloth with horizontal bands.

So far all the interlacement of warp and weft has been plain weave, the simple 'over-one, under-one' structure. This is a very large and fascinating area of weaving. But many weavers are also interested in pattern weaving: this involves other types of interlacement, such as 'over-two, under-one', and for this the weaver needs to make more than two alternative sheds, so the loom must have more than two shafts. Most table and floor looms have at least four shafts; some have as many as sixteen. In addition to plain weave, four shafts will give you several *twills* (10), *hopsack*, simple *double cloths* (235), *herringbone* (261), *overshot* patterns (265), and many weaves with names like *honeycomb* and *mock leno*.

Drafting

The weave of most of the cloth we have looked at so far doesn't need much pre-planning. Now, in order to be able to read weaving designs, or to plan your own, you need to understand the process called *drafting*. This is a way of putting down a *weave plan* – that is, a diagram representing the interlacement of threads on graph paper (usually called *point paper* by weavers) with *threading* through the heddles and the *lifting* of the shafts. Books on weaving with complicated drafts can look confusing to a beginner, and they seem even more confusing when it appears that each book uses a different method of annotating the weave. But once you have grasped one method it is easy to understand others, because the basic principles are the same.

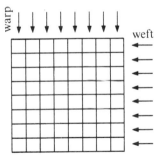

236 The gaps between the printed lines are the threads.

Weave plan

The first and essential thing to remember is that warp and weft threads are represented by the *gaps* between the printed lines on the point paper (236). This always applies. Whether the threads are thick or thin, each occupies one space between the lines on the point paper; and wherever a *warp* thread is uppermost, it is marked by blacking in the square. So a weave plan can be thought of as a diagram of a cloth which has a black warp and a white weft (237).

This is the method commonly used in books. I use another method which I find very useful for designing weaves: instead of filling in only those squares where the warp comes to the surface, draw a horizontal or vertical line in *every* square, depending on whether weft or warp surfaces at that point. This gives a very good visual impression of the actual weave (238). The diagrams show both methods.

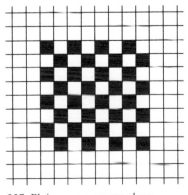

237 Plain weave, weave plan: black in the squares.

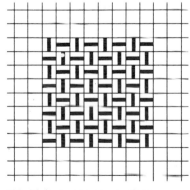

238 Plain weave, weave plan: use horizontal and vertical lines.

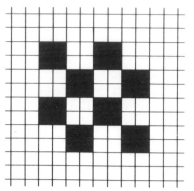

239 Hopsack on point paper, showing four repeats.

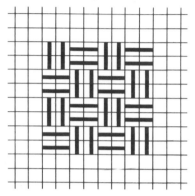

240 Hopsack on point paper, showing four repeats.

Once this is understood, weaves can be plotted on point paper. For example, 237 and 238 show plain weave. *Hopsack* is a doubling up of plain weave – that is 'over-two, under-two', in warp and weft, and is shown like this, 239, 240. In the weave plans, four repeats of this weave have been plotted, two in each direction. This is common when plotting small weaves. It is easier to see what happens at the joins of a repeat; and it is a good thing to get used to seeing where repeats begin and end.

Remember that the weave plan is a diagrammatic representation, and will not always look like the final weave, as it cannot take into account effects of colour and texture and the different relationships of warp and weft. Clearly, a balanced weave will resemble the weave plan more than an unbalanced weave where either warp or weft is hidden.

Threading plan

Having plotted down a weave in repeat on point paper, the next step is to be able to find out how to thread the loom, in order to weave that design.

To show this, let's take the weave plan of a weave called *mock leno* (241, 242), so called because it imitates *leno*, another word for gauze. One repeat of this weave is shown. And, for this diagram only, the warp threads are lettered a, b, c, d, e, f and the weft threads in the order of weaving, g, h, i, j, k, l.

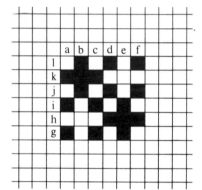

241 Three-end mock leno, weave plan.

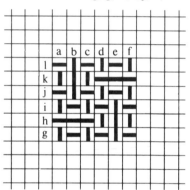

242 Three-end mock leno, weave plan.

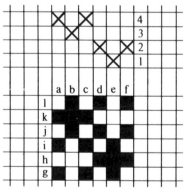

243 Mock leno, threading draft.

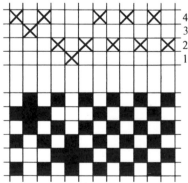

244 Draft of mock leno, with plain weave.

Above the weave plan you need a *threading diagram*, which represents the shafts on the loom. It is normal practice to number the shafts from the front to the back, with shaft no. 1 nearest the cloth. So for four shafts you use four rows on the point paper. Each row is a numbered shaft, and each square still represents the positioning of each warp thread. It is because shafts are normally used in multiples of four that weavers prefer a point paper with divisions after every 4 squares (8 squares to the inch).

Look at warp thread *a* and put an *x* above it on the line corresponding to shaft 4, indicating that it is to be threaded on shaft 4. Now look vertically all along warp thread *b* and check it against *a*. If it is interlacing in a different way (which it is) then it *must* be entered on a different shaft – say, shaft 3; so put an *x* above it on the line corresponding to shaft 3. Then check warp thread *c* against both threads *a* and *b*. You can see that its interlacement is identical with that of *a*, and it can therefore be controlled by the same shaft as that which controls *a*, and so you enter its *x* on shaft 4. Warp thread *d* is different from *a*, *b* and *c*, so you put its *x* on another shaft – say, shaft 2. Carry on like this until all the threads have been dealt with: the threading reads 4, 3, 4, 2, 1, 2, (243).

You will notice that warp threads *a* (and *c*) and *d* (and *f*) interlace in plain-weave: this means that if you wanted vertical stripes of plain weave in between blocks of the mock leno pattern, you could enter a group of warp threads exactly as *a* and *d*, that is, on shafts 4, 2, 4, 2, 4, 2, (244).

The principle of this method is that each warp thread with a different interlacement must be entered on a new shaft.

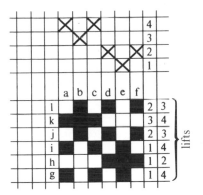

245 Draft of mock leno, with lifting plan.

Lifting plan

Now that the threading has been planned, the next step is to work out how to lift the shafts in order to produce the weave on the loom. Referring again to the draft so far (243) look this time at the weft, that is the horizontal rows *g* to *l*. Examine the first weft, *g*, and see which shafts need to be lifted to produce the shed it is lying in. In other words, wherever there is a *raised warp* – a filled-in square – look upwards to see which shaft controls that thread. In the case of *g*, it is 1 and 4, so write 1 4 beside this weft, to the right. Now look at weft *h*, and you will see that shafts 1 and 2 have to be lifted to make its shed, so write 1 2 to the right of this weft. Carry on like this for the whole pattern. The lifts will read 1 4, 1 2, 1 4, 2 3, 3 4, 2 3, (245).

So on a table loom you lift the shafts in this sequence. It is always a good idea to write out a list of liftings and fasten it to the loom.

Pedal tie-ups

On a floor loom, one pedal (1) would be tied up so that pressing it raised shafts 1 and 4, another pedal (4) would be tied to raise shafts 1 and 2, another pedal (2) would be tied to raise shafts 2 and 3, and pedal 3 would raise shafts 3 and 4. Because some lifts are duplicated you will only need four pedals. Fill in the tie-up plan on the right, level with the shafts (246).

Note: In the diagram it is assumed that a counterbalanced loom is being used, so that pedal 1 has to be tied to the lams of shafts 2 and 3 in order to raise shafts 1 and 4, and so on.

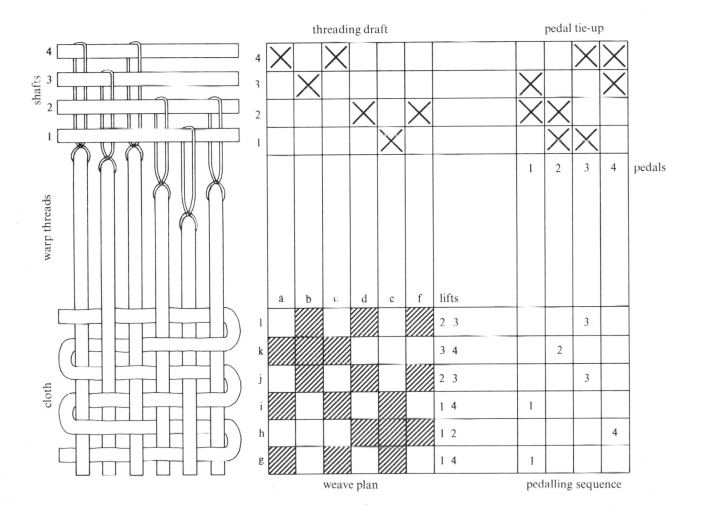

246 Draft of mock leno, with tie-up plan.

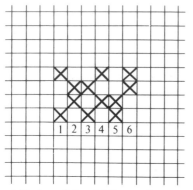

247 A useful pedal tie-up plan for a counterbalanced loom.

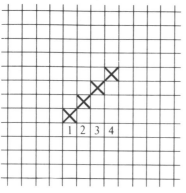

248 A skeleton tie-up for a counterbalanced loom.

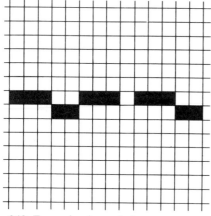

249 Example of a reed plan.

Pedal sequence

In this case, the pedals are pressed in a 1, 4, 1, 3, 2, 3, sequence, which is filled in to the right of the weave plan. Always try to design the tying up of the pedals so that the right and left foot alternately work the pedals, as in this example.

If you want to combine horizontal stripes of plain weave with mock leno, you would do it by lifting shafts 1 and 4, then 3 and 2, or by pressing pedal 1 to make one shed, then pedal 3 to make the other.

Some useful tie-ups

Many weavers with four-shaft looms often keep their six pedals tied up in six common combinations, in the convenient order of 247. (Once again this applies to counterbalanced looms.) Assuming a 1, 2, 3, 4 threading, this means that the centre two pedals are tied up to produce plain weave. The outside pedals can give a *2/2 twill* (see Page 91) if the pedals are pressed in a 6, 2, 5, 1 sequence. These are the most common liftings. If anything else is needed, some pedals must be re-tied.

No re-tying is necessary if the so-called *skeleton tie-up* is used. This applies to counterbalanced looms and entails tying each pedal to only one shaft, so only four pedals are needed (248). Then by pressing one, two or three pedals together – using both feet where necessary – every possible lift of the four shafts can be obtained. The skeleton tie-up is often used when sampling.

Reed plan

The way in which a weave is sleyed in the reed can sometimes affect its appearance, and if this is the case, a reed plan will be shown near the threading. This may look like 249, and this one would read as: enter the first three threads together in one dent, the next two threads in the second dent, three threads in the third dent, leave one dent empty, three threads together in the fifth dent, and two threads together in the sixth. Repeat. Be careful to relate the grouped threads to the groups in the threading; it is usually important to the success of the pattern.

Designing weaves

It is well worth mastering this basis of drafting, as it will enable you to read patterns in books and also to design your own weaves. It sometimes helps to see the weave if you translate it from black and white squares to the vertical and horizontal line system. By using black and white squares, however, it is easy to doodle small textured weaves, which can then be worked out for your loom. Try to make no block, black or white, horizontal or vertical, longer than three squares, and you'll have some surprising successes. Once you have discovered one which will work on four shafts try applying some colour-and-weave sequences to it: keep the same weave, but try many different colour orders. Use spots of colour around the edge of your plan to represent the colours of the warp and weft. In books a colour indication will often appear along the top and down the side of a weave plan, with a key nearby, to indicate coloured or fancy yarns in the warp and weft.

Analysing a woven fabric

If you want to analyse a piece of fabric, whether hand or machine woven, in order to see how it was made, it is possible with care to plot down its weave on point paper as above. Start by isolating one repeat of the weave. If this is large, it can be cut out carefully. More often it is better to sew around it

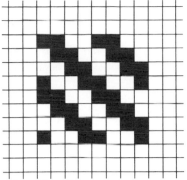

253 2/2 twill, weave plan.

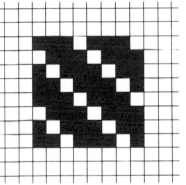

254 2/2 twill, weave plan.

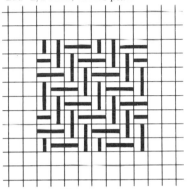

255 3/1 twill, warp faced, weave plan.

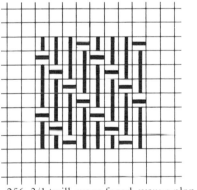

256 3/1 twill, warp faced, weave plan.

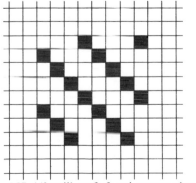

257 1/3 twill, weft-faced, weave plan.

exactly with needle and contrasting cotton, or to use pins to mark the boundary accurately. Then, taking each weft thread in turn, plot the weave on point paper. Sometimes it helps to call it out: 'Over one, under three . . .' to someone else who can concentrate on the point paper. When you have completed the repeat, the next step is to see whether it can be woven on the number of shafts available on your loom. Often it can't, but you may be able to adapt it, by making some vertical rows match each other exactly.

Twill

Twill is a large and important family of weaves. It produces a very flexible, supple cloth which drapes well. By careful weave planning its distinctive, diagonal line can be made to cross the fabric at steep or shallow angles, as well as at the common 45° (250, 10, 319, 320, 321).

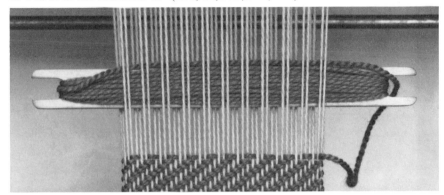

250 Weaving twill: the weft goes over two warp ends and under two warp ends.

251 Top line of hopsack, weave plan.   252 Top line of hopsack, weave plan.

If you take the top line of *hopsack* (251, 252), and repeat it, moving it along one square to the right in each row, you will get a *2/2 twill* – 2/2 means simply that the warp goes over two picks and under two picks (253, 254). A balanced 2/2 twill is a common foundation for colour-and-weave patterns, especially in tweeds, but you can try many other twills, drafting them first on point paper.

In twills, add the numbers to find how many shafts you need to be able to weave them. You can weave *3/1 twill* on four shafts: that is a weave in which the warp goes over 3 picks and under one pick, and it produces a warp-faced twill which looks like this (255, 256). *1/3 twill* is the opposite, and makes a weft-faced twill (257); it is also of course the reverse side of a 3/1 twill fabric, and many weavers prefer to weave this fabric upside-down, so that there are fewer shafts to lift for each shed.

See what patterns you get by using twill with colour-and-weave, and try cramming and spacing the ends to get undulating twills (258, 259).

258 Curved twill weave on a crammed-and-spaced warp, by Marianne Straub.

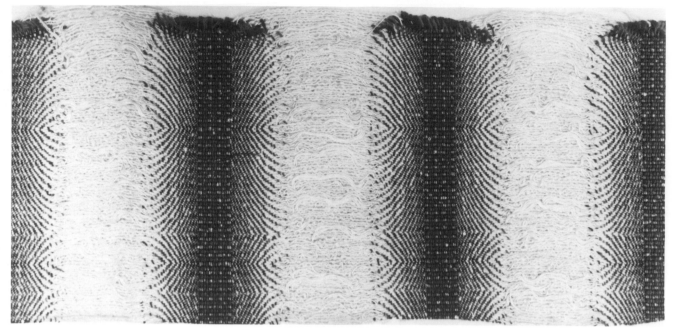

259 Crammed-and-spaced twill by Barbara Sawyer: The centre of the stripe is a 2/2 warp rib, the twill is 2/2 twill sometimes reversed.

Herringbone is one of the many variations of twill: the direction of the twill line is reversed in the cloth at intervals. This can result in broad or narrow herringbone depending on the position of reversal. If the point of reversal in the threading plan which produces this is simple, it is called a *point draft* (260, 261).

Sometimes the point is *staggered* to give a clean cut in the weave (262, 263). When a threading like this is also lifted in a reversed sequence the resulting diamond patterns are called *goose-eye* (264). The technique of reversing the threading plan and/or the lifting sequence can be applied to any twill; this gives endless possibilities, especially when more than four shafts are used.

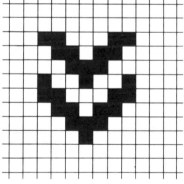

260 Point draft herringbone, weave plan.

261 Point draft herringbone weave.

264 'Goose-eye' weave.

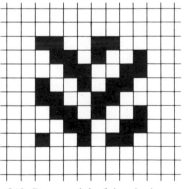

262 Staggered draft herringbone, weave plan.

263 Staggered draft herringbone weave.

Overshot weaves

Overshot weaves are another very large family of traditional weaves suitable for weaving on four shafts. At one time they were very popular, and many of the older weaving books have very interesting examples, most of which have fascinating names such as *Keep me warm one night*, and *Gertrude's fancy*. The repeats are often large and elaborate, and it may appear to the beginner that their execution on a four-shaft loom would be impossible. But they are ingeniously constructed and the weaving of one of these large overshot designs can teach you a lot about the possibilities in drafting.

These weaves consist of a warp of one thickness (usually fine, and of one colour only) and two thicknesses of weft: one, the same yarn as the warp, weaving plain and therefore called the binder, alternating with a thicker yarn which *floats* on the surface of the cloth to make the pattern. (A weft pick floats when it passes over more than one warp thread.)

By the imaginative use of yarns and colours some exotic cloths are possible using these overshot weaves (265).

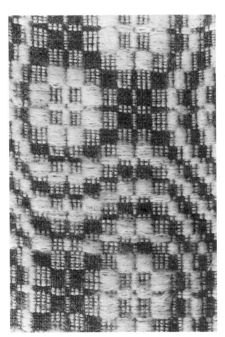

265 An overshot weave, 'Snail trail'.

Double cloth

An interesting possibility of weaving on four shafts is the simultaneous production of two plain weave cloths, one on top of the other. They can be totally separate so that they become two pieces of fabric when off the loom; or they can be joined together at both edges during weaving, to make a tube; or they can be joined down one selvedge only, which makes it possible to weave a piece of cloth which, when opened out, is twice as wide as your loom. The two layers can also be alternated during the weaving, so that

266 Detail from a wall-hanging in double cloth from Sogn, Norway; early seventeenth century.

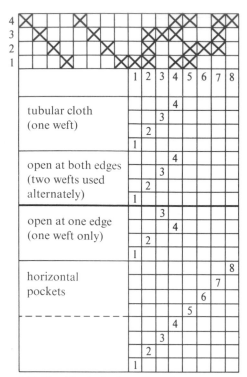

		1	2	3	4	5	6	7	8
tubular cloth (one weft)					4				
				3					
			2						
		1							
open at both edges (two wefts used alternately)					4				
				3					
			2						
		1							
open at one edge (one weft only)				3					
				4					
			2						
		1							
horizontal pockets									8
								7	
							6		
						5			
					4				
				3					
			2						
		1							

268 Double cloth, threading plan.

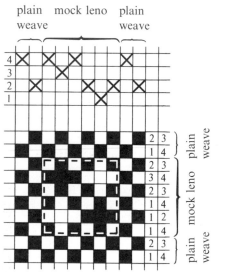

270 Three-end mock leno and plain weave, draft, threading and lifting plan.

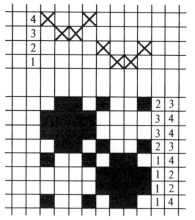

271 Four-end mock leno, draft, threading and lifting plan.

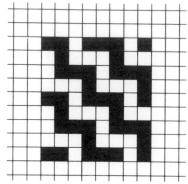

267 Double cloth, weave plan.

horizontal pockets are formed across the cloth (267, 268, 235). Any combination of these can be used in the same cloth, making it possible to construct all sorts of garments on the loom, with the minimum of sewing afterwards. Examples are tubular sleeves that open at one edge to attach to the body of the garment, which in turn can also be made as tubes with one open edge (269).

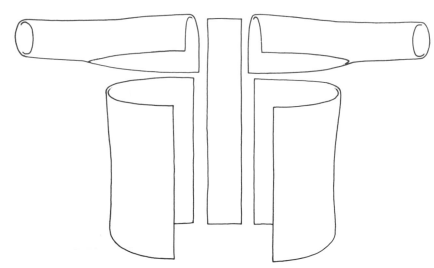

269 Garments can be constructed by weaving in double cloth with open or closed edges.

For all double cloth weaving, the warp must be set at twice the number of ends per centimetre (inch) which would be used for plain weave cloth in that yarn. If the upper and lower cloths are of a different colour, designs can be woven by making the cloths exchange places in selected areas (266).

Open weaves

As well as the hand-manipulated open weaves (see Page 84) it is possible to weave open-work areas in blocks, stripes or all over. The *mock leno* which was used as an example of drafting on Page 88 is a popular example of this. By using the plain weave rows of warp and weft which are part of the pattern, blocks of open work surrounded by plain weave can be woven even on four shafts (270).

The *four-end mock leno* makes a more dramatic texture, but it is less popular as it cannot be used to produce a plain weave as well (271).

Chapter Eleven

Designing, weaving and finishing cloth

by Geraldine St Aubyn Hubbard

Weaving a length of cloth is one of the first aims of the beginner weaver, but it is one of the most difficult things to do satisfactorily. A good floor loom is necessary in order to be able to produce a cloth of even quality, as well as the time to be able to weave for extended periods, not just the odd half-hour. Even if you are able to weave all day, there are still pitfalls: be careful not to start off in the morning with a vigorous beat which will diminish during the day resulting in a completely different cloth being woven in the evening. Also, when dressing the loom, it is much more difficult to maintain even tension on a long wide warp: it is certainly not a job for the beginner.

Designing cloth

With any hand-weaving, there is little point in doing it unless the results are something which cannot be obtained in any other way. There are some very good reasons for weaving cloth by hand:

1 to make use of rare and expensive fibres: silk, cashmere, lambswool, mohair (272, back cover 4).

2 to use unusual and special yarns – hand-spun perhaps, or dyed in a special way, or a yarn which cannot be handled by power looms (colour 1).

3 to be able to use colour and texture in a personal way.

4 to be able to place pattern, such as a stripe, where it will appear in definite parts of a garment or piece of furnishing fabric (4).

5 to create a special sort of 'handle' or feel to the cloth (273).

6 to be able to weave cloth to the exact width you require, so that there is no wastage.

272 Scarf woven of silk and cashmere by Geraldine St. Aubyn Hubbard, contrasting different qualities of lustrous and non-lustrous white yarn. Overshot weave.

It is important to get the structure and the handle of the cloth right for the purpose for which it is intended, and time spent sampling is very well spent. Once you have found a suitable structure, you may produce all sorts of designs using different combinations of colours and stripes. Always consider proportion, balance, and rhythm of stripes in a repeat. Often, very simple designs are the most effective; the exact placing of a thin line of colour adds an accent, whereas if you make the design too complicated, or put in too much, too many ideas cancel one another out.

273 Scarves of hand-spun silk woven by Elizabeth Peacock.

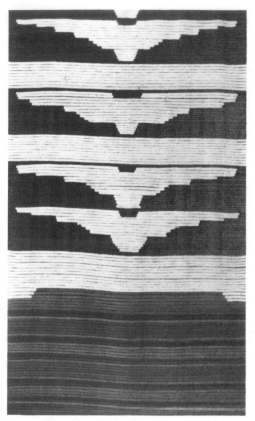

274 Banner from Dartington Hall
'Poultry', by Elizabeth Peacock;
it is handspun and vegetable dyed.

Sometimes the main quality of a cloth is in the liveliness of the hand-spun yarns used in a way that shows them to advantage. This is true of the work of Elizabeth Peacock, for example, who used hand-spun and machine-spun yarns with great sensitivity to produce cloth that had strength in its simplicity and quiet excitement (273, 274).

Look for inspiration to a number of different sources – look at the way in which colours are juxtaposed, the way in which space is divided: stripes are all around. Take the essential from the source: the design will be an abstract, not a copy. Many weavers find that their ideas are digested and distilled, and may emerge several years later.

Look at textiles from other countries and cultures. The Islamic world, India and Asia are great sources of inspiration, especially in their use of colour and stripe, not only in their textiles but in their other art forms (275, colour 14).

Look to the natural world, and also to such areas as painting for colour, calligraphy for rhythm and proportion, and photography. Old textiles are of course a constant source of ideas and a reminder of qualities of cloth that it is possible to make but that are seldom made now. An example is the beautifully draping woollen cloth for which British wool was famous, and which we see in Flemish painting (276).

Museums are treasure-houses of inspiration, with their fabrics from ancient Peru, Persian carpets, Chinese silks, and cloth and garments from ancient or ethnic cultures. Many of these pieces show the way in which the qualities of the cloth itself were considered in the planning of the work, and also show special decorative features or fine details not often seen in clothes today. There are many examples in Chapter Fifteen.

Weaving a feeler

When planning a length of cloth, weavers first of all try out ideas on a sampler. This is sometimes called a *feeler*, as it is intended to provide a large enough sample for the weaver to be able to feel the qualities, as well as to see

275 Hand towel of handspun cotton with cotton and silk inlay, from Turkey.

276 'Arnolfini marriage portrait' by Van Eyck, 1434.

them. It is a good idea to put on a three metre (yard) warp, about 18 or 20 cm (7 or 8 in) wide, and, once you have woven a square of your original idea, try out on the same warp other ideas which occur to you. These may be other weaves, using the same threading, or other yarns, or other colours, or a combination of all of these. If you are planning stripes in the warp, sample them as weft stripes, on a plain warp. It is much easier to experiment with proportions and colour in this way before committing yourself to a whole length of striped warp. The sample can be turned round when it is off the loom. But remember, if weaving it the other way you may need to re-think the sett. Don't be tempted to weave small amounts of each design and variation; a 15 cm (6 in) square is the minimum in order to be able to see and feel a cloth. And if you are designing stripes, weave two or three repeats in order to be able to see them properly.

When the feeler is completed, it must be *finished* in the same way as the cloth would be finished (see Page 99). But before you do this, make a record of the weave, the sett, the yarns, the size of the sample before finishing (and then after), weigh the feeler, note how wide the warp was in the reed, and anything else which you think will be useful for future reference (277). Finally, after finishing, the feeler can be sealed along each division between the pattern samples, either by rubbing in a tiny line of P.V.A (sold under various trade names) and allowing it to dry, or by zig-zag machining twice. The edges will then not fray when the samples are cut up through the glued line or between the machined lines.

FOR : JACKET.					
RAW MATERIAL	WARP WT. YDS. WEFT WT. YDS. WELSH – SHROPSHIRE/RADNOR X.		TYPE OF LOOM	DOUBLE COUNTERMARCH.	
SPIN method direction	Woollen singles. Z.		DRAFT TIE-UP TREADLING INTERSECTION Reeding and Colour Key		
WEIGHT OF YARN	WARP 1 lb 4 ozs. WEFT 1 lb 4 ozs CLOTH 2 lbs 8 ozs				
PLY added					
NAME OF MACHINE YARN	8s Y.S.W. 5s + 8s Y.S.W. (Dyed white + Natural Black)				
DYE	Blue = Indigo. Red = Alum Madder! Crimson = alum cochineal.				
WARP ORDER	Red-Blue x16. Blue, Red x16. repeat across width.		FINISH	Milling for ½ hour in soap. stretch dried on a roller.	
WIDTH	WARP 30" WOVEN 28" FINISHED 26"		OTHER INFORMATION		
LENGTH	WARP 4 yds. WOVEN 3 yds. FINISHED 2½ yds.		DESIGNER WEAVER DATE	Geraldine St. Aubyn Hubbard. November 1976.	
SET	warp = 20 epi. weft = 8 ppi. (4 thick 4 thin alternating)				

277 A typical record card. Information is for the colour-and-weave jacket by Geraldine St. Aubyn Hubbard.

Calculating the quantity of yarn

Once the sample is completed and approved (perhaps by a customer?), calculations must be made for weaving a longer length. The first calculation is the quantity of yarn required. You can get some indication of this by weighing the sample on very accurate scales, and multiplying by the relevant area; remember that you must allow for warp which cannot be woven, say one metre (yard). A more accurate way is to use the *count system* (see Page 12).

Making the warp

For a wide warp, it is sometimes easier to make it in up to eight parts, if there are many ends per centimetre (inch), or if the yarn is inelastic. This prevents build-up of threads on the warping mill, and loss of tension control.

Calculating the width

Use the results of measurements taken from the sample and don't forget the *reed width* – the width of the sample in the reed, which may be different from that of the finished cloth. A rough guide to the extra reed width needed to allow for shrinkage is to add 7·5 to 10 cm (3 to 4 in) per metre (yard) of the required cloth width, but it all depends on the fibre, the yarn, the weave, and the finishing process, and it is impossible to be accurate without doing a sample.

Calculating the length

Allow 15 cm (6 in) per metre (yard) extra – that is, 7·5 cm (3 in) for shrinkage plus 7·5 cm (3 in) for take-up, and between ½ to 1 metre (½ to 1 yard) 'for the loom' for warp wastage. Again this is a very rough guide, and depends on so many variables. Allow more rather than less – you can always weave a bit extra as a sample, but if the warp is too short there is little you can do.

Weaving

When a cloth wider than about 110 cm (42 in) is being woven, it becomes difficult to throw and catch the shuttle without straining both the arms and the selvedges. A fly-shuttle batten can be fitted to some looms, which enables the weaver to pull a lever in the centre of the batten which sends the shuttle, or shuttles, through the shed. But the average hand-loom does not have one of these, and most weavers will never need to use one. It is traditional for hand-woven tweeds, for instance, to be woven 'half-width', that is 76 cm (30 in) wide approximately, which will shrink to 70 cm (27 in) wide, which is still acceptable for the purpose of making up the cloth.

Taking the cloth from the loom

In most cases the warp may be cut off leaving a fringe of 2 or 3 centimetres (about one inch), and the edge machined near the edge of the fabric. Some people may prefer to oversew the edge of the fabric before cutting from the loom; others leave it as a fringe. Cut off the heading woven at the start of the weaving after wet-finishing.

Finishing cloth

278 Cloth before and after finishing.

Fabrics are very rarely complete as they leave the loom. In industry they are said to be in *loom-state*, and often bear no resemblance to their appearance after *finishing*. All fabrics need this cleaning and stabilising (278).

The process starts with any mending necessary, such as the darning in of any previously broken ends, weave mistakes, knots and so on. After that the finishing varies according to the fibre and yarns involved.

Cotton fabrics These will need washing in soap flakes or detergent – though detergent may have a bleaching effect – and stretch-drying. For small pieces, either steam-iron dry for a flatter, shinier result, or stretch on a soft board and attach with rust-free pins, making sure warp and weft are at right-angles to each other. A spin-dryer can be used to get out excess water but don't use it for too long. For larger pieces, stretch dry as for *woollens*.

Woollen fabrics (for definition see Page 10). Much of the character of a good woollen cloth is achieved in the finishing. Woollen fabrics must be *milled* or *fulled*; this is the process by which the fibres felt together and the whole fabric thickens and develops a fullness and softness of handle. To mill the cloth, prepare a strong solution of soap flakes (not detergent) in a *little* warm water, enough to wet the cloth thoroughly. Then transfer the cloth to a bath for stamping – actually getting in with bare feet and treading. For small pieces, you can do this with your hands in a bowl; put a piece of foam sheet in the bottom to save your knuckles. This action of pressure and release in warm alkaline conditions encourages the wool fibres to move towards their cut bases, because of the scale-like structure of each fibre.

If you continue this felting process for about ten minutes, the fibres will settle in the yarn but there will not be much change in the fabric, so ten minutes is really a minimum time. By continuing it longer, the cloth will felt more, shrink, and the definition of the weave and any patterning will soften. You may well decide to continue for several hours if you want to make a very dense, thickened cloth, in which case the cloth should be kept warm and soapy throughout that time. It should be turned constantly to avoid the layers felting to each other. The length of time it takes for the fibres of different breeds of sheep to felt varies: some may go much more quickly than others. The process is irreversible. Keep records of the time spent treading each sample or length, for future reference.

Rinse thoroughly until no trace of soap remains in the cloth. Remove some water, perhaps with a brief spin-dry. All fabrics should be dried under tension, either by stretching it round a slatted drying roller (279, 280) or, for samples and small pieces, by pinning them on a board. The wood should be sycamore or a non-staining wood, and the nails should be rust-proof. Take great care with warp and weft alignment and tension. Keep the drying cloth on its roller in a warm place, but not near direct heat. Keep turning it so that it dries evenly, and if it is a long length of cloth, re-roll the opposite way round to increase the drying speed. This drying roller can be used for all cloths. Woollen fabrics can also be finished by raising the surface – that is by brushing with teasles or a brush. Alternatively, the *raised* surface can be *cropped* with scissors, although, because it is difficult to do this evenly oneself, it is better to send it away for professional treatment.

279 Insert a stick into the groove in the drying roller to hold the cloth in position.

280 Wind the cloth around the roller; then tie a stick on the top to hold the end in place.

Worsted fabrics It is said that woollen cloths are made in the finishing, worsted cloths are made on the loom. A cloth woven of worsted yarn needs to have a clean finish with a clarity of definition and texture. In most cases just washing and tension-drying will cause crazing or cockling (281), especially in a plain weave with a balanced sett. To overcome this the cloth needs either *steam-blowing* – an industrial process which cannot satisfactorily be done at home – or *crabbing*. To crab the cloth, take two solid rollers made of sycamore of between 10 cm and 15 cm (4 in and 6 in) diameter, grooved down the length. Fix the cloth in the groove of one of the rollers with a rod, roll the cloth round the roller and fix the cloth again. Immerse in a bath of water, heated to between 60° and 70°C (140° to 160°F), and revolve the roller for ten minutes, by using a piece of string (282). This relaxes the fibres into a plastic state.

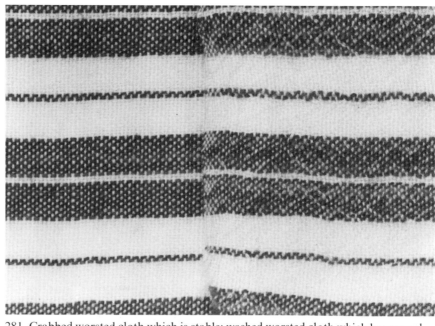

281 Crabbed worsted cloth which is stable; washed worsted cloth which has crazed.

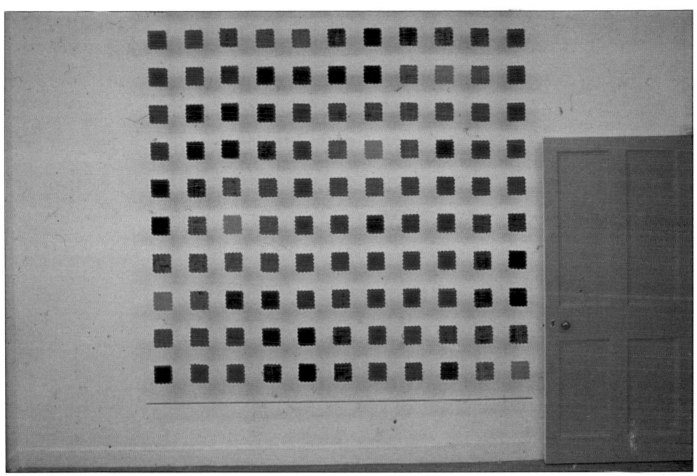

20 'Transition spectrum permutation' by Ann Sutton; small squares of wool or invisible nylon monofilament are woven separately and laced together in a colour permutation.

21 'Elizabethan manor with beech hedge'. Hanging by Margaret Smitton, woven on a dobby loom, with knotted pile 'hedges'.

22 'Arab', a three-dimensional hanging by Candace Bahouth, using tapestry and other techniques.

23 Corner of a rug, Bijar,
nineteenth century, Persian.

24 Kilim, South West Persian, Fars,
mid-nineteenth century.

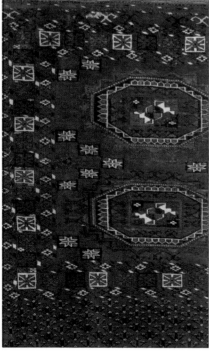

25 Detail of a Turcoman saddlebag,
nineteenth century.

26 Knotted rug found in a frozen tomb at Pazyrik, in the Altai Mountains,
about 600 BC.

27 Rya rug from Finland with the date 1711 included in the knotted design.

102

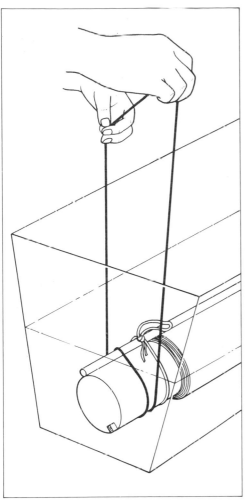

282 Revolve the roller in the hot water by pulling on a string wrapped around it.

Remove the first roller from the bath, and while still hot re-roll the cloth onto the second roller. The tension of warp and weft that you give the cloth as you roll it onto the second roller while the fibres are in this plastic state will determine the final look of the cloth. Roll the fabric directly from one roller onto the other, to avoid cooling. Again immerse in water, this time at boiling point 100°C (212°F) and revolve for ten minutes. This sets the fibres in position. Remove from the water. Allow to cool while on the roller, and keep turning to avoid water marks. When it is completely cold, re-roll the cloth onto the slatted drying roller, as for woollen cloth (279, 280).

Linen fabrics Boil linen cloth, adding a quarter of its weight of soap to the water, for about an hour to clean and soften it. Then rinse thoroughly and stretch dry. To get a smooth finish linen can be *beetled*; this means crushing and splitting the fibres so that they are no longer round but flattened out; this process gives linen a lustre, and a good drape and handle. This is done after rinsing; get rid of most of the water, and then, while it is damp, crush the linen by rolling it very firmly with a roller on a board. Then steam iron it dry, or leave it to dry naturally under some tension.

Silk fabrics If there is no gum left in the fabric, hand-wash it in hot water and soap-flakes. If the silk yarn still has gum in it (you can tell by the smell and the feel) simmer it, adding a quarter of its weight of soap-flakes to the water, for an hour or so. Repeat this process if there is still some gum in the cloth. Rinse the cloth thoroughly and stretch-dry it on a slatted roller. You may get a shinier finish if you steam-iron it dry, but it is very difficult to keep the heat and pressure even all over the cloth, and this is not necessarily the best way. You can have it steam blown by sending it to a finisher.

If all this seems difficult in home conditions – and some of these processes are difficult to control – it is often better to send the cloth away to a reputable finisher with a full description of the required result or a sample of the effect you want. Industry can apply all kinds of other specialised finishes that are often not practicable for small quantities.

283 A traditional English country smock, tightly woven in linen to be weatherproof.

Chapter Twelve

Weaving rugs

by Peter Collingwood

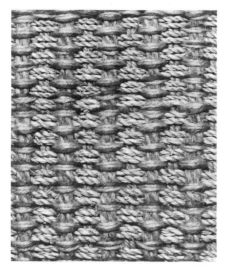

285 Matting in which both the *coir* and *sisal* warps and the *seagrass* and *jute* wefts are visible.

The history of textiles shows that the desire to decorate the floor of a tent or a house with a durable and patterned textile has existed for at least 2500 years (colour 26). That desire is still strong today and rug weaving is one of the most popular branches of hand weaving.

A rug is merely a heavy, thick textile, flexible enough to lie flat on the floor. There are three ways in which these qualities can be obtained:

1 Use a very thick warp and weft and combine them so that both these elements show in a balanced weave (285). This type of rug is just a piece of cloth, magnified or scaled up. An example is coconut fibre (coir) matting.

2 Set the warp threads very close together in the reed so that the weft is completely covered and only shows slightly at the selvedges. Such a warp-faced rug is usually restricted in design to stripes running lengthwise. As these stripes are determined during warping, making the warp is really designing the rug (291, colour 7).

3 Set the warp very openly, so that there is enough space between the ends for the weft to slide down when it is beaten and so completely cover the warp. Such weft-faced rugs offer the most scope in design, because the design is controlled by the weaver's hands or shuttles while he is weaving; the warp is reduced to an anonymous scaffolding only visible at the rug's fringes (colour 6). This chapter will therefore deal exclusively with weft-faced rugs.

Looms and other equipment

Three things are essential in order to weave weft-faced rugs with the required texture: the warp must be very tight; the beating of the weft must be very hard; and the weft must be laid in very loosely. The first two requirements dictate the sort of equipment suitable for rug weaving.

Rugs can be woven on a strong frame – even old bed frames have been used successfully. They work best if one of the cross pieces is adjustable (286). The frame has to be taller than the rug is to be long, if a simple warp is used, so the weaving begins near the floor and ends near the ceiling. If a circular warp is taken around the two cross pieces, then the weaving can occasionally be slipped round and so kept at a convenient working height. The beating is done with a heavy rug fork, either all metal or wood weighted with lead.

Vertical rug looms are available which have a warp beam at the top and a cloth beam at the bottom (287). They usually have only two shafts, sliding in grooves and controlled by two pedals. A batten which swings, or slides, up and down, is also provided, though it seldom gives a heavy enough beat, so use a metal rug fork.

The vertical rug loom is very compact and takes up no more floor space than a deep bookcase, but most weavers who make rugs in quantity prefer the much bigger horizontal floor loom (front cover). This brings the advantages of quicker weaving and a wider choice of pattern as any number of shafts can be used. But it is important to realise that a floor loom sold for normal cloth weaving will, as it stands, never be strong enough for rug weaving. It will weave samples perfectly but not full-width rugs, at least not many before it starts to break up. There are horizontal looms especially designed for rug weaving but as these are extremely expensive and of vast proportions, rug

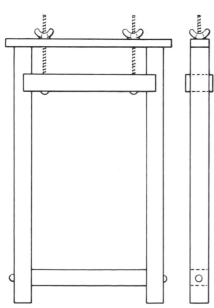

286 Frame loom with an adjustable top cross bar.

287 A typical vertical-warp rug loom with two shafts.

288 Peter Collingwood preparing to throw a ski shuttle wound with carpet wool.

weavers usually compromise by strengthening a good quality cloth-weaving loom (preferably with metal core warp and cloth beams) in the following ways.

1 The batten is weighted with a metal bar bolted beneath it to give the required heavy beat.

2 The breast beam and other cross pieces are strengthened with metal to prevent them bowing under the high warp tension.

3 The attachment between ratchets and beams are strengthened; extra pawls can be added to the cloth beam to provide finer adjustment of tension.

Remember that a loom as bought has all its parts of an appropriate strength and thickness, so altering a loom in one way may lead to the need for other alterations to preserve this balance between the parts.

Strong table looms are excellent for weaving narrow samples of rugs, but are no good for full-size rugs.

Shuttles Ordinary boat shuttles are not used as they will not hold sufficient weft. Instead, *stick shuttles* are used with vertical warps and *ski shuttles* (288) with horizontal warps. Ski shuttles are very useful tools: they carry up to 250 gm ($\frac{1}{2}$ lb) of yarn and slide easily through the shed. In some rug weaving techniques, such as soumak, the weft must be used in the form of finger-skeins (see Page 40).

Temple A *temple* is an adjustable device which stretches the rug to maintain a consistent width (289). Most weavers of weft-faced rugs use a temple: as with everything connected with rugs, it should be very strong, made either of thick wood or metal.

289 Fix the angled teeth at the ends of the temple into the edges of the rug and close it, forcing the rug out to its correct width.

Yarn winder A rug uses a large quantity of weft, perhaps 2·5 kg per square metre (5 lb per square yd) and generally this has to be wound from a skein into some other form, such as a ball, cheese, or cone, before several strands are wound together onto the shuttle. So a ball winder, as supplied with knitting machines, or some sort of electrical bobbin winder which will also take cones is very useful. A skein holder is of course essential; the traditional wooden umbrella skeiner looks decorative but a metal one lasts longer.

Yarns

Warp The first consideration in choosing warp yarn is strength; it must be capable of being held at a high tension and of withstanding repeated beating without breaking. Of the two materials most commonly used, linen and cotton, cotton is easier to handle because it has some elasticity. Linen looks better than dead white cotton at the fringes, but is harder to work with, as it demands a perfect warping and beaming technique to avoid tension problems. A home-made loom extension can help here, though it takes up a lot of space (290). Warp is drawn off the beam at the start of a rug by moving the adjustable cross-bar backwards. Whenever the weaving is *turned on* (that is, wound on on the cloth beam), this bar is simply moved forwards, and the beam is not touched at all. In this way all the linen to be used in a rug is off the beam before weaving begins and there is therefore no possibility that tension will become uneven.

A 6/10 linen and a 4/4 cotton, or slightly thinner, are commonly used warp yarns.

290 Extension on the back of Peter Collingwood's loom, which produces a perfectly tensioned warp.

Weft Almost any material can be used as weft, but wool with its good dyeing and hard-wearing properties is probably the favourite. The ideal is a worsted-spun two-ply yarn made from a long-staple fleece; although this is available, it is very expensive. Two-ply carpet wools, as used in industrial carpets, can be bought in a large range of colours; they usually contain 20 per cent nylon and vary greatly in quality.

The quality of a yarn can be judged by untwisting a section and examining the fibres of which it is made. A poor-quality yarn will have many short fibres (as it is probably made from torn-up garments) bound together with a few long fibres. A good-quality yarn will consist mainly of long fibres.

Other animal yarns, like horse, goat, and camel hair, have their own natural colours. Interesting hand spun yarns can be devised for rugs by carding, then spinning, mixtures of wool with perhaps hemp, rayon, and other materials cut to a convenient staple length.

291 Detail of a warp-faced rug by Margaret Bristow, showing the twill surface; the rug is finished with two rows of weft twining, then the warp ends are wrapped.

It is a common practice to wind several strands of weft together on the shuttle, building up the required weft thickness from thinner, usually two-ply, yarns. This kind of composite weft covers the warp better than a single thick yarn (like the six-ply wool used twenty years ago) and also allows for the possibility of blending colours. If the weaver wants a perfectly straight selvedge, all weft yarns should have the same elasticity: otherwise a stripe of highly elastic yarn will give an indentation to the selvedge, even though a temple is used in the weaving.

Warping and beaming

A warp is laid on a rug frame exactly as on a smaller frame, with the usual care to achieve equal tension all across the width. If the frame has no tension

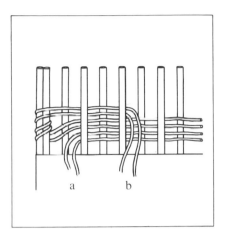

292 How to start a rug weft consisting of four threads, avoiding any extra thickness in the shed.

adjustment, then the tension must be high as well as equal; if it has a tension adjustment as in 286, the final high tension is produced by turning the butterfly screws.

A warp for a horizontal or vertical loom is made as described on Page 62, but it must be beamed at least as tightly as it is going to be used in weaving. This means that the method by which one person holds the warp under tension while another turns the warp beam is barely adequate; it is better to use a one-man method, as follows. Give the beam one turn *without* putting any tension on the warp, then take up a bunch of warp at one selvedge – perhaps 10 threads – and pull these as tightly as possible. Then pick up the next 10 threads and pull again. Working in this way across the warp from one side to the other, the weaver achieves a very tightly beamed warp. Put in a series of sticks, not paper, after every three or four revolutions of the beam in order to keep the beamed warp level and prevent the edges falling down.

Weaving

The warp is threaded, sleyed and tied to the front stick in the usual way. Take great care to tension the threads evenly, otherwise the fell of the rug will not be straight: it will curve towards the reed wherever there is a group of slacker threads.

293 Roger Oates weaving a rug: Arrange the constituent threads of the old weft so that they come out of the shed in three different places.

294 Overlap the three threads of the new weft, and arrange them in a similar manner. In this way both old and new wefts are tapered where they overlap, avoiding extra thickness.

295 After weaving another few centimetres beyond the join, darn the six weft tails one by one down into the thickness of the rug, using a packing needle.

296 Another way of darning weft tails into the rug: insert a needle into the rug with a wire loop threaded through its eye; pass the weft tail into the end of the wire loop.

In a weft-faced rug, start and join wefts in a special way so as to avoid too much extra thickness at that point. 292 shows the starting of a weft consisting of four strands. Two strands *a* never reach the selvedge; the other two *b* wrap around the selvedge thread and then re-enter the shed to be brought out two raised ends away from *a*. This ensures that there is only a slight increase of weft thickness and then only for a very short distance. 293–295 show joins between wefts consisting of three strands. Here the principle is to taper the wefts involved so that again there is as little extra thickness as possible.

It is not safe to leave the weft ends hanging out of the rug. They have to be darned in as the work proceeds. A curved packing needle and a wire loop (296) make this job quick and simple to do. Thread the loop into the eye of the needle, then push the needle down into the rug, close to a weft end, so that it slides down in front of a warp thread for about 2 cm ($\frac{3}{4}$ in) and then comes out onto the surface again. Now put the weft into the wire loop. Pull the loop to the left thus threading the weft through the eye, then pull the needle downward to darn the weft into the thickness of the rug. It is now safe to trim off any protruding weft.

Again, it must be stressed that it is important to weave with the warp as highly tensioned as possible, because the tighter the warp – the more the threads resemble rigid rods – the easier it is to beat each pick of weft close up against the previous one.

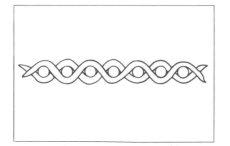

297 Cross-section of a weft-faced rug showing the weft curving over and under the straight warp threads.

In a weft-faced rug, the warp ends run straight through the centre of the woven structure, but the weft curves over and under these ends (297). To enable the weft to take this serpentine course, extra slack must be allowed when each pick is laid in. To do this in a controlled way, the weft is curved immediately after the shuttle is thrown (298–300). Usually one curve per 30 cm (12 in) width of rug is sufficient, but it will be found that an inelastic yarn is easier to control by using more and smaller curves. The weave being used also has an effect; plain weave with its many warp/weft intersections requires more slack in the weft that does a twill with the same warp setting. The whole skill in producing a well-made weft-faced rug lies in the ability to curve the weft quickly and accurately so that hour after hour, day after day, the same amount of slack goes into every pick.

298 Throw the weft to the left, and place it diagonally.

299 Begin at the right and curve the weft, drawing in slack from the free end at the left.

300 Four curves completed across the width of the rug. Marks on the batten correspond to the 'valleys' in the curves and so encourage accurate spacing.

When the weft has been curved, change the shed and then beat. Beating is the most tiring part of rug weaving as it has to be done really hard. Using a weighted batten is a great help as is the following method: hold the batten with both hands and lean back on the loom seat so that the weaver's weight is added to that of the batten (front cover); this has the effect of squeezing the last few picks together and is a far more efficient way of working than using the batten like a hammer which deals the weft a fierce blow and then rebounds.

To prevent the rug drawing in, use a temple right from the very beginning to the end. The more weft floats there are in the weave and the more elastic the weft yarn is, the greater the tendency of the rug to become narrower. So though they both need a temple, a 2/2 twill rug woven with a very springy woollen yarn needs it more than a plain weave rug woven with a non-elastic hair yarn, like goat hair. Always set the temple so that it stretches the rug to the exact width the warp has in the reed.

Plain weave rug techniques

A great deal of rug weaving is based on plain weave. It is therefore very important to find the correct relationship between *warp sett* and *weft thickness* – that is one which will give a strong yet flexible weft-faced structure. A common warp setting is 12 or 16 doubled ends per 10 cm (3 or 4 *doubled* ends per inch) – the warp is 25 or 32 ends per 10 cm (6 or 8 ends per inch) on the beam, but is used in pairs in the threading of the shafts and in sleying. The correct weft for this could be four or three two-ply carpet wools used

301 Typical pattern produced by tie-dyeing the weft when in hanks; they must be about as long as the rug is wide.

together; only experiment will show what is right. If the weft is too thick, the warp will be barely covered or, if covered, the rug will be stiff and board-like. If the weft is too thin, the rug's texture will be soft and *sleazy*, which means so loosely woven that a finger can be poked through it.

One-weft techniques Once this correct relationship is found, there are many techniques to choose from. Although the majority involve the use of two or more shuttles in turn, each bearing different coloured wefts, interesting rugs can be woven with only one weft. A mixture of different, but closely related, colours can be wound together on the shuttle and this mixture changed as weaving proceeds; hand-spun wefts of different types can be combined; tie-dyed wefts can be used in either controlled (301) or haphazard designs (336); a black and white weft can be plied and the degree of ply altered by twisting or untwisting by hand when in the shed, making possible many effects.

Cross stripes The simplest effect using two shuttles is the weaving of *cross stripes*, that is horizontal stripes, which can be very satisfying when good colours and proportions are used. The narrowest such stripe is a 2-and-2 stripe, that is two picks of colour *a* alternating with two picks of colour *b*. It shows as thin wavy lines (302).

Pick and pick stripes Alternating one pick of *a* with one pick of *b* gives narrow warp-way, that is vertical stripes, a characteristic patterning in weft-faced weaving (303). To get a neat edge to such *pick-and-pick stripes*, one weft is wrapped around the selvedge thread to compensate for the failure of the other weft to engage with the selvedge thread. Because in 303 there is an odd number of warp ends, it is the same weft which wraps at both selvedges; with an even number each weft would wrap at one side and miss the selvedge at the other.

Pick-and-pick stripes have many uses; for example, a band of them in colours *a* and *b* makes a good transition between an area of solid *a* and solid *b*. The combination of pick-and-pick stripes with cross stripes produces almost endless variations (302).

Crossed wefts There is an interesting way of weaving a shaped area of pick-and-pick stripes on a background of cross stripes (304). Working with two shuttles, *a* and *b*, start when they are at opposite selvedges. In the next shed, pass them towards each other, then bring them both out of the shed at the same point (between raised ends 8 and 10 in 304). Change the shed, re-enter one shuttle, say *b*, into the shed and carry it onto the selvedge. Then do the same for shuttle *a*. Note that in order to make a neat crossing of the two wefts, both shuttles must re-enter the shed at the same point, that is between raised ends 7 and 9.

302 Sampler woven with two colours, showing various small patterns made up from vertical and horizontal stripes and spots.

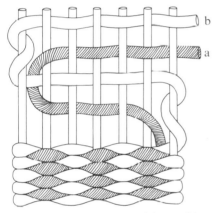

303 Pick-and-pick stripes with an add number of working ends in the warp.

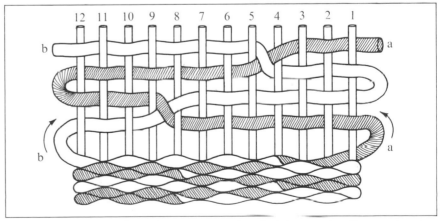

304 Crossed wefts: *top*, how the two wefts are handled; *bottom*, the effect produced when beaten down.

Change the shed and repeat the process, but this time bring the shuttles out at a different point, between raised ends 4 and 6 in 304. Change the shed and re-enter the shuttles, making a neat crossing as before. Continue the weaving, alternating the crossing points from side to side.

305 Combination of cross stripes and pick-and-pick stripes produced by the crossed weft technique.

The result is a central area of pick-and-pick stripes, bounded on each side by 2-and-2 stripes (305). The central area can be made any shape by moving the crossing points about, but they *must* alternate from one side to the other of the shape being created. This simple idea of crossing wefts in order to alter their colour sequence has many possibilities. Three or four wefts can be used leading to more complex patterns, two wefts can start at the same side and cross many times, giving several areas of pick-and-pick stripes and the possibility of reversing the striping.

Other techniques which use two or more shuttles passing from selvedge to selvedge are *skip plain weave* and *meet-and-separate weave:* for more details of these and many other possibilities, consult *Techniques of rug weaving.*

Kilim If the tapestry methods described in Chapter Five are applied to a rug, the rug is called a *kilim*, from an arabic word *kalim*, meaning 'carpet' (colour 24). Such kilims are commonly woven without any interlocking of adjacent wefts; so to avoid long slits the designs exclude long, vertical colour boundaries.

Raised surface decoration

There are several techniques, mostly traditional, in which an extra thread, inserted by hand, gives a raised decoration on the surface of one side of a plain weave rug.

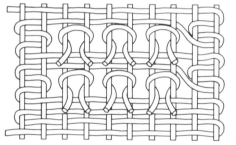

306 Diagram of the structure of a knotted rug with two rows of Turkish knots.

307 Tying a Turkish knot. Take the pile yarn down between the next two warp threads and grip with the right hand from below.

308 Take the pile yarn around the right hand warp thread and give it to the left hand.

309 With the left hand, carry the pile yarn to the left across the two raised warp threads, and then bring it up between them, *beneath* the horizontal part of the knot just formed.

310 Draw the two ends of the pile yarn down towards you, and cut to the required length. Note that scissors are held in the right hand throughout the knotting.

311 Knotted sample bent backwards
to show six picks of plain weave between
the rows of knots.

Knotted pile is the commonest (colour 23, colour 25). Although it is also
the slowest way of patterning a rug, it is the one which gives the most design
possibilities, as theoretically every knot inserted can be a different colour.
Rugs are usually knotted following a carefully prepared diagram, showing
where each colour is wanted in each row. A row of knots is tied across the
warp, around one or two warp threads, using the Turkish, Persian or Spanish
knot (306). Then two or more wefts are passed, followed by another row
of knots and so on (307–311).

This very simple plan of work has many variations such as the following:

1 The rug can vary in thickness from a heavy Swedish *rya* with a pile 10 cm
(4 in) or more long and many picks between the knot rows (colour 27)
to an eastern all-silk rug with up to 160 knots per square cm (1000 knots
per square in), and looking and feeling like velvet.

2 Areas of flat weave and pile can be combined, as can areas of cut and
uncut pile;

3 Pile can be worked on both sides of the rug, more easily done on a
vertical warp;

4 The outer few warp threads at each side, which are always left free of
knots, can be treated in many decorative ways.

Soumak, or weft wrapping, is another traditional rug technique. An extra
weft is taken across the warp, passing forwards over two warp threads, backwards under one, forwards over two and so on, giving a raised ridge (312);
this extra weft does not need to go right across the warp. This is followed by
the normal weft of the rug passing from selvedge to selvedge. Using many
extra wefts in this way, the rug can be covered with soumak patterning
(colour 17). Alternatively, a one-colour rug can be woven contrasting flat
areas with raised soumak areas. Soumak can also be worked at an angle or
even vertically (313, colour 18).

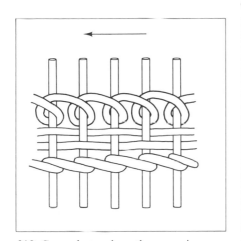

312 *Soumak: top*, how the wrapping
weft is carried around the warp threads;
bottom, how it looks in a finished rug.

313 *Vertical soumak*. Several wrapping wefts each moving vertically instead
of horizontally

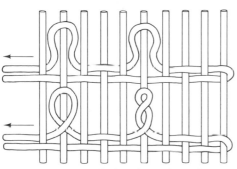

314 Loops pulled up from the weft,
lying in the shed.

Weft looping In weft looping, loops of yarn from the normal (or an extra)
weft lying in the shed are pulled up one at a time, working in the same
direction as the shuttle. Slipping the loops over a rod as they are pulled up
ensures a consistent size (314). The loops are spaced and the number of
intervening non-looped picks adjusted according to the desired density of
loops. Looped areas can be contrasted with flat areas (315). An interesting
variation with many possibilities is to chain the loops one into another
vertically (316), catching the last loop in a weft thread as shown. This
transforms the rather unstable loops into a durable structure (317).

Weft chaining In *weft chaining*, a weft is held under the warp and a loop
pulled up between two warp ends; then, *through* this loop, another loop is
pulled up a little further along the warp, and so on (318). In this way the weft

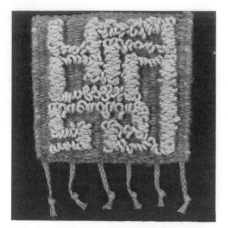

315 Combining pulled-up weft loops with flat areas in a wollen rug sample.

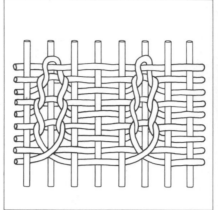

316 Pulled-up weft loops chained into each other from the bottom upwards, and secured with a weft at the top.

317 Rug sample by Kathy Hiltner, completely covered with chained weft loops in black and white wool, moving obliquely.

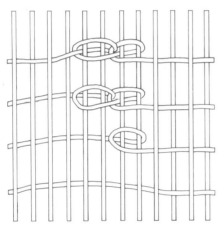

318 How to make the first and second repeat of weft chaining; how to secure the final repeat.

319 Close-up of a 2/2 twill rug being woven by Roger Oates with an *a b b* colour sequence; the last two picks are unbeaten to show their over-two, under-two course.

320 The picks beaten in; note that the colour diagonal runs in the opposite direction to the structural diagonal.

112

is chained exactly as a warp is chained when removed from the warping mill, and lies as a thick ridge across, and fixed to, the warp. Several normal picks follow each row of chaining. Chaining can be worked in two colours – two wefts under the warp and a loop of either being pulled up; it can be worked at an angle; and it can be combined with flat areas. A single row of weft chaining is sometimes used as a means of spacing the warp at the start of a rug woven on a frame.

Four-shaft weaves

Although plain weave techniques can produce endless designs and textures, they are of necessity very slow, as they depend on the weaver's hands controlling the wefts in special ways. If more complex weaves are used, such as twills and blockweaves, the design is controlled by the extra shafts brought into play, and so the work is correspondingly quicker. Such multi-shaft rug weaves form a very large group, and it is only recently that they have begun to be explored (colour 16, colour 19). Two examples follow, both of which can be woven on a warp set at 16 ends per 10 cm (4 ends per in) used either singly or double, depending on the thickness of the warp.

a 2/2 twill The shafts are lifted as for normal 2/2 twill – that is, 1 2, 2 3, 3 4 and 4 1 (see Page 91) but the result is quite different as the weave here is weft-faced. If one colour only is used, little is seen except faint diagonal ridges, or *wales*. But by using two or more colours in a definite sequence, a great variety of small-scale effects can be woven. Calling the two colours *a* and *b*, here are some good sequences to try.

1 *a, a, b* and *a, b, b*, which give diagonal stripes of the two colours (319, 320).

2 *a, a, b, a, a, b, b, b, b*, which gives rhomboids of *a* surrounded by *b* (321).

3 *a, b, b, a, a, b, a, a, a, b, b, b*, which gives triangles of the two colours (321).

Remember that the sequence of shaft lifts continues, unaffected by the various shuttle sequences.

b Other designs result from using the lifts for **broken 2/2 twill** which are 1 2, 2 3, 4 1, 3 4. Good sequences to use here are *a, b, a, b, a* and *a, a, a, b, a, b, b, b* which gives diamonds of *a* and *b*. Sequences such as *a, a, a, b* and *b, a, a, a*, give thin warp-way lines which can be built up into complex designs (322). There is much scope for individual exploration in these and other twills, especially when a third or even fourth colour is introduced as in this example.

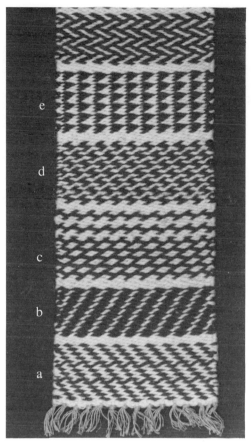

321 2/2 twill sampler woven with normal lifts and with colour sequences as follows:
a *a b b b a*, occasionally *a b a b a*
b *a a b a a a b*
c *a a b a a b b b b*, plus a variation
d *a b b a b a b b a a*
e *a b b a a b a a a b b b*

322 Sampler using broken twill lifts and simple four-pick colour sequences, like *a a a b* and *a b a b*; occasionally using three colours.

In all these methods, the weft will fail to catch automatically at the selvedge, so either the shuttle has to be carried around the selvedge thread or a *floating* selvedge must be used.

The floating selvedge

A floating selvedge is one which is *not* entered in a heddle, but is sleyed normally through the reed; so when a shed is opened, all the other warp threads rise or fall but the floating selvedge stays unaltered, lying horizontally in the neutral position of the warp, bisecting the angle of the shed. It is shown as a dotted line (323). The shuttle is always entered *over* the floating selvedge (in opening *x*), and it naturally leaves the shed at the opposite side *under* the floating selvedge (opening *y*). When next needed the shuttle is again entered over the floating selvedge and so on. In this way the weft cannot fail to catch around the selvedge thread at both sides.

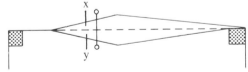

323 Floating selvedge, (dotted line), remaining horizontal when the shed is opened.

Blockweaves

Whereas twills give small areas of colour which appear repeatedly across the rug, a blockweave gives large rectangles or blocks of one colour against the background of another (324, colour 16). When such a rug is turned over, the same pattern of rectangles is seen but with the colours reversed.

This effect is achieved by threading the warp in two different ways. Where the blocks are wanted, it is threaded on shafts 1, 4, 2, repeated as many times as desired, and where the background is wanted it is threaded on shafts

1, 3, 2 again repeated as desired. Lift the shafts in the sequence 1 3, 1 4, 2 3, 2 4 and use two wefts, *a* and *b* alternately. This will give blocks of colour *a* lying on a background of *b*, on the front of the rug as woven.

Notice that the threading of the warp decides the width of the blocks and the spacing between them. How far they stretch in the warp direction can be decided while weaving. At any point, the lifts can be changed to 1 3 4, 1, 2 3 4, 2 (the colour sequence remaining *a, b, a, b*), and the blocks will disappear, giving a rug which shows colour *b* right across on the front, and *a* right across on the back.

The weft will catch at both selvedges as long as they are used alternately as just described. But they will fail to do so if other sequences are employed, such as *a, b, b, b*, which converts the block from a solid colour to stripes. Several such sequences exist, enabling the blocks to be varied in their colouring. Also a third colour can be introduced: for example, a sequence of *a, b, c, b* gives a block striped with *a* and *c* on a background of *b*.

Shaft switching

There exists a method (evolved by the writer and described in his book *Techniques of rug weaving*) of moving warp threads between shafts 3 and 4 during the weaving itself, and thus converting at will an area which showed colour *a* into one showing colour *b*, and vice versa (325, 326). This shaft-switching technique means that any two-colour design can be woven with ease and so gives the weaver great scope (back cover 1, 327). The method involves adding a system of cords controlled by levers above the shafts (288). Other ways are possible.

324 Two samples of blockweaves, each using two colours; colours reverse on the back.

325 The rug seen on the loom in 326, wool and horsehair wefts on linen warp.

326 A rug by Peter Collingwood, with the design controlled by shaft switching; the last two picks unbeaten to show the structure.

Rug fringes

When a rug is cut from the loom it does not need to undergo any of the wet or heat treatments applied to woven cloth. But the exposed warp ends must be treated in some way, both to prevent them fraying and to stop the first and last picks of weft from becoming unwoven. Many methods can be used, some purely functional, others which are very decorative as well. A simple way is as follows:

Start with the rug on a table, with its warp ends hanging over the edge. Imagine that these are numbered from right to left. Pick up thread 1 and knot it around 2; hold 2 under tension so that 1 bends around it (328). Now knot 2 in a similar way around 3 (329), and so on. In this way a continuous fastening is made right across the rug edge, finally ending at the left. Make sure it is straight; the table edge can act as a good guide.

Now plait the warp ends beyond this finish, using three groups of four threads for each plait. End each with an overhand knot, pulling separately on each warp end beyond the knot to make sure it is really tight and can withstand the hard wear to which it will be subjected.

To avoid a fringe, weave each warp end into the other adjacent warps (330, 331), and finish with a tassel (colour 16).

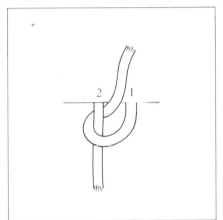

328 Knotted rug finish: knot warp thread 1 around thread 2.

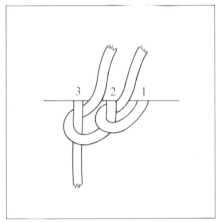

329 Now knot thread 2 around 3, and so on, moving across the rug edge to the left.

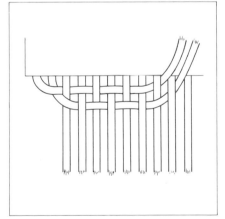

330 Woven rug finish: weave the warp into the warp.

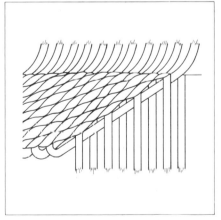

331 This gets rid of the fringe altogether.

Weaving rag rugs

Another way of getting a thick, heavy texture in a rug is to use a thick weft, such as a rag strip, in a plain weave or twill. Cut or tear the rags into strips – some weavers like the hairy chenille-like effect of using rags torn rather than cut. Wind them onto ski-shuttles, and weave normally, using a heavy beat (332).

327 Shaft-switched rug by Peter Collingwood, in which the design follows diagonals, which occur naturally in the weave.

332 Roger Oates weaving a rag rug: note the ski shuttles wound with weft ready for use in the basket.

333 Cut the ends of the rag strips diagonally, to ensure a neat join, and lay the tapered ends in the shed.

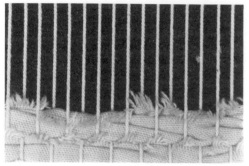

334 A rag rug weft join, beaten down.

If a weft runs out a new one can be started in the middle of a pick, by cutting the ends of the rags diagonally and laying them together in the shed to avoid a build-up of thickness in the weft at that point (333, 334).

Roger Oates gets interesting effects by the use of contrasting textures and plain and patterned fabrics. For example a rag strip torn from a cloth with a large flowered design will give repeated spots of colour when beaten down (335).

As well as making flat rugs, rags can also be used to give a thick pile (see Page 132 and colour 4).

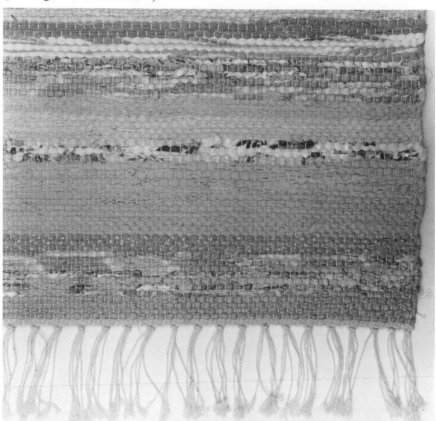

335 Detail of a rag rug, in which Roger Oates has used both one-colour and printed rags.

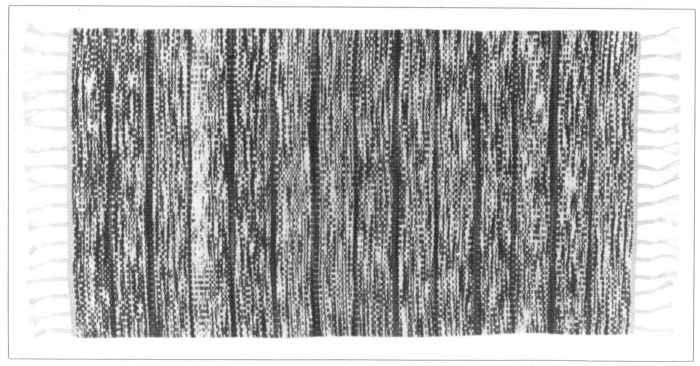

336 Tie-dyed rug by Vanessa Robertson.

Chapter Thirteen

The backstrap loom, inkle weaving, tablet weaving

The backstrap loom is one of the simplest and most portable of looms, and for this reason is found all over the world from the Far East to South America (337, 402). It is very versatile, and is able to produce all weights of cloth, patterned or plain, from mats to fine woollen garments. There is no frame in a backstrap loom: the warp is stretched between two rods, one of which is fastened to an immovable post, such as a tree and the other to a strap which passes around the back of the weaver who sits, kneels or stands; most prefer to wear it around the hips. In another type of backstrap loom the far rod, instead of being fastened to a post, is lodged behind the weaver's feet – so she herself becomes the frame of the loom (338). The body of the weaver thus controls the tension of the warp, and can respond to its needs.

337 Traditional position for backstrap weaving.

338 Backstrap weaver in Vietnam using her feet to tension the warp.

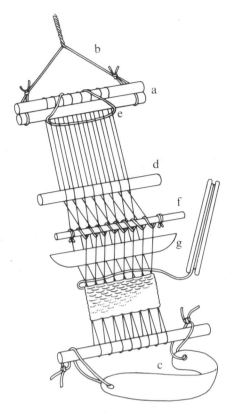

339 The backstrap loom:
a warp- and cloth-beams, *b* tie cord,
c backstrap, *d* shed stick, *e* lease-string,
f leash rod, *g* sword.

Each backstrap loom has a *cloth-beam* and a *warp-beam, tie cords,*
and a *backstrap*. It also has some way of making a shed. This may be:
1 A leash rod and a shed stick,
2 Two or more leash rods, or
3 A rigid heddle (see Page 41).

Making a backstrap loom

Because it is so simple, it can be made very easily. You will need five lengths
of 1 cm (half-inch) dowelling, at least 40 cm (15 in) long. The ends of four of
these must be notched, to stop the loops of the tie-cord and strap falling off.
Set two of these aside as **warp-beam** and **cloth-beam** (339a, 340a).

The tie-cord Take six strands of heavy jute, or something similar, each
3 metres (yards) long; knot the ends together, and, working the threads
in pairs, plait for 120 cm (4 ft). Divide in two, and plait with single strands
for 50 cm (20 in). Tie the ends back in a loop (339b, 340b).

The backstrap This can be made of webbing or leather, or it can be made on
a backstrap loom. It is a band 40 × 5 cm (16 × 2 in) with a cord about 30 cm
(12 in) long attached to each end, ending in loops (339c, 340c).

The shed stick is a length of 2·5 cm (1 in) diameter dowel or bamboo (339d).

Lease strings, two of them, each about 10 cm (4 in) more than twice the
width of the warp (339e).

The leash rod is another of the five original dowels (339f). There are two
ways of attaching the heddles: like this, for a close warp (344a), or like this
for a widely spaced warp, or one with gaps in it (344b). The heddle cord
must be firm, smooth cotton.

The cloth roll and warp roll are the remaining two dowel rods. They are used
to roll up with the warp- and cloth-beams to store the warp or cloth.

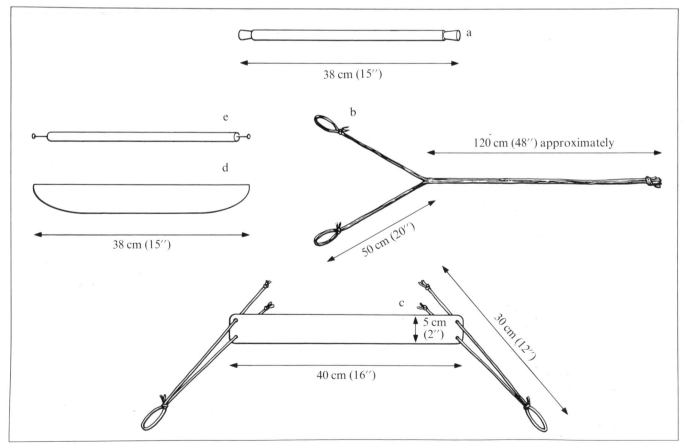

38 cm (15″)

120 cm (48″) approximately

50 cm (20″)

38 cm (15″)

5 cm (2″)

30 cm (12″)

40 cm (16″)

340 *a* warp- or cloth-beam, *b* tie cord, *c* backstrap, *d* sword, *e* tenter.

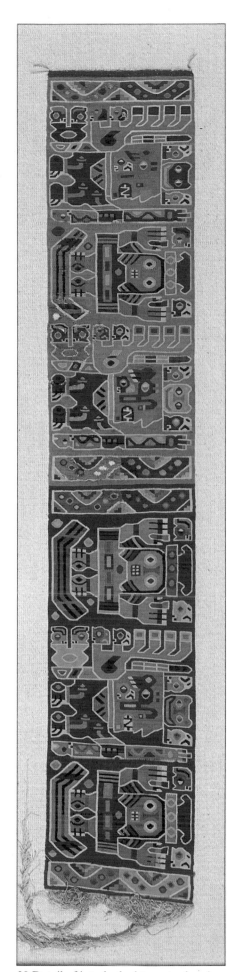

29 'The hunting velvet', intended as the interior of a tent ceiling, woven during the Safavid dynasty, Persia; sixteenth century.

30 Raffia cloth from Bakuba, Zaire, with areas of raffia pile and thin lines worked in oblique soumak.

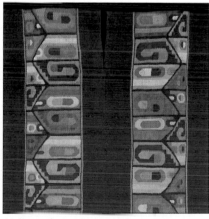

28 Detail of interlocked tapestry band, showing a figure appearing to stand on a raft; Tiahuanaco, Peru; AD 550–700.

31 Part of a tunic, tapestry woven with alpaca on cotton warp, Tiahuanaco, Peru; sixteenth century.

32 Two lion hunters on a silk textile, perhaps from Syria; about seventh century.

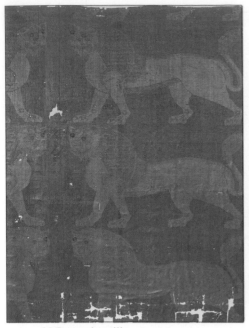

33 Byzantine silk,
showing very large opposed lions.

36 'The beast from the sea', part of one of the seventy scenes in the famous
'Apocalypse' tapestries in Angers, France; from the workshop of Nicholas Bataille;
end of the fourteenth century.

34 The 'senmurv', a mythical beast
within a string of pearls, on Sassanian
silk; sixth to seventh century.

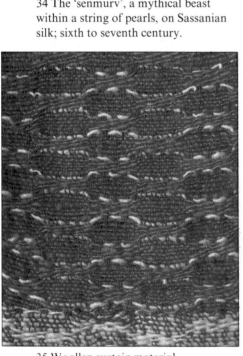

35 Woollen curtain material
by Ethel Mairet; machine spun warp,
hand-spun weft, both dyed with madder.

37 'April' from a tapestry found in Baldishol church, Norway; about 1180.

120

The sword is a flat piece of thin but strong wood about 5 × 38 cm (2 × 15 in), shaped at each end (339g, 340d).

A tenter may be useful: this is traditionally a stick 5 mm ($\frac{1}{4}$ in) in diameter, as long as the width of the cloth to be woven, with a fine nail or pin pushed into each end (340e). The pins are pushed through the edge of the weaving to maintain the width of the cloth.

Making the warp for a backstrap loom

Although it is possible, with care, to wind a long warp onto the warp beam, it is so easy to set up these looms (no threading up is necessary) that most weavers prefer to set up for each piece of, say, a garment, and weave them separately, rather than using a long warp. To begin with it is wiser to plan an item measuring not longer than one metre (yard) in length. Set up two warping pegs, the required distance apart, and attaching the warp thread loosely but firmly (not by means of a slip knot), wind in a figure-of-eight until the warp is complete. Try not to build up the threads on top of one another, in order to maintain even tension. Count the threads in the middle at the cross, well away from the posts, so that there is no chance of counting only one half. Tie the final end, again loosely, to a post (341).

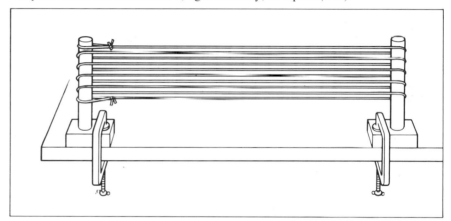

341 Making a warp for a backstrap loom: there is only one cross, in the centre.

Setting up a backstrap loom

1 Tie a lease string on each side of the cross, long enough to allow the warp to spread out fully (342).

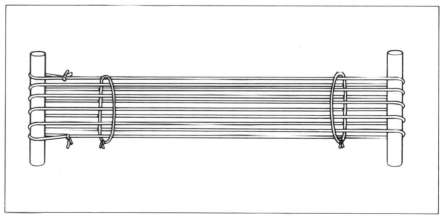

342 Tie a loose lease-string on either side of the cross.

2 Take the warp- and cloth-beams and slip one down alongside the post at one end of the warp, and the other one at the other end. Gently and carefully remove the warp from the posts and lay it on a table, with the lease strings on the top. Arrange the warp in the centre of the rods. At the far end, place another rod *on top* of the warp, next to the warp-beam.

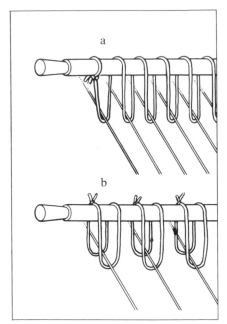

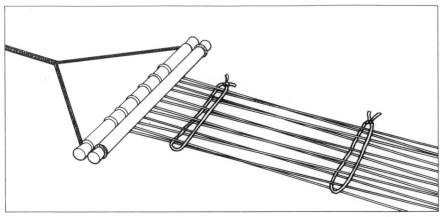

343 Transfer the warp to the warp-beam, place the extra rod on top, attached to the tie cord.

344 Two types of leashes *a* and *b*, *b* is more suitable for a spaced warp.

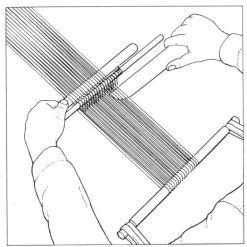

345 To weave, pull the shed stick forward to the back of the leash rod and insert the sword in front of the leashes, tipping it to form a shed for the shuttle.

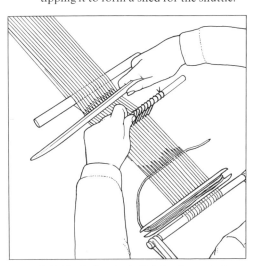

346 Push the shed stick back, and raise the leash rod; push down the threads behind the heddles with the sword, which is then used again to hold open the shed.

3 Tie the tie cord to a tree, pillar, or hook, very firmly, and attach the two loops to the rod which is laid on top of the warp threads, passing them underneath the warp-beam. This will hold the warp very firmly in place (343).

4 Put the backstrap around your hips and attach the loops to each end of the cloth beam, wriggling backwards until the warp is taut. If one edge of the warp appears slacker than the other at any stage, just pull the backstrap around a little to adjust it.

5 *Insert the shed stick* Lift the far lease string up, and insert the 2·5 cm (1 in) diameter shed stick. Push the string right to the back of the loom, but don't remove it. Lift the near lease string and insert the sword. *Push the sword and the shed stick together at the cross.*

6 *Inserting the leash rod* This will be attached to the warp threads which are now on top of the sword. Take a ball of smooth twine and insert the end through the shed from right to left. Tie a 2·5 cm (1 in) loop, and slip it over the end of the leash rod. Starting at the left, with the leash rod in the left hand, bring a loop of the twine up between each raised thread and slip over the rod (344). Continue along to the right, trying to make all the loops of the same length, about 6 cm (2½ in). Adjust the length if necessary, from left to right. (If the twine is given two half hitches as it is slipped onto the rod, the leashes cannot alter in size during weaving.) Wrap the end tightly around the leash rod, about six times, cut it and tie firmly. Remove the sword and the front lease string. For safety, you can tie a tight string from one end of the shed-stick to the other.

Weaving on a backstrap loom

Wind the weft yarn onto a *stick shuttle* (346, 355).

1 Pull the shed stick forward, to the back of the leash rod, and insert the sword in front of the leashes (345).

2 Tip the sword on edge, and insert the shuttle. Remove the sword.

3 Push the shed stick back. With the left hand, raise the leash rod. Push down the threads *behind* the heddles with the sword, held in the right hand (346). Lean forward slightly at this point to relax the tension.

4 Insert the sword in front of the leashes and tip it on edge; insert the next weft and beat with the edge of the sword. (Some Mexican weavers wind the weft into a small ball which rolls downhill through the shed, which is alternately tilted to right and to left by the weaver.)

The leashes can be slid back on the warp as weaving progresses. Towards the end of the weaving, if you wish to weave right up to the warp-beam, it will be necessary to remove the leashes and shed-stick and darn in the last few picks with a needle. Remove the finished cloth from the loom by taking out all the rods.

348 Motif from a Mexican belt woven in black and white cotton.

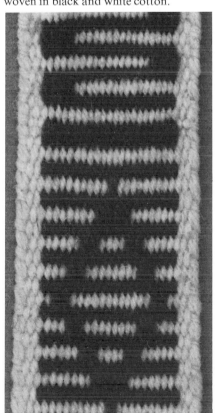

349 Inkle-woven band by Lavinia Bradley.

Longer warps are possible on this sort of loom – the warp is stored by tying a rod to the warp-beam and winding it up. Wind stiff paper in between the layers of thread (347). It is useful to have another person to help when winding. As the weaving progresses, the cloth can be wound around the cloth-beam in the same way with the aid of a flat stick which can be strapped to it.

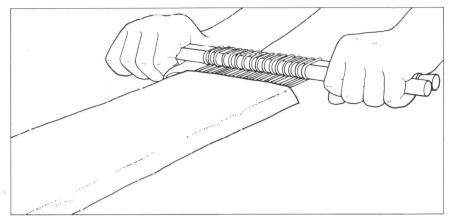

347 A longer warp can be wound onto the warp-stick.

Using a rigid heddle on a backstrap loom

The warp threads must be cut at the front – it is better to cut them in tens to avoid confusion. Put the loop over the warp-beam, and thread the ends through the rigid heddle, which should be supported so that it stands upright on the table. Tie the threads in bunches. At the front, attach the two outside bunches to the cloth beam first. Then, with these under body tension, finish tying up to the cloth beam and adjust the tension in the way used for normal loom weaving (see Pages 69–70).

Pattern weaving on a backstrap loom

Backstrap looms can be used for many patterning techniques from the finest gauze (403) to picked-up patterns on heavy warp-faced cloth. The following methods are found in Central America today (348).

Choose a pattern weft which is heavier than the background weft, doubling or tripling the thread if necessary. In many of the Guatemalan cloths the pattern weft is inserted in a closed shed, and in this case a finger skein (see Page 40) is the most convenient way of holding the weft thread. The thick pattern weft can be woven in and out in a 'brocaded' way – that is with the weft thread passing under one warp, then *floating*, or passing, over two or more, then under one, over several, so that the floating weft makes the pattern. More usually, the pattern weft is wrapped over and under large groups of threads, giving the same pattern on both sides of the cloth. Alternatively, a *soumak* technique can be used (see Page 111).

Other ways of pattern weaving will occur to you, but it is usually necessary to use the background weft thread in a plain weave shed in between each pattern weft.

Weaving narrow fabrics

Narrow fabrics, such as braids, can be woven on any loom in the normal way, just by setting up a narrow warp. But there are two special weaving techniques which do not need a conventional loom and which produce braids up to about 10 cm (4 in) wide. These methods are called *inkle weaving* and *tablet weaving* (sometimes called *card weaving*). Both produce warp-faced braids, but there the similarity ends. Inkle weaving produces a plain weave fabric with the possibility of picking up patterns by hand, and is perhaps

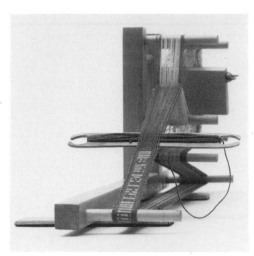

350 Small inkle loom
with lettered band being woven.

the easiest weaving technique for incorporating lettering (349, 350). Tablet weaving produces a structure consisting of groups of twisted warp threads with the weft holding the twists in place; elaborate patterns can be achieved by the way in which the warp is coloured and the tablets handled (361, 363).

Only non-fluffy yarns should be used, such as worsted or cotton. Remember that these braids are warp-faced, so that all colour in the design is provided by the warp. The weft should be the same colour as the edge threads, as the selvedge is the only place where it will show.

Inkle weaving

An inkle loom consists of a series of pegs inserted at right angles to a frame (351). Sometimes the frame is floor-standing, but more often it sits on a table. These looms are made in several sizes; the largest will make about 3 metres (3 yards) of braid. Some inkle looms have *tensioners*, blocks of wood which can be swung out on a screw to hold the warp out fully at the beginning of weaving, to be lowered gradually as the warp is taken up by the weaving process, so that even tension can be maintained for the whole length of warp.

Unlike most looms, the warping and threading processes on an inkle loom take place at the same time, so there is no need for any warping equipment. A continuous warp is made on the loom: breaking the thread is unnecessary even when changing colour. The principle of inkle weaving is that alternate threads are tied down permanently with leashes, while the others are free to be lifted and lowered through them to make the shed. There is no reed. As the weaving progresses and nears the leashes, the whole warp is pulled carefully around the loom to expose a fresh area. As in all weaving, keep a record of each braid with warp yarn samples, number of ends and leashes, and the resulting width, with a small sample cut off the end of the weaving. This will be a great help when planning future braids.

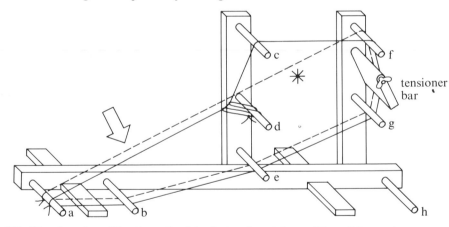

351 Warping: *dotted line* the path of the first end, and the position of the tensioner bar is for this first thread – a longer warp could be made by zig-zagging $g - e - h - b$; *solid line* the path of the second thread. The *arrow* shows the point at which weaving takes place, the *star* is the point at which your hand makes the shed, by depressing or lifting these threads.

Making the leashes

The leashes can be made of any smooth cotton or linen yarn: they do not move when on the loom, and therefore do not need to have special strength. They can be re-used for another warp; remember to tie them up, with a label stating how many there are in the bundle. To find out how many leashes are needed for a particular warp, calculate the sett in the usual way, remembering that the braid will be warp-faced, and halve the resulting number of threads to find the number of leashes required.

On some inkle looms the pegs above and below the tensioner bar (pegs *f* and *g*) are the right distance apart to use as a gauge to make the leashes.

When you have wound the leash thread round them the right number of times (once for each leash you need), cut through the hank, and tie each leash in a loop. On the same looms the vertical pair of pegs to the left (pegs c and d) are the right distance apart to use as a gauge for actually tying the leashes.

When the right number of leashes have been made, you can begin to dress the loom.

Dressing the inkle loom

It is difficult to get good selvedges on an inkle-band, and because it is so narrow, the selvedges show very clearly. It will help if you make the first and last threads slightly tighter than the rest of the warp: when winding them, tip the tensioner bar to an angle of 45 degrees; push it out to right angles when winding the rest of the warp.

Do not tie the warp threads to the pegs or the warp cannot be moved round the loom. The very first thread can be tied temporarily to peg a, then taken directly to peg f, and then back over the tensioner bar, by any route which will give the required length of warp, to peg a. Untie the temporary knot and tie the thread to itself at that point.

If the next thread is to be the same colour, start to wind it; if it is to be a different colour, tie the second colour to the first and wind that. If you will not be using the first colour again, cut it off, but if you will need it again later just leave it hanging and pick it up again and use it when required.

Take a leash loop; fold it over, with the knot at the end so that it cannot get in the way of the warp threads. As you fold it over, enclose the second warp thread, and with the help of your finger, slip the two leash loops onto peg d (352). The warp thread then goes over peg c, and then follows the path of the previous warp thread, back to peg a. These two warping actions are repeated until the warping is completed. Every alternate end is now passing directly to peg f, with the ones in between secured by leashes to peg d, then passing up and over peg c. Weaving can now begin.

Weaving on an inkle loom

The weft must be wound onto a *stick shuttle* (353), or a *belt shuttle* as this is also used to press the weft into place. The action of creating the shed is unique to inkle weaving: the weaver's hand presses alternately up and down that layer of warp which passes directly to peg f (marked with a star on 351) so that it passes through the other layer held down by the leashes (353). Weaving takes place at the point indicated by the arrow on 351.

When the weaving gets too close to the leashes, put the shuttle in the shed, slacken the warp by dropping the tensioner bar, and pull the shuttle with the weaving gently towards you. Then re-tighten the warp and continue to weave. Towards the end you will find it impossible to weave the last 20 to 30 cm (9 to 12 in), and the braid can be cut off.

Pattern weaving

There are many ways of making patterns. The following is one simple technique which, like all inkle patterning methods, involves the picking up of warp threads with the fingers. The results can be lettering or geometric designs and motifs. It is better done on a very fine warp, in order to get extra detail. Traditionally, the patterned or lettered braids are warped with coloured borders, and the central area, where the pattern is, is warped in alternating black and white ends – the black being *open* and the white *leashed*. Use the *down* shed for the pattern weft, passing right to left. Use the *up* shed for the plain weft, passing left to right.

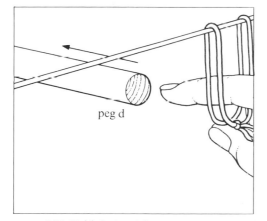

peg d

352 Fold the leash loop over the second warp end and transfer it to peg d with your finger.

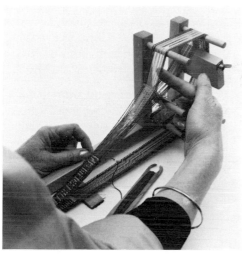

353 One shed is made by lowering these threads with the right hand, the other is made by raising *the same threads.*

125

To pick up a pattern open the down shed; insert the left hand. Beginning at the right-hand selvedge, with the *right* hand, pick up the desired pattern threads from the layer of black threads below, and *also* all the raised white threads, slipping the hand along until the left-hand edge is reached, and the new shed is on the right hand. Insert the shuttle and weave (354, 355). Return the weft on the next plain shed, the up shed. Alternate these pattern and plain sheds.

It may be helpful to plan the desired pattern first using squared paper.

354 Pattern weaving: pick up the pattern threads from below on the right hand.

355 Transfer the pattern threads to the left finger and insert the shuttle.

Tablet weaving

Tablet weaving doesn't need any loom at all, but it does need tablets – small square plates with a hole in each corner. Traditionally they were made of bone or wood – the earliest wooden tablet found has been dated at 400 BC – but more recently old playing cards have been used, cut into squares. You can buy plastic or cardboard tablets: they have rounded corners, and the four punched holes are lettered *a, b, c, d* or numbered 1, 2, 3, 4 in a clockwise direction. The tablets sometimes also have a central hole, and this can be used to tie them together during a pause in the weaving. You can make your own tablets; use an office punch to make smooth holes (356).

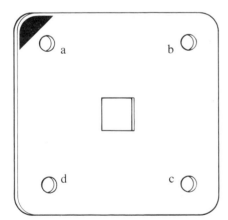

You will need about 30 of these tablets, depending on the width of the braids being woven, and the fineness of yarns used. The yarn used for tablet weaving must be smooth: it is a good idea to use cotton to begin with, but worsted, linen, and some embroidery and metallic threads also produce good braids.

Although no loom is needed, tablet weaving needs to have the warp under tension, and the easiest way to achieve this is to tie the far end of the warp to a tree or a door knob, and the near end to the back of your chair. Your weight on the chair will stop it moving, and you can also adjust the tension easily by shuffling the chair slightly one way or the other.

If long braids are needed, a loom can of course be used, with the warp beamed in the usual way but threading taking place through tablets instead of through shafts and reed. An inkle loom can also be used for tablet weaving, but one of the joys of this sort of weaving is its freedom from the necessity for equipment. Another of the pleasures of tablet weaving is that, because of its special structure, in which the warp twines around the weft, all sorts of elaborate patterns can be woven which are impossible to weave on a loom.

The two methods of tablet weaving

There are two ways of tablet-weaving:

1 Thread the holes in each card with different colours according to a *pattern*, then turn all the tablets together between each weft.

356 Tablets can be bought, or made at home.

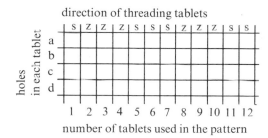

number of tablets used in the pattern

359 Reading a tablet weaving draft.

2 Thread all the holes with the same colour arrangement, but turn each tablet separately, or in groups, according to a set of instructions, between each weft.

Method 1

For this method it is necessary to be able to read a pattern;
once the principles have been grasped it will be possible to design your own.
You will find that tablet-weaving patterns for four-holed tablets have four rows; it is possible, however, to use tablets with fewer or more holes.
Each denotes a lettered hole in the tablet. The number of tablets used in that pattern is shown by the length of the pattern, each row representing a separate tablet. At the top of each column is an *s* or a *z*. This shows which way that particular tablet is to be threaded; s-threaded or z-threaded (357, 358, 359). The pattern in the centre will indicate the number of colours to be used, how many threads there are in each colour, and where they will need to be threaded.

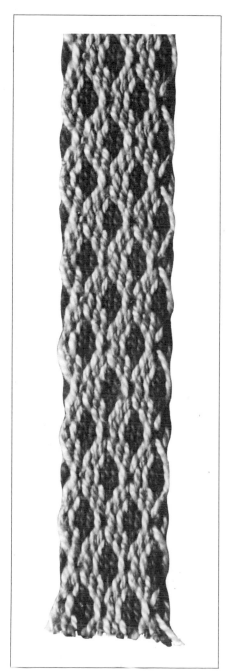

361 Diamond-patterned braid
by Pat Holtom.

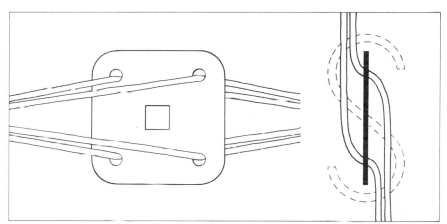

357 'S' threaded tablets, side and top views.

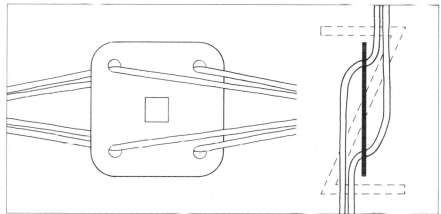

358 'Z' threaded tablets, side and top views.

Here is a typical pattern, giving a small diamond (360, 361).

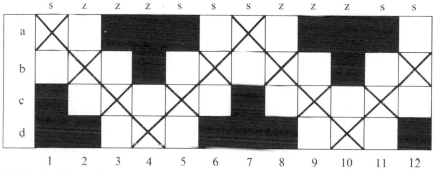

360 A draft for a diamond-patterned braid.

Method 1: Preparation

Cut lengths of yarn for the warp, each 120 cm (4 ft) long: this design will need sixteen dark threads, twelve medium threads, and twenty light threads. Lay them down the length of a table, and sit facing the ends. Have twelve tablets in a pile, on your right (number them temporarily, in pencil). Pick up the first one, collect one light thread, one medium, and two dark from the warp, and thread them through the holes (medium in *a*, light in *b*, dark in *c* and *d*) according to the symbol (in this case *s*, from the bottom upwards). Once it is threaded, lay the tablet down on your left. Take up the second tablet and thread it according to the pattern, noting that the direction of threading must change according to the symbol, in this case *z*. Lay it on top of the first tablet. After carefully following the pattern and threading all the tablets correctly, and knot the warp ends nearest you, first getting them even in order to avoid wastage. Smooth out the warp, tie the far end to a support and the near end to your chair (362).

362 The warp is stretched between the weaver's chair and a fixed object.

Method 1: How to weave

You are now ready to weave. The ingenious shedding action in tablet weaving is quite unlike that in any other form of weaving. By taking hold of the suspended pack of tablets in both hands and rotating them, one quarter turn at a time, a succession of new sheds is obtained. Pass a weft in each of these, and beat the pick with the shuttle.

So, if the pack starts off with holes *d* and *a* uppermost, it must be turned away from you so that *c* and *d* are at the top. You will find this easier to do if you don't squeeze the tablets tensely, but keep them under control. When this action is repeated and four picks have been woven, *d* and *a* will once again be at the top. *The rotating action must now be reversed*, turning the cards towards you for the next four turns. This will prevent any build-up of twist at the back of the warp, and is essential for the completion of the other half of this particular design. With some patterns, it can be effective to turn six, eight, or ten times before reversing – or not to reverse at all. Another solution for the building-up of twist is to have two weavers working together, one at each end of the warp, with one set of tablets in the middle which can then rotate in the same direction all the time.

It is important, if you leave the work, to tie the tablets firmly together and to make a note of the point you have reached in turning.

363 Details from silk tablet-woven garters, Greece, nineteenth century.

Method 2

The above method embodies the very simplest of tablet weaving techniques. By turning and manipulating tablets *separately* (not altogether in a pack), designs and structures of an extraordinary diversity and complexity can be woven, some of them very similar to those produced on a multi-shaft loom, some of them unique to tablet weaving.

This method usually requires all the tablets to carry the same arrangement of coloured warp threads, so a threading diagram is unnecessary. An arrangement with many possibilities is for each tablet to carry two dark threads in two adjacent holes and two light threads in the other adjacent holes. This can be quickly set up as follows; the tablets are threaded before the warp is made.

Method 2: Preparation

Stack the tablets into a neat pack so that their holes tally exactly, and thread the four warps through the whole pack, the two dark and the two light threads coming from four packages or spools. Knot these four threads

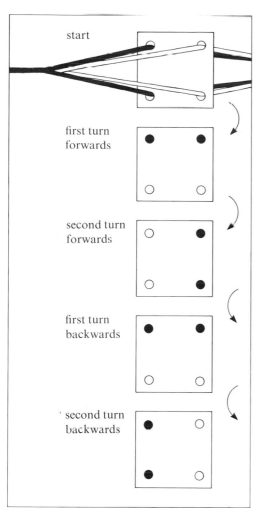

start

first turn
forwards

second turn
forwards

first turn
backwards

second turn
backwards

366 Turn all the tablets two quarter turns forward and two quarter turns backward, inserting a weft after each quarter turn.

together at one end and fasten to a warping post of some kind (364). Now, drawing the warp through the pack, lay it between two posts, releasing a tablet each time you pass the midway point. When all the tablets have been released, cut the warp and tie the four threads to the nearest post. The warp is now ready for weaving (365).

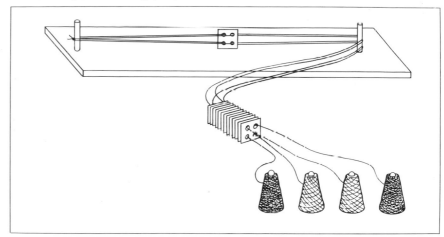

364 Thread through the pack of tablets, two dark and two light threads coming from four packages of yarn; fasten them to a post.

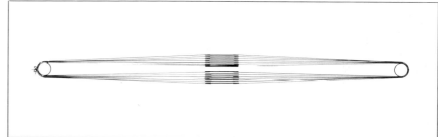

365 *Top view* The tablets threaded and ready for weaving.

Method 2: How to weave

For a much-used patterning technique, arrange the tablets so that they are alternately s- and z-threaded, and so that the dark threads in all the tablets are in the holes nearest the end of the warp where weaving is to start. Then weave with two quarter-turns forward, two quarter-turns backward, inserting a weft after each quarter turn (366). This frequent reversal of turning direction naturally prevents the warp threads from twining round each other, instead something very like a loom-woven warp-faced fabric is produced (363).

The dark colour will show only on the top surface, and the light colour only on the back. Now, to make a pattern – say, an inverted triangle of light on a dark ground – you must begin to move the tablets individually. Before either the two forward or the two backward turns, slide the two central tablets out of the pack, a little distance towards the far end of the warp (367, 368). For the next two picks, turn these in the *opposite* direction to the main pack. As a result, a light coloured spot will appear in the centre of the weaving, the point of the triangle. Now slide out the next tablet on each side to make four in the far pack, and again turn this pack in the opposite direction to the main pack for the next two picks (369). Take care that the shed made by the far pack reaches the fell of the weaving. Continue adding a tablet at each side of the far pack, and the triangle you are weaving will gradually increase in width. Reversing the procedure at some point – that is, sliding back a tablet from each side of the far pack before either the two forward or two backward turns – will diminish the width of the triangle, eventually forming a diamond.

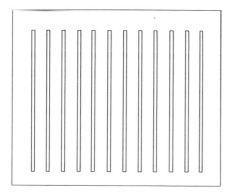

367 *Top view* Warp threads omitted; start with one main pack

With practice, this technique becomes very flexible, and you can weave letters, numbers, animals and flowers, as seen on the old Persian bands (370). The weave does not give a neat selvedge, so turn several tablets at each side of the pack continuously in the same direction to make a firm, warp-twined edge.

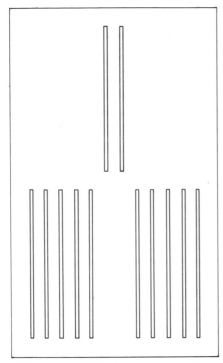

368 *Top view* Slide the centre two tablets out along the warp to make a far pack, and turn them in the opposite direction to the main pack for two picks.

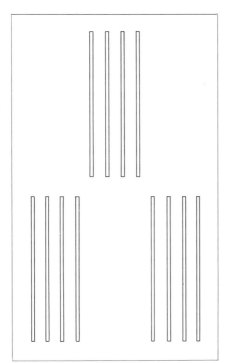

369 *Top view* Slide out the next tablet on each side and add to the far pack; turn the far pack in the opposite direction to the main pack for two picks.

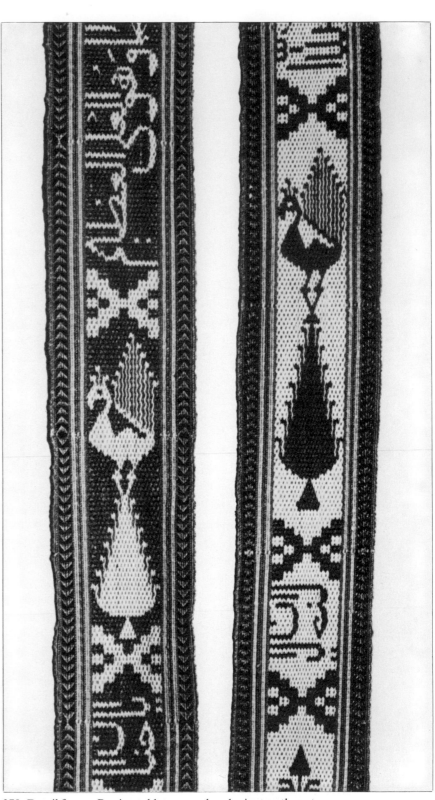

370 Detail from a Persian tablet-woven band, nineteenth century.

Chapter Fourteen

Woven hangings

Weavers use the techniques described in this book in many ways. Most professional handweavers tend to specialise in their products, choosing to make either garments or rugs, furnishings, or tapestries or other forms of wall-hanging. Once learned, techniques can often be put aside, and, especially in the field of wall-hangings, innovation may take over. Practically, the wall-hanging has few limitations: it does not have to drape, be cut, lie flat on the floor, wear well, wash well or perform any normal cloth function. So it is in this field, more than any other, that the weaver's imagination and ingenuity can be exercised. Within this freedom lies danger, however, and a few years ago 'novelty' was of paramount importance, resulting in much wild work of little value. Now, more weavers are realising the value of the technical disciplines, not only for their own sakes but for the controlling element which they can contribute to a concept, ideally refining it in the process. The weaving process is attracting more and more serious artists, who see in it an integral and inherent discipline not to be found in the use of paint or the traditional materials of sculpture.

Re-thinking may well start at the yarn stage: uncommon yarns, sometimes invented yarns, can often demand a new technique, which may also have to be invented. This technique may in some cases even suggest a form for the resulting hanging. Many weavers, however, take their inspiration from the study of natural forms: plants, animals, people and landscape, and they will do much drawing and painting or take colour notes. These studies are rarely translated directly into textile form, except by some tapestry weavers, but serve to extend the weaver's knowledge of form and colour, suggesting personal ways of working with weaving.

What follows is a small 'gallery' of work – it is in no way comprehensive – which may give an idea of the range and variety of woven hangings in this country.

Theo Moorman is an established weaver who has been working for many years in her own inlay technique. Continually inventive, she breaks away from the conventional square or rectangle of woven fabric by weaving this hanging in several bands, each of which is tapered towards beginning and end (371). She achieves this by using a small, fan-shaped reed of her own devising. The strips are assembled in a twisted state, so that light is reflected by the lustrous, silvery-grey yarn in the weft.

Margaret Smitten uses a dobby loom (149, 150) for many of the repeated elements on her hangings of houses and gardens. She programmes the loom to weave rows of windows, roof tiles, and trees in orchards, which she then assembles into the large buildings with their formal grounds which is one of her favourite themes (colour 21). This technique is ideally suited to the dobby loom, which is designed to produce repeats of weaves (372, 373) and is generally used for industrial designing. Margaret Smitten is one of only a few weavers to use it in this way to produce hangings.

Tadek Beutlich started weaving in the traditional Gobelin tapestry technique, but later, in the 1960s, developed the use of unusual materials in his woven hangings. Linen was combined with charred wood, X-ray film and honesty pods in an extensive series of transparent hangings. He also pioneered the use of large quantities of unspun jute in dramatic and huge pieces such as 'Eruption', which is 280 cm × 325 cm (9 ft 4 in × 10 ft 10 in), (16). More recently his work has become small in scale, and the square hanging illustrated (colour 15) measures only 30 cm (12 in), although it is 20 cm (8 in) deep, with brilliantly coloured yarns of all fibres, matt and shiny, wrapping

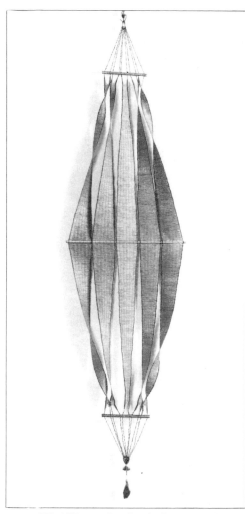

371 'Silver twisted strips' by Theo Moorman; a fan-shaped reed produces the tapered panels.

372 Part of a dobby-woven panel, 'Orchard', by Margaret Smitten.

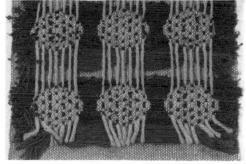

373 Reverse side of Margaret Smitten's 'Orchard'.

374 The reverse side of Tadek Beutlich's panel 'Burning moss', showing the wrapped and woven foundation.

375 'Roots' by Maggie Riegler, incorporating weaving and wrapping.

around loops of esparto grass. These loops are interwoven at the back, to form a woven foundation, into which is looped and bound the 'pile' (374). He does not use a loom for this type of weaving, but works it all in his hands.

John Hinchcliffe's rag rugs (colour 4) are woven in strips on the loom, using the double-corduroy technique. This is a weave developed by Peter Collingwood in order to speed up the insertion of a weft pile. The pile yarn (in this case cloth cut into long strips) weaves in for several ends and then floats for several centimetres (inches), to be woven in again. The floats can then be cut, so that the ends stand up as a pile, which is automatically anchored by the woven areas. A few picks of plain weave are inserted between the pile weft. (For more details, see Peter Collingwood's book *The techniques of rug weaving*.) His exotic but subtle colouring is obtained by carefully controlled dyeing and over-dyeing of the cloths used. Although these rugs are sturdy enough to be used on the floor, most of them are designed as wall-hangings.

Maggie Riegler works on an upright loom in a mixture of weaving techniques as well as macramé, plaiting and wrapping, to produce free two- and three-dimensional forms. In 'Roots' (375), inspired by the roots of a birch tree, she has recreated the 'grotesque and reptilian' qualities which attracted her to the subject.

Archie Brennan is the doyen of British tapestry weavers, and for many years he ran the Edinburgh Tapestry Company at the Dovecot Studios. His tapestries are often humorous in subject (5) and he uses, as part of his imagery, devices which are technically useful in tapestry weaving: the narrow lines flickering across a television screen in his portraits of Mohammed Ali, or in 'The runner' (385).

Candace Bahouth uses the classical tapestry technique for her work, but develops it into shaped and three-dimensional forms – often portraits – adding unusual materials for extra dynamism: hair for beards, feathers, beads or tinsel (colour 22).

David Hill uses a traditional tapestry technique also, but changes the usual flat surface subtly with variations in yarn. In this tapestry (376) he has been inspired by the repetitive elements in African patterning, and by the way in which slight variations ensure that the design does not become a simple, perhaps boring, repeat.

376 Tapestry by David Hill; the imagery comes from geometric African designs.

377 A detail of 'Zig-Zag three' by Ruth Harris, showing diagonal soumak on a tapestry ground.

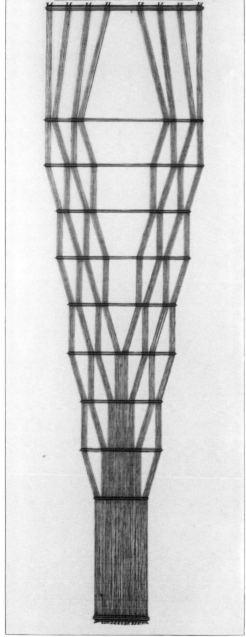

378 Macrogauze hanging by Peter Collingwood; the warp threads do not cross, space is introduced between them.

Maureen Hodge also works in tapestry technique. In 'A hill for my friend' (124), she has used the medieval device of *mille fleurs*, in which small flowers were woven all over the ground. Her tapestries often include lettering, and have mystical and private themes.

Using a diagonal soumak technique, **Ruth Harris** weaves hangings based on 'man's mark on the earth's surface' – such as ploughed fields, excavations and quarrying (colour 18, 377).

A normal loom produces a textile in which each warp thread must of necessity lie parallel to the selvedge, but **Peter Collingwood** has invented a loom which frees the warp from this limitation and in his macrogauze hangings the warp threads lie at various angles (378). He achieves this by dispensing with the usual shafts and reed, and having in their place a number of narrow rigid heddles housed side by side in a special rigid batten. Each rigid heddle is threaded with its own separate linen warp, which is wound on a weighted bobbin and hung over the back bar of the loom (379). The light-weight batten is on springs, and so can move up and down to give the two plain weave sheds. At any point in the weaving, the top of the batten can be raised on its hinges, and the rigid heddles rearranged, in order to give angled crossings of warp threads (380). He uses the minimum of linen weft, combined with fine steel rods to keep the hanging flat (381, 382). Sometimes Peter Collingwood also adds rods after weaving to open out the textile into a three-dimensioned structure (383), but in all cases it is the warp which is dominant, and it is from the movement of the warp that macrogauzes derive their original designs.

379 Macrogauze loom, showing many small warp bobbins hanging from the back.

380 Crossing over the separate rigid heddles in the batten, with their warp.

381 Steel rod entering the shed beyond the clamp which holds the crossed warp in position.

382 Weaving the few picks of linen weft which follow the rod.

384 A cube measuring 8 cm (3 in) woven in tiny panels on a loom by Ann Sutton.

"........I AM NOT EVEN THE GREATEST. DISTANCE RUNNER IN GATESHEAD."

385 'The runner', a tapestry by Archie Brennan.

Ann Sutton In my work, I explore permutations and systems of colour placing: in 'Transition spectrum permutation' (colour 20), I also use the mixing of colours thrown up by the permutation – often they appear to be bizarre combinations of colour. The structure is a collection of woven squares – not woven on a loom, but darned on nails on a small board, so that I can obtain a selvedge on each side of every square. The coloured ones are wool – the transparent ones (which are there for invisible structural support, not decorative shadows) are made of nylon monofilament. As well as working on a large scale, I also work in miniature, and in 'Primary unit cube', which measures 7·5 cm (3 in) (384), I have investigated a way of joining small squares (woven on a loom) so that warp is linked to weft, to become a cube. The resulting form is stiff – the cube is not filled in any way.

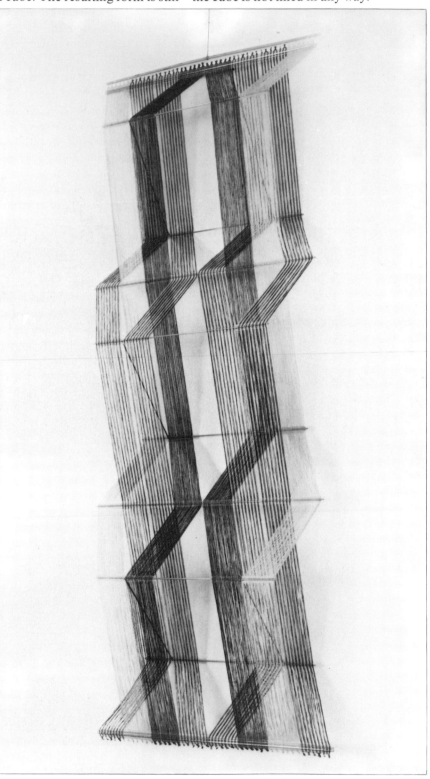

383 Macrogauze hanging by Peter Collingwood, made three-dimensional by inserting stretch rods after the weaving is cut from the loom.

Chapter Fifteen

Historical textiles

by Peter Collingwood

Textiles have been woven for at least 10,000 years. Such historical textiles are always a source of great interest and inspiration to the modern weaver, because they show him how, in the past, the raw material of his craft, the thread, has been manipulated into an incredible variety of techniques and patterns. Every culture has had its own special textiles, recognisably distinct from all others, some functional, some ceremonial, some simply woven, some amazingly complex. One might therefore think that a history of textiles is nothing less than a history of mankind, but this is to forget their perishability. Unlike pottery, which though easily broken is practically indestructible, old textiles are easily destroyed by bacteria, moths and chemical action: the great majority of all textiles ever woven have unfortunately rotted away.

So there are many gaps preventing the telling of a continuous story, and these gaps naturally become longer the further back in time one goes. In fact, the few textiles which survive from very early times owe their preservation to freak conditions, resulting, for instance, from burial in very dry, sandy soil (as in Egypt, 5000 BC, and in Peru, 8000 BC); or from submersion in water or boggy ground (as in Switzerland, 2500 BC and Denmark, 1400 BC; North Germany, AD 200); or from being permanently frozen (Siberia, 600 BC); or being converted into metallic rust or carbon (Catal Huyuk, 6000 BC; Susa, 3000 BC). This small quantity of evidence makes immensely valuable each blackened textile fragment recovered from an archaeological site; some researchers spend all their time trying to wrest the maximum of information from such unpromising artefacts.

The history of the earliest textiles is therefore patchy, a disconnected list of chance survivals. Later on, the history is still unbalanced as it concerns only rich and expensive textiles, because these were the ones consciously preserved. Luxurious silks and velvets were treasured as works of art and were used for burial clothes for kings, for gifts and as wrappings for sacred relics. On the other hand, the common everyday textiles which formed the majority of woven fabrics were used until worn out, then discarded. So from about AD 500 to 1500 the history of textiles in Europe is largely concerned with silk textiles, owned or worn by an elite minority. It is only from very recent times that we have a complete record of *all* textiles woven.

The beginnings

The interworking of two sets of materials at right angles is found in basketry and mat-making, as well as in weaving. In early finds, as in Guitarrero Cave, Peru, dated from 8000 BC, it is often difficult to distinguish between them because the difference lies more in the method of production than in the result. Basketry uses stiff materials and so can be worked with the hands alone; weaving uses soft spun threads and so needs a loom to tension and make manageable one set of materials, the warp. In fact, one theory for the origin of the loom could be that early man evolved it in order to give his flexible threads the rigidity, and therefore ease of handling, that he found in his basket-making materials. But it is an over-simplification to suggest one path by which the thread-stretcher, the loom, was invented. Civilisation is said to have evolved independently in at least six places in the world, and the loom may have come into being by a different combination of chance discoveries and logical steps in each place.

Weaving can be done with natural threads, such as raffia, but more usually the threads are spun – which suggests that the discovery of spinning preceded that of weaving. The twisting and plying of raw material to make

386 Steatite spindle whorl; Mycenaean. 1400–1200 BC.

thread or cord is hinted at by the fine bone needles found in Europe from 10,000 BC, probably used for sewing skins together; it is first actually seen in a fragment of a fishing net from mesolithic times. A wooden stick can be used for spinning, and this of course leaves no archaeological trace. Adding a stone or clay whorl increases its efficiency, and such whorls often survive (386). Eight thousand were found in the earliest level at Troy (3000 BC), though not a single item of weaving.

In the earliest finds of interworking two sets of spun threads at right angles, the majority were made by weft-twining – that is, by twisting two wefts around each other enclosing a warp thread in each twist (387). At Huaca Prieta, a Peruvian village of 2500 BC, over three-quarters of the textiles found in the rubbish dump were weft-twined, and less than a twentieth were interlaced – that is, truly woven. In both of these techniques, short wefts were used, just long enough to cross the warp once and then be tied in pairs at the selvedge. This is thought to represent a moment in history before the invention of leashes. At that stage, it was just as quick and easy to twine two threads across a stretched warp as to darn them across with a needle; but once leashes were invented and combined with a shed stick, two clear plain-weave sheds for the weft could be opened up all across the warp. This crucial invention immediately made interlacing far quicker than twining, and all later archaeological finds show that weaving became the most popular method of fabric production. It continues in that position today, although weft-twining still lingers on for certain specialised uses.

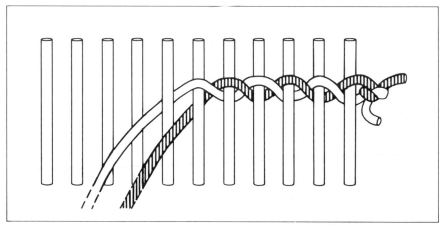

387 Weft-twining.

The Huaca Prieta fabrics were mainly warp-faced, the obvious construction to choose if the passage of the weft is slow and difficult, because this method needs fewer picks per centimetre (inch). But with easily produced sheds, the weaving of weft-faced fabrics became practical and new techniques like tapestry could develop. The existence of the shed also meant that a shuttle, instead of a needle, could be passed, carrying enough weft for many rows of weaving, and that a sword could be introduced for beating the weft.

The shed is therefore absolutely basic to weaving. Many subsequent loom innovations can be seen as efforts to refine the shed, so that the weaver, always seeking new textures and patterns, gradually achieved a more direct control over the raising of each individual thread. Perhaps this mainly occurred where weaving became a profession, when there was an economic advantage in being able to weave fabrics your rivals could not. But it may also have resulted from a desire to explore and experiment which seems to have possessed weavers from all times and places. Such innovations included the use of several sets of leashes so that twill could be woven, the development of shafts which could both raise and lower threads and, being worked by pedals, left the hands free for shuttle throwing and beating, and finally, the invention of the draw loom and jacquard.

Other shed-making devices were developed for the weaving of narrow bands, such as tablets (known from 600 BC) and rigid heddles (known from Roman times), both of which still exist in their original forms up to the present day.

136

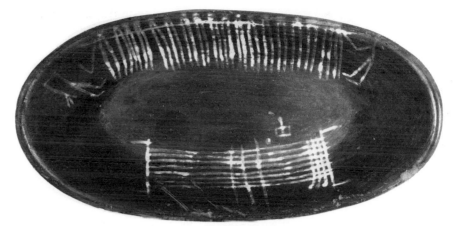

388 Horizontal ground loom depicted on a dish from Badari, Egypt, about 4500 BC.

389 Horizontal ground loom as painted on a tomb at Beni Hasan, Egypt, about 1900 BC; the person on the right is plying.

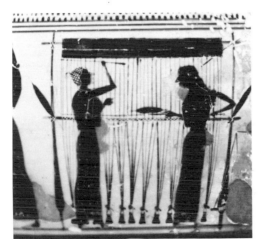

390 Warp-weighted loom on a Greek vase painting, 560 BC.

Like the textiles woven on them, most early looms have rotted away. The earliest representation of a loom exists on an Egyptian dish from 4500 BC, which clearly shows a warp stretched out between two beams pegged to the ground (388). This is the typical horizontal ground loom still used today by nomadic tribes. Egyptian tomb paintings of a later date also show this type (1900 BC, 389), and a vertical frame loom (1500 BC), being used by weavers working singly or in pairs.

The warp-weighted loom was another very important type, which was used for cloth weaving from earliest times. As Greek vase paintings from 600 BC show, the warp was tensioned with weights at ground level; weaving began at the top and progressed downwards, the weft being beaten upwards (390). The loom weights, made of stone or clay and pierced for attaching to the warp, have survived in large quantities, occasionally lying in two neat rows exactly as they would have fallen from the loom. They are found all over Europe and as far east as the Urals. As some date from 3000 BC, they constitute the earliest surviving *physical* evidence of a loom.

391 Beating the weft upwards with the fingers on a warp-weighted loom, while weaving a wool blanket; North Norway, 1955.

392 Part of a Navaho blanket in grey, brown, black and white.

The warp-weighted loom is still in use in Scandinavia (391), but it was superseded in many places around AD 1000 by the horizontal floor loom, probably an import from the East, the type still used by most hand-weavers today.

Summary of world textiles

Despite gaps in our knowledge, there is still enough known about textiles from the past and from recent times to give us a wealth of material to discuss. What follows is a summary of the highlights of weaving from various parts of the world, and then a closer look in greater detail at three particular areas: textiles in Egypt, weaving in Peru, and silk weaving in the Middle East and Europe.

A simple listing of highlights is a formidable task. Even excluding textiles in complex techniques unfamiliar to most hand-weavers it is still a long list, but it would have to include the following:

The Americas

Early cottons from the Southwest United States in a large range of very interesting techniques, made from AD 1300 onwards.

Blankets woven by Navaho Indians from about 1850 onwards, (392, 103). They were tapestry woven, with four selvedges, by women who never repeated their designs; the designs are usually geometric and beautifully coloured.

Costumes of Mexico and Guatemala; brilliantly coloured, still very much a part of life today, especially in the Highlands.

Textiles of Colombia, Bolivia and, of course, Peru (see separate section, Page 143).

The Far East

Silk warp-faced weaves in two or more colours, with freely curving designs; geometric gauzes (404) and simple float weaves from the Han Dynasty (205 BC to AD 220) in China.

Meticulous kasuri (tie-dye) work on cotton and silk, and simple striped plain weaves, often resembling tartans, from Japan, a country of inventive and skilled weavers (79). The contents of the Shoso-in, an Imperial treasury founded in AD 756, which has the world's finest collection of eighth-century textiles, many from China.

Incredible geometric warp ikats from Borneo, Sumatra and Bali (78), the many supplementary warp and weft designs from Sumba and Sumatra and the Javanese and Balinese batiks. These Indonesian textiles, usually of cotton, have designs of a staggering richness and complexity; every inch of the cloth is covered with motifs or little background patterns, yet all is so perfectly organised that there is no suggestion of muddle.

Extraordinarily fine cotton muslins from Dacca (with names like 'woven air'), gold-brocaded silks from Benares and flowered muslins from Bengal are all examples of the outstanding textiles from India woven in the great Moghul dynasty in the sixteenth century.

Kashmir shawls, tapestry woven from very fine wool in 2/1 twill (not the more normal plain weave) with their intricate and distinctive patterns (12). These Indian products were imported into Europe and resulted in the setting-up of shawl industries in Paisley and Norwich, and in Lyons in France where imitations were woven on draw looms.

393 Bag used by nomads for carrying salt, in skip plain weave technique, Baluchistan.

394 Roll of narrow cotton cloth as sold in the market, Africa; strips like these are then sewn together to make clothes.

The patola (colour 3); a large silk double-ikat (a fabric in which both warp and weft have been tie-dyed to a very careful design – an extremely skilful technique) is still made in Gujarat on a loom with a strangely tilted breast beam.

Bold and dazzling warp ikats from Central Asia.

The Middle East

Knotted rugs (a technique known from 500 BC, colour 26) with a bewildering range of place and tribal names, the Persian usually being floral (colour 23), the Caucasian and Turkestan geometric (colour 25).

Flat, woven kilim rugs and hangings (see Page 110, colour 24), a technique known from 2500 BC, varying from boldly patterned and coloured Caucasian and Anatolian to the darker and exceedingly fine Sehna.

Rarer rugs in the soumak technique, often copying designs of local knotted rugs.

As well as producing these famous rugs, this area is the source of many other textiles used by nomadic tribesmen in their everyday life: these include grain bags, salt bags (393), tent hangings, camel trappings, cushions, saddlebags (colour 17), shoulder bags and even Koran bags. All are satisfyingly sturdy, made of wool or goathair with simple but time-consuming decorative weaving techniques; often embellished with beads, shells and elaborate tassels.

Africa

A vast range of textiles varying in material (mostly cotton, wool and raffia, but also silk and bast fibres in some areas), in technique (practically every method based on plain weave) and in use (everyday clothing, ceremonial and funerary cloths, dance costumes). Outstanding are the very narrow strips (394), with indigo dyed stripes, woven in Ghana and Nigeria, which are sewn together to make clothing (14); the Bakuba raffia cloths, decorated with soumak and raffia pile (colour 30); the white wool blankets from Mali with brocaded patterns in madder and black (6); the shaped Berber cloaks; and the intriguing *liar's cloth* from Ghana which embodies threads which act now as warp, now as weft.

The long series of Egyptian textiles from 4000 BC to AD 1200 (see separate section, next page).

Europe

Stone Age linens with very complicated soumak designs from the Swiss Lake dwellings, dated 2500 BC onwards. (A similar but later lake site at Glastonbury, England, yielded only spindle whorls and loom weights, no textiles.)

Danish oak coffin burials from 1150 BC contain the most perfect record of prehistoric clothing in the world, including seven complete outfits of male and female clothing, all in wool. They are mostly plain weave, but with tablet weaving, sprang and looping as well.

Impressive woollen cloaks from North German bog burials, AD 200 to 300, woven in twill, with not only the starting border worked on tablets, which is typical of textiles made on the warp-weighted loom, but with wide side and finishing borders worked on tablets as well.

The great parade of tapestries intended as wall decorations; 'April and May' from Baldishol, Norway (twelfth century, colour 37); the amazing 'Apocalypse' series from Angers cathedral (fourteenth century, colour 36);

395 Typical detail from one of the 'Lady and the unicorn' tapestries; about 1400.

396 'L'Astrapate', a tapestry by Jean Lurçat, France, 1948

the 'Lady and the unicorn' at Cluny sixteenth century, (395, colour 11), right up to those inspired by Jean Lurçat in this century (396), which rejected the detailed copying of artists' designs and returned to a mediaeval simplicity.

Rich and endlessly elaborate silk weaving, which dominates the museum collections (see separate section, Page 146).

Linen textiles woven in the flax-producing areas of northern Europe, from 1500 onwards; especially the exceedingly fine damask tablecloths, up to 2×4 metres (7×14 feet) in size, with central designs such as battle scenes and banquets.

'Peasant' weaving, especially from eastern Europe, including double cloths (266) and rya rugs (colour 27), from Scandinavia, Bulgarian aprons, tablet-woven belts and other items of clothing from Yugoslavia.

Egypt

Egypt's climate is hot and dry, and therefore ideal for the preservation of textile materials, and the country has yielded a wealth of textiles, dated from 4500 BC onwards. The earliest are burial shrouds which were wrapped around mummified bodies. Like all Egyptian textiles until the end of the Dynasties in 332 BC, they are exclusively of linen. Wool may have been used for clothing, but being considered impure, was prohibited from burials, although a few balls of red and blue wool have turned up in some tombs. The first shrouds are unpatterned plain weave, but they represent feats of weaving, being up to $1 \cdot 5 \times 18$ metres (5×60 feet) in size, and of spinning. The fineness of the spinning is shown by thread counts which could be as high as 64 ends per cm (160 ends per inch) and 48 picks per cm (120 picks per inch). Such an incredibly fine linen fabric has an almost silky softness and is worlds away from the tough and sturdy linen used, for instance, in an English smock (283).

It was not until 2600 BC that any patterning appeared, and then it only consisted of blue warp and weft stripes and, later, pulled-up weft loops. Our knowledge from this time is not only dependent on the surviving textiles, but also on the detailed tomb paintings, such as those at Beni Hasan, which show the cultivation, spinning and weaving of linen (389). Even more instructive are the amazing miniature models of textile workshops found in tombs from about 2000 BC (397). In these, doll-like wooden figures spin on spindles with the whorl uppermost, warp on wall pegs and weave on the ground

397 Wooden model of a spinning and weaving workshop, found in a tomb at Deir-el-Bahri, Egypt, about 1800 BC.

loom. The weavers squat in a cramped position on the floor, recalling the contemporary comment, 'The weaver in the workshops, he is worse than a woman, with his thighs against his belly. He cannot breathe the open air. If he cut short the day of weaving, he is beaten with fifty thongs.' These conditions, and those of the 'Chosen women' in Peru (see Page 143) would seem to show that although weavers were reduced to the condition of slaves, they still managed to produce textiles of great beauty and craftsmanship.

The first elaborate patterning technique to appear was tapestry; it is interesting that this coincides both with the arrival of weavers from Syria and with the first tomb paintings of a vertical frame loom – the type traditionally associated with tapestry weaving. The earliest tapestry is a rather crude representation of the name of Thotmes III found on a cloth in a tomb dated 1405 BC. But one-and-a-half centuries later, as shown in the exceedingly rich collection of textiles from Tutankhamun's tomb, tapestry was well developed, being used there for belts, hangings and a complete tunic.

This find also included a linen fabric with an incredible 112 warp threads per cm (280 per in) and many separately woven braids sewn onto the edges of textiles. The technique of these braids seems to be related to that of a unique and beautiful belt, the so-called 'Girdle of Rameses III', dated 1197 BC (398). This masterpiece is woven in four colours of linen, using a type of warp-face double cloth never recorded elsewhere; it was previously believed to have been made on tablets. By means of dropping off warp threads, the belt gradually tapers throughout its length of 5 metres (5½ yards).

After Alexander the Great conquered Egypt and the Dynasties came to an end, the country came under the Greek Ptolemies. The use of wool now made possible the dyeing of bright colours, which are found in more elaborate patterns. This period now seems like an interlude between the great textiles of dynastic Egypt and those to follow them from the Coptic weavers.

Christianity became the official religion of Egypt about AD 380 and its adherents were known as Copts. Believing in the resurrection, the Copts no longer mummified their dead but buried them in complete outfits of everyday clothes, sometimes badly worn and even patched. These textiles have survived in a truly remarkable condition, due to the siting of the graves in dry regions, well above the level of the Nile's annual flood. This practice continued until about the twelfth century, and has resulted in a mass of excavated textiles, mainly from Akhmim and Antinoe, which provide

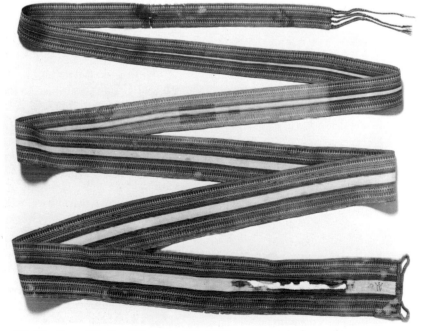

398 The linen 'Girdle of Rameses III', 1197 BC, woven in four colours; the dropping-off of warp threads makes the belt taper gradually over 5 m (5½ yd).

a stylistic progression unparalleled in any other medium. The immense numbers involved are such that practically every museum has a collection of Coptic textiles: the Victoria and Albert Museum, for example, has over 2,500 pieces. Unfortunately, many were dug up in an unscientific manner, or bought from dealers, so their dating presents a problem. This difficulty is increased by the fact that the styles were successively influenced by Byzantine, Islamic and Persian invaders. Indeed, it is doubtful if those woven after the Islamic conquest of AD 650 were really woven by or for Copts.

Without doubt the favourite technique of the Coptic weavers was tapestry. The many small separate pieces in museums were originally an integral part of large, rectangular Coptic tunics, which they decorated in the form of neck bands, panels and roundels. A few such tunics have survived complete and are very impressive cloak-like garments (399). Though some were all wool or all linen, the majority were woven of wool across a linen warp. In the tapestry areas, the warp threads were grouped into twos or threes to reduce the effective ends per centimetre (inch), and so make the structure weft-faced. The main tunic weft floated behind such areas if they were small, but turned back at the edge of large areas. Some fragmentary but impressive tapestries, intended just as decoration, have also survived (138).

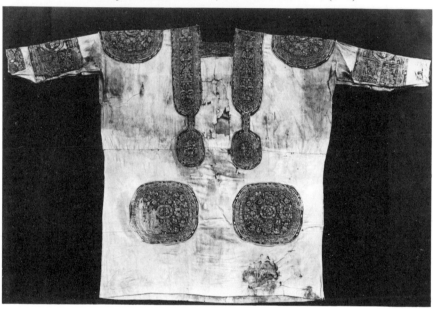

399 Linen tunic with tapestry areas woven in wool, probably from Akhmim, Egypt, sixth to eighth century.

The tapestries used many subjects, often human figures, animals or fish, taken from classical, Christian and Persian traditions (406). These were interpreted, at least initially, in a characteristically lively way, the weavers often using wefts lying not at the usual 90-degree angle to the warp, but obliquely. This in turn led to the warps being pulled sideways out of their normal alignment. In fact, seen under magnification, the textiles show an incredible degree of movement of both warp and weft and this helped the weavers to achieve lifelike curves and contours even on the small scale at which they were working. This immensely skilful but free method of weaving makes Coptic tapestries instantly recognisable. Though many colours were used in some pieces, perhaps the most satisfying are those which rely only on purple and natural wool yarns, alone and in mixtures. One such type has entirely geometric designs worked in fine white lines on a purple background.

For decorative panels the Copts used another and quicker technique, pulled-up loops (400), but as it did not lend itself to fine detail, it was suitable only for large scale designs. In some cases the loops covered the surface completely, in others only the motifs showed as loops, the remainder being flat plain weave. The wool weft for looping was much thicker than the background weft and was dyed in many colours. One such pattern pick, perhaps consisting of many overlapping yarns of different colours, would be followed by several picks of the background weft.

400 Linen cloth with figure of running boy worked in pulled-up loops of coloured wool; Egypt, fourth to fifth century.

142

These two textiles, tapestries and pulled-up loops, were in all probability woven on vertical frame looms. However, far more sophisticated equipment was required for textiles of another type excavated from the same graves. These show small motifs exactly repeated in two colours, woven from woollen wefts taking an over-3, under-1 course across a linen warp. Such a textile could be produced only with some sort of *draw* apparatus, presumably housed over a horizontal frame loom. The *draw loom* is one where the weaver has individual control of every thread in each repeat, and is similar to a Jacquard loom today. Incidentally, this is the same structure as that found in the earliest Persian silks, suggesting that Persian weavers were employing an existing Coptic technique for the newly imported eastern yarn.

The Egyptian textile achievement lay in two quite different fields: the production of austere, extremely fine linen cloths in the Dynastic period; and the weaving of very lively and colourful small tapestries in the Coptic era. In both fields the Egyptian weavers were outstanding.

Peru

Peru holds a unique position in weaving history in that its artistic expression was concentrated in its textiles. The very earliest are too fragmentary to base judgements on, but at least from 2500 BC until the Spanish conquest in AD 1532, Peruvian weavers poured out a range of textiles whose beauty and daring technical innovation overawe any hand-weaver who studies them. The inhabitants of Huaca Prieta, a village on the north coast of Peru around 2500 BC, could not make pottery or work metal and they relied on simple stone tools, yet, though virtually living in the Stone Age, they were able to make intricately structured cotton fabrics, with patterns of eagles and snakes in red, blue and natural brown. Huaca Prieta has yielded at least three thousand of these warp-faced fabrics which testify to this strange imbalance of skills. These skills persisted, because through the following centuries Peruvian weavers seem to have tried every possible technique in weaving, often both in a warp-faced and a weft-faced version – also many techniques which with our time-scale of working we would classify as extremely impractical, such as warp-interlock tapestry. They carried every one of these weaves to its uttermost limit of complexity – with the remarkable exception of twills, which occur only rarely. They also delighted in juxtaposing several methods in one fabric as if to demonstrate the ease with which they could move from one to another. Their use of a great range of natural and dyed colours is also exceptional, and was sometimes based on rules and sequences which present-day scholars are still deciphering and analysing.

The superlatives which Peruvian weaving unfailingly invokes are reinforced by further study, because this always uncovers new and unrecorded variations. One's admiration is further increased by the realisation that they were pre-eminent not only in weaving, but also in sprang, braiding and embroidery – in fact all types of thread work. They even used knots on cords as their only way of recording numbers, having no system of writing.

The spinning and weaving was the work of women. Under Inca rule, girls were officially classified at the age of ten, the most beautiful, the 'Chosen women' being sent away to learn weaving, cooking and to study religion. After this education, they were again classified and some were directed to shrines, such as the Sun Temple at Cuzco, to weave the fine ceremonial textiles. Presumably the humbler textiles were woven by women at home under less coercive conditions. Work-baskets containing spindles, balls of yarn and other small implements are often found in the graves of women.

Huaca Prieta is on the north coast of Peru, but the great majority of textile finds come from the extremely arid regions of the south coast. Here, as in Egypt, the conditions were ideal for the preservation of organic material, and textiles remarkable for their fresh appearance and colouring have been excavated in large quantities from the Paracas Necropolis and the Nazca

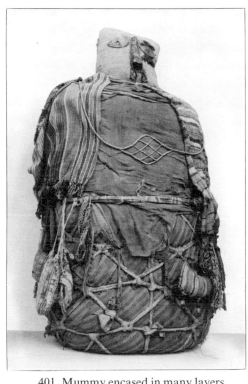

401 Mummy encased in many layers of cloth and hung about with bags, from a burial ground on the North coast of Peru, 1200–1400.

143

cemeteries (500 to 300 BC). Bodies were buried here (401), seated in baskets and wrapped around with cotton cloths into which were tucked new and unworn articles of clothing, such as mantles, capes, skirts and head bands, as many as a hundred and fifty in one case. The cloths were sometimes exceedingly large, in one instance measuring 4 metres wide by 25 metres long (13 feet wide by 84 feet long). These may have been woven on a much narrower backstrap loom (the typical Peruvian tool) (402), by working several interconnected layers which were later opened out. The garments were mostly woven of yarn spun from llama and vicuña wool. Starting with such very fine fibres, the Peruvian spinners were able to spin the finest and most perfect wool yarns ever made; they were occasionally as much as three times finer than the finest worsted yarn spun industrially today. For this work, very small spindles, presumably supported in a cup, were needed.

402 Backstrap looms depicted around the edge of a pottery dish from the Mochica period, Peru; before 1000.

The techniques which were pioneered by the Peruvians and which are often found nowhere else in the world, are really too complex to be explained here, but you can read more about them in a number of books (see Booklist). We will just look at two methods which they developed to a high degree.

Tapestry Tapestry seems to have been one of the favourite Peruvian techniques and the best Peruvian tapestries are certainly among the masterpieces of textile art. The method appears early, about 850 BC, and was then worked entirely in cotton. In the Paracus and Nazca finds it is also present, now made of wool, but it is overshadowed by the many embroideries of those periods. It reached its peak in the Tiahuanaco period (colour 28 and 31, AD 700–1000) in the southern highlands of Peru, but was still carried on throughout the subsequent Chancay (back cover 2), and Inca periods.

The warp was always cotton and sometimes set as closely as 25 ends per cm (64 ends per in); the weft was finely spun llama or vicuña wool, and counts of up to 200 picks per cm (500 picks per in) have been recorded. The corresponding figures for an average European tapestry might be 6 ends per cm (15 epi) and 32 picks per cm (80 ppi). This amazing fineness of texture was not merely a technical *tour de force*; it was essential, because these tapestries were articles of clothing, not wall decorations, and so had to be as fine and flexible as ordinary cloth. The tapestries were seldom cut, so the garments were usually rectangular, like ponchos; but they could be slightly shaped in the weaving.

The vertical slit which appears at colour boundaries in tapestry weaving was dealt with in three ways: the wefts were interlocked; or the slit was sewn up after weaving; or a fine cotton weft was passed selvedge to selvedge after every so many tapestry wefts. This hidden weft neatly sealed up the slits; it is a method not found elsewhere. As many as a hundred and ninety shades

144

403 Flying bird woven in plain weave on a background of gauze; warp and weft pink cotton; Paracas, Peru.

have been identified in Paracas tapestries, but they were usually limited to ten or fewer in one piece. The Chancay tapestries have a very distinctive range of cheerful yellows and reds.

The imagery used in the designs is still the subject of much study. For instance, a Tiahuanaco shirt might have a falcon-headed figure bearing a staff as a recurring motif, but the elements in this design would be compressed or expanded in each repeat according to certain rigid rules. In this way the weaver could achieve a rich variety of effects while still maintaining the symbolic meaning required in such garments.

As with all Peruvian techniques, tapestry was often combined with other structures, such as plain weave, gauze and twill.

A technique called warp interlock tapestry was a Peruvian speciality: a warp was made on scaffolding threads stretched on a frame, following a plan and using different colours for different areas. Sometimes the warps from adjoining areas were interlocked, sometimes they just went around the same scaffolding thread. The discontinuous warp was then woven, either with a single weft which went right across, giving a warp-faced structure (so the fabric was just like a conventional tapestry turned through a right angle) or a separate and appropriately-coloured weft was used for each coloured area. In the latter case, the result was a patchwork of areas in which both warp and weft showed equally. The weave here could be very open, so a patterned textile even lighter than a tapestry was produced; this may have been the reason for using such a time-consuming method. The scaffolding threads were pulled out when the weaving was complete. This method was used for complex patterns for several centuries but reached its peak in the Nazca period.

Gauze The technique of gauze has always been important in hand weaving. The regular crossing and uncrossing of pairs of warp threads, held in place by successive wefts, was the best way to make an openwork, yet stable, textile on the hand loom. Amongst the world's gauzes, the Peruvian are undoubtedly the most interesting and varied, their closest rival probably being the Chinese.

The technique first appeared in the Paracas Cavernas period, 500 to 300 BC, and technically it was fully developed from the start (403). The gauzes were usually woven only 30 cm (12 in) wide and then seamed together if additional width was required, for example for the large mantles. Other uses included head cloths and small shirts.

The yarn was always cotton, but with a variable degree of twist. Sometimes it was a very highly twisted single ply (in reality, overspun), whose spring-like twists and curls gave good adhesion between warp and weft and added elasticity to the already very stretchable fabric. Sometimes a softer, thicker yarn enabled a more compact gauze to be woven. The two types could be combined to give textural contrast. Later gauzes used two-ply cotton; a few were made entirely of wool.

The colours were often limited to the large range available from natural cotton – browns, beiges and white – but exciting effects were also produced by tie-dying the fabric after weaving.

All the techniques depend on picking up threads from the lower layer of an open plain weave shed, using the point of a stick. They were brought up on the wrong side of the raised warp thread in the upper layer so as to cause a twisting between adjacent pairs or groups of warp threads. The weft was passed through this picked-up shed and was followed by another weft in the opposite plain weave shed. Opening the latter shed had the effect of uncrossing the threads, so in this way only every other shed had to be picked up.

Designs were worked by combining two or more types of gauze crossings (one giving a more dense effect than the other) or by combining gauze and plain weave. The fact that they were woven on a backstrap loom meant that

145

perfect control over warp tension, so necessary in this technique, was easily achieved. Also, the absence of any reed meant that the warp threads could become markedly diverted from their normal alignment and so lead to the very open areas seen in the beautiful Chancay head-cloths.

It is probably true to say that of all old textiles, it is the Peruvian which speak most directly to weavers today. Seeing what can be produced with an extremely skilful and imaginative use of simple equipment is a constant source of inspiration.

404 Patterned silk gauze found on the 'Silk Road' at Noin-Ula; Han dynasty.

Silk weaving in the Middle East and Europe

Silk is really the ideal textile fibre; it combines practical features like length, strength, fineness, elasticity and regularity with aesthetic ones like high lustre, exciting handle, and the beautiful way it takes dye. These make possible the weaving of luxurious fabrics, intricately patterned by means of complex and many-layered interlacements, which are still light enough for clothing. Right from the start silk was used in this way.

The story begins in China. Though a silkworm cocoon has been found there at a site dated 2000 BC, the earliest surviving silk textiles are from the Han Dynasty (206 BC – AD 221) (404). These have mostly been excavated from points along the trade route from China to the West, the so-called 'Silk Road'. They are warp-faced, need a draw loom to weave them, and show patterns in two or three colours. It was such imported fabrics which first gave the West a glimpse of the luxury and beauty of silk. In addition to textiles, the Chinese traded silk yarn with the West; early in the Christian era there is evidence from Persia of locally woven silk fabrics, and by the fourth century there was an Imperial silk-weaving factory in Byzantium.

The earliest Persian silks were made under Sassanian rule – third century AD onwards – and usually showed a single animal set in a roundel of small circles, the 'string of pearls' (colour 34). This motif proved to be an enduring one and was still being used in the eleventh century. However, the Persian weavers were quick to see that, by slightly altering the threading of their draw looms, they could weave a mirror image, two symmetrically opposed animals or figures, thus enlarging the woven repeat without increasing the work in setting up or weaving (colour 32). In some such designs, a king appears as twins! The background space between such opposed images was carefully designed to form shapes, sometimes called 'void patterns', perhaps showing mythical or religious motifs which could not be depicted overtly, sometimes for religious reasons. Much ingenuity was exercised in introducing these concealed references, which persisted for centuries after they were truly relevant.

These Persian silks also required a draw loom but they were from the start weft-faced and so resembled a Han silk turned through a right angle. This simple structure had already been woven in wool by Syrian weavers before the coming of silk; it is very like the structure of some block weaves used by rug weavers today. (As very few weavers now use draw looms, these intricacies are really understood today only by museum specialists and then often only in a theoretical way.) This structure was later altered by the addition of a ground weft which did not appear on the surface; this had the effect of reducing the preparatory tie-up work needed on the draw loom. In time, the techniques became more varied and complex as the weavers tried to find ways of increasing the size of the woven repeat and the character of the textures produced.

Two large centres for silk weaving, as for other trade, were Antioch and Alexandria, but when these were overrun by the Islamic invasion in AD 640, Byzantium came into its own. By this time sericulture (the raising of silk-worms and the production of silk from their cocoons) was practised in the West, reputedly because two monks (at the instigation of Emperor Justinian) had smuggled silkworm eggs out of China hidden in their staffs. Thus silk weaving no longer depended on importing yarn from the East. It became highly organised in the Byzantine weaving factory and was protected by laws. At one time an exhibition displaying the factory's wares was even illuminated at night. Only certain higher ranks were allowed to wear silk dyed purple, and an illicit market developed in purple cloth for humbler people, woven by slaves escaped from the factory. Nevertheless, visitors attested to the general magnificence of Byzantine clothes: 'All the people look like princes', one wrote.

Three Byzantine silks from AD 900 onwards are outstanding for the width of the woven repeat; in one case the motif of a single lion measures 75 cm (30 in) across, so must have demanded an incredible number of simple cords to control the warp threads in each repeat (colour 33).

Silks were still produced in Persia after Islamic rule was established there in AD 642, although its use and the representation of living forms were at first prohibited. But the most important silks woven under Arabic influence came from Spain. After the Arabs introduced silk and sericulture to Spain, the craft developed to a very high level at centres like Almeria. These Hispano-Moresque textiles, generally garments, had exuberant and sometimes heraldic designs. Like other Islamic textiles, they often included some inscription from the Koran, called a *tiraz*. Eventually the textiles themselves were called *tiraz* and every high official had his own tiraz workshop, often within his own house.

Such production was carried on until the fifteenth century in Spain, but in Persia silk weaving stopped abruptly in 1220 when Genghis Khan invaded the country, making it the western limit of his vast empire, which stretched eastward as far as Korea. However, from 1550 onwards, Persia had a second great textile period under the Safavid dynasty. Stimulated by a nationalist revival and under such famous rulers as Shah Abbas, textiles of great luxury and elegance were woven, including silk tents and hangings. But the real summit of the Persian weavers' art was the production of figured silk velvets. Velvet has a cut silk pile, the pile threads coming from an extra warp, wound on a separate beam. One-colour velvets are known from the thirteenth century onwards. It is difficult enough to make even such a simple velvet, as it involves adjustment of warp tensions and delicate manipulation of the pile wires and cutting tool; in fact only one man still weaves velvet by hand in England. But to weave velvet with naturalistic scenes of animals and hunters in eight colours, as in the famous 'Hunting velvet' used to decorate the ceiling of a sixteenth-century tent, is a task beyond the skill of any weaver today (colour 29). Each of the threads of pile yarn had to come from a separate bobbin mounted in a vast creel, below or above the main warp, so the setting up was a prodigious feat. It is strange that no earlier 'tentative' velvets have survived: the earliest known already show elaborate, large-scale patterns.

Like other silk textiles, velvet was often used as a gift, and one reads of a royal letter delivered in a velvet envelope. 'The hunting velvet' was probably woven in Kashan. Other Persian textile centres were Isfahan, which specialised in the use of a silver thread which still shines today, and Yazd where double and triple cloths and warp twill were woven. Yazd was also the home of Ghiyath ed-din Ali, probably the greatest silk weaver in Asian history to whom a name can definitely be given; his signed silks appeared around AD 1600.

Sicily, like Spain, became a silk weaving centre only after its conquest by the Arabs and in the ninth century a *tiraz* factory was set up at Palermo. Two centres later, Sicily was again conquered, this time by Roger of Hauteville, a patron of the arts who introduced silk weavers from Greece. Gradually, pre-eminence in silk weaving shifted from Byzantium to Palermo. Here fabrics with a greater freedom of design were woven, the motifs being continuous, no longer separated by frames or medallions. When the last of Roger's descendants died in 1266, it was natural for Palermo silk weavers to move to

Lucca, a town famous for wool weaving from Roman times and which had always had close links with Palermo. Here they produced sumptuous silks with a lavish use of gold and silver thread, many of which have been preserved because they were made for the Church. The style became more naturalistic, with animals running about, not opposed to each other in pairs. It is interesting that recently the notebook of a seventeenth century Lucchese weaver has been discovered, containing his analyses of many simple patterns with names like 'Rosa doppia', which means double rose. Such a direct link with a weaver from the past is very rare.

When the Florentines captured Lucca in 1315, many weavers again migrated, either to Florence itself or to Genoa and Venice. Venice was already a well-established silk weaving centre, but it was the arrival of the Lucchese weavers which brought it to full development. Venetian velvets became famous, some being designed by artists (such as Crivelli and Pisano); this sort of participation contributed to the leading position that velvet held in the textiles of the sixteenth and seventeenth centuries. New types were developed, one in which the pattern pile stood up higher than the background pile and another with an uncut pile of gold thread. In fact the technique became so complex that the Guild of Velvet Weavers had to be split into five sections because the journeymen complained that they could not master the complete craft.

All this time, France had been importing silks and velvets from Italy and Spain, despite the efforts of the French kings to be independent in this field. Such efforts included the granting of many privileges to foreign silk weavers who settled in Lyons. It was only in the seventeenth century, and especially with the organising help of Colbert, Louis XIV's finance minister, that the Lyons weavers finally outstripped Italian competition. Claude Dandon's new draw loom, invented around 1600, was crucial in this connection as it made possible the weaving of really large repeats. The demands of the trade stimulated other inventions, culminating in Jacquard's revolutionary loom, which substituted punched cards for the previously used drawboy; it was in use in Lyons by 1808. After an obvious slump during the French Revolution, the silk and velvet trade was partly revived by Napoleon who used expensive fabrics to cover his palace walls.

Silk weaving in England was an offshoot of her willingness to accept refugees. In 1585 about 30,000 Flemish refugees landed, many of them silk weavers, and they set up in Spitalfields, Norwich and Canterbury. Many of the Huguenot refugees who arrived exactly a century later were from Lyons, and they joined the Spitalfields silk weavers in London. This group soon became a serious rival to Lyons, and, by the end of the eighteenth century, England was said to be the leading silk- and velvet-producing country. Eventually the Spitalfields weavers dwindled as mechanical weaving increased in importance. The few who remained at the start of the Second World War moved to Braintree and worked with the firm of Warners. When this firm was finally closed, some of the unique looms, and their operators, were established in a small workshop at Castle Hedingham, Suffolk, where they can still be seen working today.

Unlike the silks just described, those produced by weavers today such as Geraldine St Aubyn Hubbard are often woven in plain weave (back cover 4). That this was done in the past is shown by the derivation of the word 'tabby', frequently used word for 'plain weave'; it comes from 'Attābiy', a district of Baghdad where such simple silk weaving was once carried out from the twelfth century onwards.

The very complex weave structures to which silk is so well suited are now no longer in the hand-weaver's vocabulary. But a contemporary revival of interest in dobby and Jacquard hand looms could possibly lead to their re-introduction – an interesting prospect.

The revival in Britain

The Industrial Revolution in Great Britain really started in the textile trade with inventions like the flying shuttle, spinning and carding machines and finally, the power loom, at first reducing the hand workers to dreadful levels of poverty and eventually replacing them. Being the first country to suffer such an upheaval, Britain had no experience to guide it. So through this ignorance, coupled with an apparent lack of concern, it allowed to become irretrievably lost those hand skills which had been taken for granted for centuries, and on which the past wealth of the country had almost totally depended. It is true that in isolated areas, like the north of Scotland, hand-weaving and spinning still managed to persist on a small scale, but never again would it be the means of providing the clothing and household textiles for the masses. So when the inevitable reaction to machine-made goods came, based on both philosophical and aesthetic grounds, there was no great living tradition of textiles to plug into and draw strength from. Thus we find William Morris, the founder of the Arts and Crafts Movement, rising at 5 am each morning in 1879 to weave his very first tapestry sample, and having no other tutor but a small eighteenth-century book in French.

405 Design for a tapestry 'The orchard' made by William Morris in 1890.

Despite this emphasis on handwork, Morris's gift lay more in designing. His company, which produced a wide range of carefully designed and hand-made objects from furniture and stained glass to door-knobs, produced large, decorative double cloths, as well as tapestries (405) and knotted rugs; but he had little direct effect on the revival of hand-weaving. However he had a link with Ethel Mairet (colour 35), the greatest figure in that revival, because a book by her and her husband on the art of Ceylon was published by his Kelmscott Press in 1908. Two years later, she returned to England, filled with enthusiasm for the spinning, weaving and dyeing she had seen in Ceylon, and, finding someone who had learnt these skills in Scotland, set up house close by to learn the skills herself. It was when she later remarried and moved to 'Gospels' that she really began to make her influence felt. Few weavers who made the pilgrimage to that house in Sussex came away unaffected by her enthusiastic and critical attitude. The latter was necessary to combat a sort of cosiness which perhaps infects all revivals at some stage – a celebration of old techniques and implements simply because they were old, and a tolerance of muddy colours just because they were vegetable dyed. Ethel Mairet was far more concerned that weaving should be of its time and should contribute to contemporary art, industry and education, a message which she wrote into her several books and which is still relevant today.

It was through such clear-headed guidance from Ethel Mairet and her pupils, and with another strand of influence coming from the Bauhaus-trained

Margaret Leischner, that hand-weaving in this country managed to steer a fairly healthy course. It had to absorb the great knowledge of wool still residing in the textile industry, from the selection of fleece to the choosing of a weave structure for a specific yarn; it had to find its own balance between the aesthetic and the practical; and it had to resist the pressure to absorb, undigested and wholesale, the influence of countries such as Sweden, where hand-weaving was still a living force in a different context. The many active Guilds and their organ, *The Weavers Journal*, show the degree of enthusiasm which carries it forward today.

Britain may not shine on the world stage in exhibitions such as the International Biennale of Tapestry, as do America, Poland and Japan, but she still exerts a considerable influence. Her art school textile courses are judged to be among the best in the world; her leading weavers export a large proportion of their work and as much of their teaching time as they can spare; their books exert a stabilising force in the over-commercial realm of craft book publishing; and, through Ann Sutton, Britain gave the concept of the miniature textile to the world (384).

Strongly influenced by the surfacing of textiles as an art form in America, we are beginning to lose our notion of weaving as a separate, self-sufficient, activity. We are being persuaded that it is just one of the many skills with which any creative person dealing with threads should be conversant, along with crochet, knitting, embroidery, felting and so on. It is difficult to see where this breaking of age-long barriers will lead; will there be a compensatory intensification of vision as the skills become mixed and diluted?

Whatever happens, the future certainly looks full of interest.

406 Portrait bust tapestry woven in dyed wools, Akhmim, Egypt, fourth to fifth century.

Book list

Books out of print are marked op. but may be obtained from a library. Specialist weaving books may be obtained from a supplier such as Miss K. Drummond, 30 Hart Grove, London W5. Callers by appointment only.
Telephone 01-992 1974

Heavy type means especially recommended

General

ALBERS, Anni **On weaving** Wesleyan U.P., 1965; Studio Vista, 1966; paperback 1974.
ALBERS, Anni **On designing** Wesleyan U.P., 1962. Two notable books by an ex-Bauhaus weaver who writes revealingly about textiles and their place in society.
BURNHAM, Dorothy *Warp and weft. a textile terminology* Royal Ontario Museum, 1980. An illustrated dictionary of textile terms; well-researched.
EMERY, Irene **The primary structures of fabrics** Washington, DC: Textile Museum, 1966. op. An illustrated classification of all fabric structures, both woven and non-woven, with special attention to terminology – a very important book.
MAIRET, Ethel *Hand-weaving today* Faber, 1939. op. Deals with many of Mrs Mairet's favourite topics, including handweaving and education, handweaving and industry, fibres and their properties.
WALLER, Irene *Fine-art weaving: a study of the work of artist weavers in Britain* Batsford, 1979. The only book devoted to living textile artists of Great Britain; a chapter on each of seventeen weavers with an excellent historical introduction.

Wools and spinning

BAINES, Patricia **Spinning wheels: spinners and spinning** Batsford, 1977. A well-researched book dealing with the great variety of spinning wheels and their uses.
BRITISH WOOL MARKETING BOARD *British sheep breeds: their wool and its uses* The Board, 1967.
DAVENPORT, Elsie G. **Your hand-spinning** Mountain View, MO: Select Books, paperback 1964.
FANNIN, Allen A. *Hand-spinning: art and technique* Van Nostrand Reinhold, 1971. A very technical book applying to hand-spinning the expertise derived from industrial practice; full of information.
HAIGH, H. and NEWTON, R. A.
The wools of Britain Pitman, 1952. op.
LEADBEATER, Eliza *Hand-spinning* Studio Vista, 1976. A standard well-illustrated book, especially detailed on preparation and spinning of flax.
RYDER, Michael L. *Sheep and wool for handicraft workers* 1978. A useful pamphlet available from the author, White Rose, 23 Swanston Place, Edinburgh, EH10 7DD.
RYDER, Michael L. and STEPHENSON, S. K. **Wool growth** Academic Press, 1968. Standard reference work.

TEAL, Peter *Hand wool-combing and spinning* Blandford Press, 1976. A unique book on making and using wool combs and worsted spinning; very exact, uncrafty approach.

Making equipment

ABRAMS, A. J. and C. W. *Building craft equipment* Pitman, 1977. Has chapters on making floor and inkle looms, also warping frame, shuttles and spool rack.
HJERT, J. and von ROSENSTIEL, P. *Loom construction* Van Nostrand Reinhold, cased and paperback 1978. How to make inkle, tapestry and four-shaft table and floor looms, with good instructions on setting them up for weaving.
KILBRIDE, Thomas *Spinning and weaving at home: expert advice on constructing and using your own low cost spinning wheel and loom* Thorsons, 1980. How to make a spinning wheel and loom from junk metal.

Dyeing

ADROSKO, Rita J. *Natural dyes and home dyeing* Dover Publ. n.e. 1971. Practical guide with recipes, some illustrations.
DAVENPORT, Elsie **Your yarn dyeing** Mountain View MO: Select Books, paperback 1970. Deals with natural and synthetic dyes, many recipes.
EDWARDS, A. Cecil *The Persian carpet* Duckworth, n.e. 1975; Totowa, NJ: Biblio Distribution Centre, 1975. Good section on dyes.
LARSEN, Jack Lenor *The dyer's art: ikat, batik and plangi* Van Nostrand Reinhold, 1977. Expensive book, lavishly illustrated, on dyed and resist-dyed textiles.
MAIRET, Ethel **A book on vegetable dyes** 1916. Faber, latest edn. 1938. op. A standard work on vegetable dyeing, containing instructions and recipes.
PARTRIDGE, William *A practical treatise on dyeing of woollen, cotton and skein silk* 1823. Edington, Wiltshire: Pasold Research Fund, 1st edn. reprinted 1973.
ROBINSON, Stuart **A history of dyed textiles** Studio Vista, 1969. Useful and well illustrated.
THURSTAN, Violetta **The use of vegetable dyes** Dryad Press, n.e. 1977. Useful little book of recipes.
WULFF, Hans E. *The traditional crafts of Persia* Massachusetts Institute of Technology Press, 1966. Good section on natural dyes and dyeing of carpets.
Dye plants and dyeing Vol. 20 No.3 and **Natural plant dyeing** Vol. 29 No. 2 pub. Brooklyn Botanic Gardens, obtainable from American Museum, Claverton Manor, Bath. Collections of practical, illustrated articles.

History

BURNHAM, Harold B. and Dorothy K. **Keep me warm one night: early handweaving in Eastern Canada** University of Toronto Press, 1973. Fine study of early Canadian weaving and equipment.
HOFFMAN, Marta **The warp-weighted loom** (Studia Norvegica no. 14) University of Oslo, 1964; paperback 1975.

A definitive and highly detailed account of this loom, but also touches on most of the early history of European textiles; a great source book.
GEIGER, Agnes **A history of textile art** Sotheby Parke Bernet, 1979. Deals mainly with history relating to Scandinavia, but is outstanding in this area.
JENKINS, J. G. ed. *The wool textile industry in Great Britain* Routledge and Kegan Paul, 1972. A good survey, well illustrated, including latest findings.
SINGER, C. ed. **A history of technology** 7 volumes OUP, 1954–1978. Each volume has a chapter on textiles with accurate information and many references.
THURSTAN, V. *A short history of decorative textiles and tapestries* Ditchling: Pepler, 1934. 2nd edn. *Ancient decorative textiles* 1954. op.
Entries in *Encyclopaedia Britannica* under tapestry, carpets etc.
Ciba Review: magazine published 1937–1975 by Chemical Industry of Basel. Each number was a monograph written by the acknowledged expert on the subject. Sets exist in some libraries; a few numbers have been reprinted.
Textile History: annual magazine, Pasold Research Fund Ltd, 23 St James's Square, Bath, Avon BA1 2TT. Serious thesis-like articles, often on post-industrial revolution history; reviews the year's textile literature.
Textile Museum Journal: annual magazine, Washington DC. Usually contains about four well researched articles – strong on carpets, Peruvian textiles and conservation.

Technical

ATWATER, Mary M. **Byways in handweaving** (inkle and tablet weaving) New York: Macmillan, 1968. Contains good technical and historical information.
BEUTLICH, Tadek **The technique of woven tapestry** Batsford, 1967. A standard book on tapestry techniques including the making of simple equipment, illustrated with the author's early work.
BROWN, Rachel *The weaving, spinning and dyeing book* Routledge and Kegan Paul, cased and paperback 1979. A good all-round book, information well presented with many clear sketches.
CASON, M. and CAHLANDER, A. A. **The art of Bolivian highland weaving** Watson-Guptill, 1976. Exceptional textbook on very interesting methods, many not described elsewhere.
COLLINGWOOD, Peter **The techniques of rug weaving** Faber, 1968. Exhaustive exploration of rug weaving, covering traditional and new methods, both finger and shaft-controlled.
FANNIN, Allen A. *Handloom weaving technology* Van Nostrand Reinhold, 1979. A companion volume to the author's book on spinning; analyses every aspect of handweaving and suggests many ways to improve efficiency.
HALSEY, Mike *Introducing tapestry weaving* Halbar Press, 2 paperbacks 1980. 89a Grosvenor Avenue, London N5 2NL.

HALSEY, Mike and YOUNGMARK, Lore **Foundations of weaving** David and Charles, 1975. Detailed instruction book explaining everything right from the beginning, based on the authors' teaching experience.

d'HARCOURT, Raoul et al **Textiles of ancient Peru and their techniques** University of Washington Press, 1966. op; paperback 1974. The greatest book devoted to Peruvian textiles and their analysis, still used constantly, though written in 1934.

HELD, Shirley E. **Weaving: A handbook of the fiber arts** Holt Rinehart & Winston, n.e. 1978. The art side of textiles.

HOOPER, Luther **Handloom weaving** Pitman, 1979. A great book full of detailed technical information derived from the English silk-weaving tradition; describes some devices not mentioned anywhere else.

KIRBY, Mary **Designing on the loom** Mountain View, MO: Select Books, paperback 1973. Highly regarded book, taking the weaver from plain weave right through to Jacquard weaves; exact details given of every fabric illustrated.

KNIGHT, Brian *Technique of rug weaving* Batsford, 1980. Concentrates on a few techniques, but has useful advice on colour and design.

MATTERA, Joanne *Navajo techniques for today's weaver* New York: Watson-Guptill, 1975; Pitman, 1976.

MOORMAN, Theo *Weaving as an art form* Van Nostrand Reinhold, 1975; paperback 1980. Combines autobiography and a personal view on textiles with description of the author's special technique for fine hangings. Many illustrations.

NEHER, Evelyn *Inkle* published by the author, 1974, USA. Without doubt the best book on inkle weaving, covering all the many patterning methods; ends with 100 pages showing old and modern looms.

OELSNER, G. H. **A handbook of weaves** Dover Publications, n.e. 1975. 400 pages of weaves, but only shown as weave plans, no pictures of woven cloth; very specialised information, eg 342 crepe weaves are described.

PICTON, John and MACK, John **African textiles** British Museum Publications, cased and paperback 1979. Excellent illustrated survey with many technical details and historical background.

REDMAN, Jane *Frame-loom weaving* Van Nostrand Reinhold, 1976; paperback 1980.

REICHARD. Gladys A. *Weaving a Navaho blanket* Dover Publications, n.e. 1974. Unsurpassed account written by a weaver who learnt directly from the Navaho.

SNOW, M. and W. *Step-by-step tablet weaving* New York: Golden Press, 1973. op. Contains some advanced methods.

STRAUB, Marianne **Hand weaving and cloth design** Pelham Books, 1977. op. Very clear instruction book, excellent on structure especially multi-layered weaves.

SUTTON, Ann and HOLTOM, Pat **Tablet weaving** Batsford, 1975. A good clear introductory textbook, well illustrated.

TABER, Barbara and ANDERSON, Marilyn **Backstrap weaving** Pitman, 1975. Probably the best book on the subject.

TOMITA, J. and N. **The techniques of Kasuri** Japan, 1979. Very clear practical account of Japanese warp and weft tie-dye methods.

TOVEY, John *The technique of weaving* Batsford, n.e. 1975. Extremely detailed book dealing with every phase from warp preparation onwards, illustrated with many photos of the author at work; unique section on loom mountings.

TOVEY, John *Technique of weaves and pattern drafting* Batsford, 1978. Good coverage of most weaves used by handweavers, including gauze.

WATSON, William **Textile design and colour** 7th rev. edn. Z. Grosicki. Newnes-Butterworth, 1975. The industrial designer's bible, packed with technical information; over 400 diagrams.

Magazines

The Weavers' Journal see Association of Guilds of Weavers, Spinners and Dyers.
Crafts see Crafts Council.

Useful addresses

Crafts Council
12 Waterloo Place, London SW1Y 4AU
Telephone 01-930 4811
Exhibitions, information, slide collection. Publishes *Crafts* magazine, bimonthly, available from booksellers and crafts shops or by post from *Crafts* magazine, 8 Waterloo Place, London SW1Y 4AT

Association of Guilds of Weavers, Spinners and Dyers
BCM 963, London WC1N 3XX
Has a list of local Guild secretaries. Publishes *The Weavers Journal*. Annual subscription (4 issues) from The Secretary, *The Weavers Journal*, at the above address. Also publishes a useful booklet listing suppliers of materials.

BBC tapestry weaving pack and spinning pack available from The Yarn Store, 89A Grosvenor Avenue, Highbury, London N5 2NL
Telephone 01-354 0985

Residential Short Courses published by the National Institute of Adult Education, is available from Research Publication Services, Victoria Hall, East Greenwich, London SE10 0RF

Britain: Holiday Courses published by the British Tourist Authority and available from BTA Sales Counter, 4 Bromells Road, London SW4 0BJ

Floodlight published by the Inner London Education Authority, is available through newsagents and bookshops. It lists courses in London starting each year in September.

Try your local Public Library and your Local Education Authority for details of weaving courses in your area.

Museums and galleries
(where weaving past and present can be seen)

Museum of Mankind (Ethnography Department of the British Museum)
6 Burlington Gardens, London W1X 2EY

The Victoria and Albert Museum
Cromwell Road, South Kensington, London SW7 2RL

Horniman Museum
London Road, Forest Hill, London SE23 3PQ

Crafts Council Gallery
12 Waterloo Place, London SW1Y 4AU
Telephone 01–930 4811
Slide index by appointment. Various crafts exhibitions.

British Crafts Centre
43 Earlham Street, Covent Garden, London WCH 9LD

Whitworth Art Gallery
University of Manchester, Whitworth Park, Manchester

Portsmouth City Museum
Museum Road, Old Portsmouth

Leeds Art Galleries
Lotherton Hall, Aberford, Leeds

York Castle Museum
Tower Street, York

Piece Hall Museum
Halifax, Yorkshire

Museum of English Rural Life
University of Reading, Whiteknights, Reading

Royal Scottish Museum
Chambers Street, Edinburgh 1

The Burrell Collection
Pollok Park, Glasgow
(opens 1983/4)

Welsh National Folk Museum
St. Fagans, Cardiff, Glamorgan

The photograph on the *front cover* is of Peter Collingwood.

Key to photographs on back cover

1 Shaft-switched rug by Peter Collingwood, intended to be used as a draughts or chess board.

2 Section of a poncho shirt, interlocked tapestry with alpaca wefts on a cotton warp; probably Chancay; about 1400.

3 Tapestry woven by Linda Green, used as the title for the BBC television series, 'The craft of the weaver'.

4 Silk and cashmere scarves by Geraldine St Aubyn Hubbard, using natural and synthetic dyed yarns of various thicknesses in plain weave and 2/2 twill.